Max Mueller

Essays on the science of religion

Max Mueller

Essays on the science of religion

ISBN/EAN: 9783742895134

Manufactured in Europe, USA, Canada, Australia, Japa

Cover: Foto ©Thomas Meinert / pixelio.de

Manufactured and distributed by brebook publishing software
(www.brebook.com)

Max Mueller

Essays on the science of religion

CHIPS

FROM A GERMAN WORKSHOP.

BY

MAX MÜLLER, M.A.

FELLOW OF ALL SOULS COLLEGE, OXFORD.

VOLUME I.

Essays on the Science of Religion.

SECOND EDITION.

LONDON:

LONGMANS, GREEN, AND CO.

1868.

To the Memory

OF

BARON BUNSEN,

MY FRIEND AND BENEFACTOR.

et quanto diutius
Abes, magis cupio tanto et magis desidero ~

PREFACE.

———◆———

MORE than twenty years have passed since my revered friend Bunsen called me one day into his library at Carlton House Terrace, and announced to me with beaming eyes that the publication of the Rig-veda was secure. He had spent many days in seeing the Directors of the East-India Company, and explaining to them the importance of this work, and the necessity of having it published in England. At last his efforts had been successful, the funds for printing my edition of the text and commentary of the Sacred Hymns of the Brahmans had been granted, and Bunsen was the first to announce to me the happy result of his literary diplomacy. 'Now,' he said, 'you have got a work for life—a large block that will take years to plane and polish.' 'But mind,' he added, 'let us have from time to time some chips from your workshop.'

I have tried to follow the advice of my departed friend, and I have published almost every year a few articles on such subjects as had engaged my attention, while prosecuting at the same time, as far

as altered circumstances would allow, my edition of
the Rig-veda, and of other Sanskrit works connected
with it.   These articles were chiefly published in the
'Edinburgh' and 'Quarterly Reviews,' in the 'Oxford
Essays,' and 'Macmillan's' and 'Fraser's Magazines,'
in the 'Saturday Review,' and in the 'Times.'
In writing them my principal endeavour has been
to bring out even in the most abstruse subjects
the points of real interest that ought to engage
the attention of the public at large, and never to
leave a dark nook or corner without attempting to
sweep away the cobwebs of false learning, and let
in the light of real knowledge.   Here, too, I owe
much to Bunsen's advice, and when last year I
saw in Cornwall the large heaps of copper ore
piled up around the mines, like so many heaps of
rubbish, while the poor people were asking for
coppers to buy bread, I frequently thought of
Bunsen's words, 'Your work is not finished when
you have brought the ore from the mine: it must
be sifted, smelted, refined, and coined before it can
be of real use, and contribute towards the intellectual
food of mankind.'   I can hardly hope that in this
my endeavour to be clear and plain, to follow the
threads of every thought to the very ends, and
to place the web of every argument clearly and
fully before my readers, I have always been successful.   Several of the subjects treated in these
essays are, no doubt, obscure and difficult: but there
is no subject, I believe, in the whole realm of human

knowledge, that cannot be rendered clear and intelligible, if we ourselves have perfectly mastered it. And now while the two last volumes of my edition of the Rig-veda are passing through the press, I thought the time had come for gathering up a few armfulls of these chips and splinters, throwing away what seemed worthless, and putting the rest into some kind of shape, in order to clear my workshop for other work.

The first and second volumes which I am now publishing contain essays on the early thoughts of mankind, whether religious or mythological, and on early traditions and customs. There is to my mind no subject more absorbing than the tracing the origin and first growth of human thought;— not theoretically, or in accordance with the Hegelian laws of thought, or the Comtian epochs; but historically, and like an Indian trapper, spying for every footprint, every layer, every broken blade that might tell and testify of the former presence of man in his early wanderings and searchings after light and truth.

In the languages of mankind, in which everything new is old and everything old is new, an inexhaustible mine has been discovered for researches of this kind. Language still bears the impress of the earliest thoughts of man, obliterated, it may be, buried under new thoughts, yet here and there still recoverable in their sharp original outline. The growth of language is continuous, and by continuing our researches backward from the most modern to the most ancient strata, the very elements and roots of human speech have been reached, and with them the elements and roots of human thought. What lies beyond the beginnings of language, however interesting it may be to the physiologist, does not yet belong to the history of man, in the true and original sense of that word. Man means the thinker, and the first manifestation of thought is speech.

But more surprising than the continuity in the growth of language, is the continuity in the growth of religion. Of religion, too, as of language, it may be said that in it everything new is old, and everything old is new, and that there has been no entirely new religion since the beginning of the world. The elements and roots of religion were there, as far back as we can trace the history of man; and the history of religion, like the history of language, shows us throughout a succession of new combinations of the same radical elements. An intuition of God, a sense of human weakness and dependance, a belief in a Divine government of the world, a distinction between good and evil, and a hope of a better life, these are some of the radical elements of all religions. Though sometimes hidden, they rise again and again to the surface. Though frequently distorted, they tend again and again to their perfect form. Unless they had formed part of the original dowry of the human soul, religion itself would have remained an impossibility, and the tongues of angels would have been to human ears but as sounding brass or a tinkling cymbal. If we once understand this clearly, the words of St. Augustine which have seemed startling to many of his admirers, become perfectly clear and intelligible, when he says[1]: 'What is now called the Christian religion, has existed among the ancients, and was not absent from the beginning of the human race, until Christ came in the flesh: from which time the true religion, which existed already, began to be called Christian.' From this point of view the words of Christ too, which startled the Jews, assume their true meaning, when He said to the centurion of Capernaum: 'Many shall come from the east and the west, and shall sit down with Abraham, and Isaac, and Jacob, in the kingdom of heaven.'

During the last fifty years the accumulation of new and authentic materials for the study of the religions of the world, has been most extraordinary; but such are the difficulties in mastering these materials that I doubt whether the time has yet come for attempting to trace, after the model of the Science of Language, the definite outlines of the Science of Religion. By a succession of the most

---

[1] August. Retr. 1, 13. 'Res ipsa, quæ nunc religio Christiana nuncupatur, erat apud antiquos, nec defuit ab initio generis humani, quousque Christus veniret in carnem, unde vera religio, quæ jam erat, cœpit appellari Christiana.'

fortunate circumstances, the canonical books of three
of the principal religions of the ancient world have
lately been recovered, the Veda, the Zend-Avesta,
and the Tripitaka. But not only have we thus
gained access to the most authentic documents
from which to study the ancient religion of the
Brahmans, the Zoroastrians, and the Buddhists, but
by discovering the real origin of Greek, Roman, and
likewise of Teutonic, Slavonic, and Celtic mythology, it has become possible to separate the truly
religious elements in the sacred traditions of these
nations from the mythological crust by which they
are surrounded, and thus to gain a clearer insight
into the real faith of the ancient Aryan world.

If we turn to the Semitic world, we find that
although but few new materials have been discovered
from which to study the ancient religion of the
Jews, yet a new spirit of inquiry has brought new
life into the study of the sacred records of Abraham,
Moses, and the Prophets; and the recent researches
of Biblical scholars, though starting from the most
opposite points, have all helped to bring out the
historical interest of the Old Testament, in a manner
not dreamt of by former theologians. The same may
be said of another Semitic religion, the religion of
Mahommed, since the Koran and the literature connected with it were submitted to the searching
criticism of real scholars and historians. Some new
materials for the study of the Semitic religions have
come from the monuments of Babylon and Nineveh.

The very images of Bel and Nisroch now stand before our eyes, and the inscriptions on the tablets may hereafter tell us even more of the thoughts of those who bowed their knees before them. The religious worship of the Phenicians and Carthaginians has been illustrated by Movers from the ruins of their ancient temples, and from scattered notices in classical writers; nay, even the religious ideas of the Nomads of the Arabian peninsula, previous to the rise of Mohammedanism, have been brought to light by the patient researches of Oriental scholars.

There is no lack of idols among the ruined and buried temples of Egypt with which to reconstruct the pantheon of that primeval country: nor need we despair of recovering more and more of the thoughts buried under the hieroglyphics of the inscriptions, or preserved in hieratic and demotic MSS., if we watch the brilliant discoveries that have rewarded the patient researches of the disciples of Champollion.

Besides the Aryan and Semitic families of religion, we have in China three recognised forms of public worship, the religion of Confucius, that of Laotse, and that of Fo (Buddha); and here, too, recent publications have shed new light, and have rendered an access to the canonical works of these religions, and an understanding of their various purports, more easy, even to those who have not mastered the intricacies of the Chinese language.

Among the Turanian nations, a few only, such as the Finns and the Mongolians, have preserved some remnants of their ancient worship and mythology, and these too have lately been more carefully collected and explained by d'Ohson, Castrèn, and others.

In America the religions of Mexico and Peru had long attracted the attention of theologians; and of late years the impulse imparted to ethnological researches has induced travellers and missionaries to record any traces of religious life that could be discovered among the savage inhabitants of Africa, America, and the Polynesian islands.

It will be seen from these few indications, that there is no lack of materials for the student of religion; but we shall also perceive how difficult it is to master such vast materials. To gain a full knowledge of the Veda, or the Zend-Avesta, or the Tripiṭaka, of the Old Testament, the Koran, or the sacred books of China, is the work of a whole life. How then is one man to survey the whole field of religious thought, to classify the religions of the world according to definite and permanent criteria, and to describe their characteristic features with a sure and discriminating hand?

Nothing is more difficult to seize than the salient features, the traits that constitute the permanent expression and real character of a religion. Religion seems to be the common property of a large community, and yet it not only varies in numerous

sects, as language does in its dialects, but it escapes
our firm grasp till we can trace it to its real habitat,
the heart of one true believer. We speak glibly of
Buddhism and Brahmanism, forgetting that we are
generalising on the most intimate convictions of
millions and millions of human souls, divided by half
the world and by thousands of years.

It may be said that at all events where a religion
possesses canonical books, or a definite number of
articles, the task of the student of religion becomes
easier, and this, no doubt, is true to a certain extent.
But even then we know that the interpretation of
these canonical books varies, so much so that sects
appealing to the same revealed authorities, as, for
instance, the founders of the Vedânta and the
Sânkhya systems, accuse each other of error, if not
of wilful error or heresy. Articles too, though drawn
up with a view to define the principal doctrines
of a religion, lose much of their historical value by
the treatment they receive from subsequent schools;
and they are frequently silent on the very points
which make religion what it is.

A few instances may serve to show what difficulties
the student of religion has to contend with, before
he can hope firmly to grasp the facts on which his
theories are to be based.

Roman Catholic missionaries who had spent their
lives in China, who had every opportunity, while
staying at the court of Pekin, of studying in the
original the canonical works of Confucius and their

commentaries, who could consult the greatest theologians then living, and converse with the crowds
that thronged the temples of the capital, differed
diametrically in their opinions as to the most vital
points in the state religion of China. Lecomte,
Fouquet, Prémare, and Bouvet thought it undeniable
that Confucius, his predecessors and his disciples, had
entertained the noblest ideas on the constitution of
the universe, and had sacrificed to the true God in
the most ancient temple of the earth. According
to Maigrot, Navarette, on the contrary, and even
according to the Jesuit Longobardi, the adoration
of the Chinese was addressed to inanimate tablets,
meaningless inscriptions, or, in the best case, to coarse
ancestral spirits and beings without intelligence[2]. If
we believe the former, the ancient deism of China
approached the purity of the Christian religion; if
we listen to the latter, the absurd fetichism of the
multitude degenerated amongst the educated, into
systematic materialism and atheism. In answer to
the peremptory texts quoted by one party, the other
adduced the glosses of accredited interpreters, and
the dispute of the missionaries who had lived in
China and knew Chinese, had to be settled in the
last instance by a decision of the see of Rome.

There is hardly any religion that has been
studied in its sacred literature, and watched in
its external worship with greater care than the

---

[2] Abel Rémusat, ' Mélanges,' p. 162.

modern religion of the Hindus, and yet it would
be extremely hard to give a faithful and intelligible description of it.   Most people who have
lived in India would maintain that the Indian
religion, as believed in and practised at present
by the mass of the people, is idol worship and
nothing else.   But let us hear one of the mass of
the people, a Hindu of Benares, who in a lecture
delivered before an English and native audience
defends his faith and the faith of his forefathers
against such sweeping accusations.   'If by idolatry,'
he says, 'is meant a system of worship which confines our ideas of the Deity to a mere image of clay
or stone, which prevents our hearts from being
expanded and elevated with lofty notions of the
attributes of God, if this is what is meant by
idolatry, we disclaim idolatry, we abhor idolatry, and
deplore the ignorance or uncharitableness of those
that charge us with this grovelling system of worship. . . . . But if, firmly believing, as we do, in the
omnipresence of God, we behold, by the aid of our
imagination, in the form of an image any of His
glorious manifestations, ought we to be charged
with identifying them with the matter of the image,
whilst during those moments of sincere and fervent
devotion, we do not even think of matter ?   If at
the sight of a portrait of a beloved and venerated
friend no longer existing in this world. our heart
is filled with sentiments of love and reverence; if
we fancy him present in the picture, still looking

upon us with his wonted tenderness and affection,
and then indulge our feelings of love and gratitude,
should we be charged with offering the grossest
insult to him—that of fancying him to be no other
than a piece of painted paper? . . . . We really lament
the ignorance or uncharitableness of those who con-
found our representative worship with the Phenician, Grecian, or Roman idolatry as represented by
European writers, and then charge us with polytheism in the teeth of thousands of texts in the
Purânas, declaring in clear and unmistakeable terms
that there is but one God who manifests Himself
as Brahma, Vishnu, and Rudra (Siva) in His func-
tions of creation, preservation, and destruction [3].'

In support of these statements, this eloquent
advocate quotes numerous passages from the sacred
literature of the Brahmans, and he sums up his
view of the three manifestations of the Deity in
the words of their great poet Kalidâsa, as translated by Mr. Griffith:

> In those Three Persons the One God was shown,
> Each First in place, each Last,—not one alone;
> Of Siva, Vishnu, Brahma, each may be
> First, second, third, among the Blessed Three.

---

[3] The modern pandit's reply to the missionary who accuses
him of polytheism is: 'Oh, these are only various manifestations
of the one God; the same as, though the sun be one in the
heavens, yet he appears in multiform reflections upon the lake.
The various sects are only different entrances to the one city.'—
See W. W. Hunter, *Annals of Rural Bengal*, p. 116.

If such contradictory views can be held and defended with regard to religious systems still prevalent amongst us, where we can cross-examine living witnesses, and appeal to chapter and verse in their sacred writings, what must the difficulty be when we have to deal with the religions of the past? I do not wish to disguise these difficulties which are inherent in a comparative study of the religions of the world. I rather dwell on them strongly, in order to show how much care and caution is required in so difficult a subject, and how much indulgence should be shown in judging of the shortcomings and errors that are unavoidable in so comprehensive a study. It was supposed at one time that a comparative analysis of the languages of mankind must transcend the powers of man: and yet by the combined and well directed efforts of many scholars, great results have here been obtained, and the principles that must guide the student of the Science of Language are now firmly established. It will be the same with the Science of Religion. By a proper division of labour, the materials that are still wanting will be collected and published and translated, and when that is done, surely man will never rest till he has discovered the purpose that runs through the religions of mankind, and till he has reconstructed the true Civitas Dei on foundations as wide as the ends of the world. The Science of Religion may be the last of the sciences which man is destined to ela-

borate; but when it is elaborated, it will change
the aspect of the world, and give a new life to
Christianity itself.

The Fathers of the Church, though living in much
more dangerous proximity to the ancient religions
of the Gentiles, admitted freely that a comparison
of Christianity and other religions was useful. ' If
there is any agreement,' Basilius remarked, ' between
their (the Greeks') doctrines and our own, it may
benefit us to know them: if not, then to compare
them and to learn how they differ, will help not a
little towards confirming that which is the better of
the two[4].'

But this is not the only advantage of a comparative study of religions. The Science of Religion
will for the first time assign to Christianity its
right place among the religions of the world; it
will show for the first time fully what was meant
by the fulness of time; it will restore to the whole
history of the world, in its unconscious progress
towards Christianity, its true and sacred character.

Not many years ago great offence was given by
an eminent writer who remarked that the time
had come when the history of Christianity should
be treated in a truly historical spirit, in the same
spirit in which we treat the history of other reli-

---

[4] Basilius, ' De legendis Græc. libris, c. v. Εἰ μὲν οὖν ἐστί τις
οἰκειότης πρὸς ἀλλήλους τοῖς λόγοις, προὔργου ἂν ἡμῖν αὐτῶν ἡ
γνῶσις γένοιτο. εἰ δὲ μὴ, ἀλλὰ τό γε παράλληλα θέντας καταμαθεῖν
τὸ διάφορον, οὐ μικρὸν εἰς βεβαίωσιν βελτίονος.

gions, such as Brahmanism, Buddhism, or Mohammedanism.   And yet what can be truer?   He must
be a man of little faith, who would fear to subject
his own religion to the same critical tests to which
the historian subjects all other religions.   We need
not surely crave a tender or merciful treatment for
that faith which we hold to be the only true one.
We should rather challenge for it the severest
tests and trials, as the sailor would for the good
ship to which he entrusts his own life, and the
lives of those who are most dear to him.   In the
Science of Religion, we can decline no comparisons,
nor claim any immunities for Christianity, as little
as the missionary can, when wrestling with the
subtle Brahman, or the fanatical Mussulman, or the
plain speaking Zulu.   And if we send out our
missionaries to every part of the world to face
every kind of religion, to shrink from no contest,
to be appalled by no objections, we must not give
way at home or within our own hearts to any
misgivings, lest a comparative study of the religions
of the world could shake the firm foundations on
which we must stand or fall.

To the missionary more particularly a comparative
study of the religions of mankind will be, I believe,
of the greatest assistance.   Missionaries are apt to
look upon all other religions as something totally
distinct from their own, as formerly they used to
describe the languages of barbarous nations as
something more like the twittering of birds than

the articulate speech of men.   The Science of Language has taught us that there is order and wisdom
in all languages, and that even the most degraded
jargons contain the ruins of former greatness and
beauty.   The Science of Religion, I hope, will produce
a similar change in our views of barbarous forms
of faith and worship; and missionaries, instead of
looking only for points of difference, will look out
more anxiously for any common ground, any spark
of the true light that may still be revived, any
altar that may be dedicated afresh to the true
God [5].

And even to us at home, a wider view of the
religious life of the world may teach many a useful lesson.   Immense as is the difference between
our own and all other religions of the world—and
few can know that difference who have not honestly

---

[5] Joguth Chundra Gangooly, a native convert, says: 'I know
from personal experience that the Hindu Scriptures have a great
deal of truth. . . . If you go to India, and examine the common
sayings of the people, you will be surprised to see what a splendid
religion the Hindu religion must be.   Even the most ignorant
women have proverbs that are full of the purest religion.   Now I
am not going to India to injure their feelings by saying, "Your
Scripture is all nonsense, is good for nothing ; anything outside the
Old and New Testament is a humbug."   No; I tell you I will
appeal to the Hindu philosophers, and moralists, and poets, at the
same time bringing to them my light, and reasoning with them in
the spirit of Christ.   That will be my work.'—'A Brief Account of
Joguth Chundra Gangooly, a Brahmin and a Convert to Christianity.   *Christian Reformer*, August, 1860.

examined the foundations of their own as well as
of other religions—the position which believers and
unbelievers occupy with regard to their various
forms of faith is very much the same all over the
world. The difficulties which trouble us, have
troubled the hearts and minds of men as far back
as we can trace the beginnings of religious life.
The great problems touching the relation of the
Finite to the Infinite, of the human mind as the
recipient, and of the Divine Spirit as the source
of truth, are old problems indeed; and while
watching their appearance in different countries,
and their treatment under varying circumstances,
we shall be able, I believe, to profit ourselves, both
by the errors which others committed before us,
and by the truth which they discovered. We shall
know the rocks that threaten every religion in this
changing and shifting world of ours, and having
watched many a storm of religious controversy
and many a shipwreck in distant seas, we shall face
with greater calmness and prudence the troubled
waters at home.

If there is one thing which a comparative study
of religions places in the clearest light, it is the
inevitable decay to which every religion is exposed.
It may seem almost like a truism, that no religion
can continue to be what it was during the lifetime
of its founder and its first apostles. Yet it is but
seldom borne in mind that without constant reforma-
tion, i.e. without a constant return to its fountain-

head, every religion, even the most perfect, nay
the most perfect on account of its very perfection,
more even than others, suffers from its contact
with the world, as the purest air suffers from the
mere fact of its being breathed.

Whenever we can trace back a religion to its
first beginnings, we find it free from many of the
blemishes that offend us in its later phases. The
founders of the ancient religions of the world, as
far as we can judge, were minds of a high stamp,
full of noble aspirations, yearning for truth, devoted
to the welfare of their neighbours, examples of purity
and unselfishness. What they desired to found upon
earth was but seldom realised, and their sayings, if
preserved in their original form, offer often a strange
contrast to the practice of those who profess to be
their disciples. As soon as a religion is established,
and more particularly when it has become the
religion of a powerful state, the foreign and worldly
elements encroach more and more on the original
foundation, and human interests mar the simplicity
and purity of the plan which the founder had conceived
in his own heart, and matured in his communings
with his God. Even those who lived with Buddha
misunderstood his words, and at the Great Council
which had to settle the Buddhist canon, Asoka,
the Indian Constantine had to remind the assembled
priests that 'what had been said by Buddha, that
alone was well said ;' and that certain works ascribed
to Buddha, as, for instance, the instruction given

to his son, Rāhula, were apocryphal, if not heretical[6].
With every century, Buddhism, when it was accepted by nations, differing as widely as Mongols
and Hindus, when its sacred writings were translated into languages as wide apart as Sanskrit
and Chinese, assumed widely different aspects, till
at last the Buddhism of the Shamans in the steppes
of Tatary is as different from the teaching of the
original *Samana*, as the Christianity of the leader
of the Chinese rebels is from the teaching of Christ.
If missionaries could show to the Brahmans, the
Buddhists, the Zoroastrians, nay, even to the Mohammedans, how much their present faith differs from
the faith of their forefathers and founders, if they
could place in their hands and read with them
in a kindly spirit the original documents on which
these various religions profess to be founded, and
enable them to distinguish between the doctrines
of their own sacred books and the additions of
later ages, an important advantage would be gained,
and the choice between Christ and other Masters
would be rendered far more easy to many a truth-
seeking soul. But for that purpose it is necessary
that we too should see the beam in our own eyes,
and learn to distinguish between the Christianity of
the nineteenth century and the religion of Christ.
If we find that the Christianity of the nineteenth
century does not win as many hearts in India and

---

[6] See Burnouf, 'Lotus de la bonne Loi,' Appendice, No. x. § 4.

China as it ought, let us remember that it was the
Christianity of the first century in all its dogmatic
simplicity, but with its overpowering love of God
and man, that conquered the world and superseded
religions and philosophies, more difficult to conquer
than the religious and philosophical systems of
Hindus and Buddhists. If we can teach something
to the Brahmans in reading with them their sacred
hymns, they too can teach us something when
reading with us the Gospel of Christ. Never shall
I forget the deep despondency of a Hindu convert,
a real martyr to his faith, who had pictured to himself from the pages of the New Testament what a
Christian country must be, and who when he came
to Europe found everything so different from what
he had imagined in his lonely meditations at Benares!
It was the Bible only that saved him from returning
to his old religion, and helped him to discern beneath
theological futilities, accumulated during nearly two
thousand years, beneath pharisaical hypocrisy, infidelity, and want of charity, the buried, but still
living seed, committed to the earth by Christ and
His Apostles. How can a missionary in such circumstances meet the surprise and questions of his
pupils, unless he may point to that seed, and tell
them what Christianity was meant to be; unless he
may show that like all other religions, Christianity,
too, has had its history; that the Christianity of
the nineteenth century is not the Christianity of the
Middle Ages, that the Christianity of the Middle

Ages was not that of the early Councils, that the Christianity of the early Councils was not that of the Apostles, and 'that what has been said by Christ, that alone was well said?'

The advantages, however, which missionaries and other defenders of the faith will gain from a comparative study of religions, though important hereafter, are not at present the chief object of these researches. In order to maintain their scientific character, they must be independent of all extraneous considerations : they must aim at truth, trusting that even unpalatable truths, like unpalatable medicine, will reinvigorate the system into which they enter. To those, no doubt, who value the tenets of their religion as the miser values his pearls and precious stones, thinking their value lessened if pearls and stones of the same kind are found in other parts of the world, the Science of Religion will bring many a rude shock ; but to the true believer, truth, wherever it appears, is welcome, nor will any doctrine seem the less true or the less precious, because it was seen, not only by Moses or Christ, but likewise by Buddha or Laotse. Nor should it be forgotten that while a comparison of ancient religions will certainly show that some of the most vital articles of faith are the common property of the whole of mankind, at least of all who seek the Lord, if haply they might feel after Him, and find Him, the same comparison alone can possibly teach us what is peculiar to Christianity, and what has secured to it that pre-eminent position which now it holds in spite of all obloquy. The gain will be greater than the loss, if loss there be, which I, at least, shall never admit.

There is a strong feeling, I know, in the minds of all people against any attempt to treat their own religion as a member of a class, and, in one sense, that feeling is perfectly justified. To each individual, his own religion, if he really believes in it, is something quite inseparable from himself, something unique, that cannot be compared to anything else, or replaced by anything else. Our own religion is, in that respect, something like our own language. In its form it may be like other languages; in its essence and in its relation to ourselves, it stands alone and admits of no peer or rival.

But in the history of the world, our religion, like our own language, is but one out of many; and in order to understand fully the position of Christianity in the history of the world, and its true place among the religions of mankind, we must compare it, not with Judaism only, but with the religious aspirations of the whole world, with all, in fact, that Christianity came either to destroy or to fulfil. From this point of view Christianity forms part, no doubt, of what people call profane history, but by that very fact, profane history ceases to be profane, and regains throughout that sacred character of which it had been deprived by a false distinction. The

ancient Fathers of the Church spoke on these subjects
with far greater freedom than we venture to use
in these days. Justin Martyr, in his 'Apology' (A.D.
139), has this memorable passage (Apol. i. 46): 'One
article of our faith then is, that Christ is the first
begotten of God, and we have already proved Him
to be the very Logos (or universal Reason), of which
mankind are all partakers; and therefore those who
live according to the Logos are Christians, notwithstanding they may pass with you for Atheists ; such
among the Greeks were Sokrates and Herakleitos, and
the like ; and such among the Barbarians were
Abraham, and Anan'as, and Azarias, and Misael, and
Elias, and many others, whose actions, nay whose
very names, I know, would be tedious to relate, and
therefore shall pass them over. So, on the other
side, those who have lived in former times in defiance
of the Logos or Reason, were evil, and enemies to
Christ and murderers of such as lived according to
the Logos ; but *they who have made or make the*

---

⁷ Τὸν Χριστὸν πρωτότοκον τοῦ Θεοῦ εἶναι ἐδιδάχθημεν, καὶ
προεμηνύσαμεν Λόγον ὄντα, οὗ πᾶν γένος ἀνθρώπων μετέσχε · καὶ οἱ
μετὰ Λόγου βιώσαντες Χριστιανοί εἰσι, κἂν ἄθεοι ἐνομίσθησαν, οἷον
ἐν Ἕλλησι μὲν Σωκράτης καὶ Ἡράκλειτος καὶ οἱ ὅμοιοι αὐτοῖς, ἐν
βαρβάροις δὲ Ἀβραὰμ καὶ Ἀνανίας καὶ Ἀζαρίας καὶ Μισαὴλ καὶ
Ἠλίας καὶ ἄλλοι πολλοί, ὧν τὰς πράξεις ἢ τὰ ὀνόματα καταλέγειν
μακρὸν εἶναι ἐπιστάμενοι, τανῦν παραιτούμεθα. ὥστε καὶ οἱ προ-
γενόμενοι ἄνευ Λόγου βιώσαντες, ἄχρηστοι καὶ ἐχθροὶ τῷ Χριστῷ ἦσαν,
καὶ φονεῖς τῶν μετὰ Λόγου βιούντων · οἱ δὲ μετὰ Λόγου βιώσαντες
καὶ βιοῦντες Χριστιανοὶ καὶ ἄφοβοι καὶ ἀτάραχοι ὑπάρχουσιν.

*Logos or Reason the rule of their actions are Chris-
tians*, and men without fear and trembling.

'God,' says Clement (200 A.D.), ' is the cause of all
that is good: only of some good gifts He is the primary
cause, as of the Old and New Testaments, of others
the secondary, as of (Greek) philosophy. But even
philosophy may have been given primarily by Him
to the Greeks, before the Lord had called the Greeks
also. For that philosophy, like a schoolmaster, has
guided the Greeks also, as the Law did Israel,
towards Christ. Philosophy, therefore, prepares and
opens the way to those who are made perfect by
Christ [8].'

And again : 'It is clear that the same God to
whom we owe the Old and New Testaments, gave
also to the Greeks their Greek philosophy by which
the Almighty is glorified among the Greeks [9].'

And Clement was by no means the only one who
spoke thus freely and fearlessly, though, no doubt,
his knowledge of Greek philosophy qualified him

---

[8] Clem. Alex. Strom. lib. I. cap. v. § 28. Πάντων μὲν γὰρ αἴτιος
τῶν καλῶν ὁ Θεός, ἀλλὰ τῶν μὲν κατὰ προηγούμενον, ὡς τῆς τε
διαθήκης τῆς παλαιᾶς καὶ τῆς νέας, τῶν δὲ κατ᾽ ἐπακολούθημα, ὡς
τῆς φιλοσοφίας· τάχα δὲ καὶ προηγουμένως τοῖς Ἕλλησιν ἐδόθη τότε
πρὶν ἢ τὸν κύριον καλέσαι καὶ τοὺς Ἕλληνας. Ἐπαιδαγώγει γὰρ καὶ
αὐτὴ τὸ Ἑλληνικὸν ὡς ὁ νόμος τοὺς Ἑβραίους εἰς Χριστόν. προ-
παρασκευάζει τοίνυν ἡ φιλοσοφία προοδοποιοῦσα τὸν ὑπὸ Χριστοῦ
τελειούμενον.
[9] Strom. lib. VI. cap. v. § 42. Πρὸς δὲ καὶ ὅτι ὁ αὐτὸς Θεὸς
ἀμφοῖν ταῖν διαθήκαιν χορηγὸς, ὁ καὶ τῆς Ἑλληνικῆς φιλοσοφίας
ἰστὴρ τοῖς Ἕλλησιν, δι᾽ ἧς ὁ παντοκράτωρ πῦρ· Ἕλλησι δοξάζεται,
παρέστησεν, δῆλον δὲ κἀνθένδε.

better than many of his contemporaries to speak
with authority on such subjects.

St. Augustine writes : ' If the Gentiles also had
possibly something divine and true in their doctrines,
our Saints did not find fault with it, although for
their superstition, idolatry, and pride, and other evil
habits, they had to be detested, and, unless they
improved, to be punished by divine judgment. For
the apostle Paul, when he said something about
God among the Athenians, quoted the testimony of
some of the Greeks who had said something of the
same kind : and this, if they came to Christ, would
be acknowledged in them, and not blamed. Saint
Cyprian, too, uses such witnesses against the Gentiles.
For when he speaks of the Magians, he says that
the chief among them, Hostanes, maintains that the
true God is invisible, and that true angels sit at
His throne ; and that Plato agrees with this, and
believes in One God, considering the others to be
angels or demons ; and that Hermes Trismegistus
also speaks of One God, and confesses that He is
incomprehensible.' (Augustinus, ' De Baptismo con-
tra Donatistas,' lib. VI, cap. xliv.)

Every religion, even the most imperfect and
degraded, has something that ought to be sacred
to us, for there is in all religions a secret yearning
after the true, though unknown, God. Whether we
see the Papua squatting in dumb meditation before
his fetish, or whether we listen to Firdusi exclaim-
ing : ' The height and the depth of the whole

world have their centre in Thee, O my God! I do not know Thee what Thou art: but I know that Thou art what Thou alone canst be,'—we ought to feel that the place whereon we stand is holy ground. There are philosophers, no doubt, to whom both Christianity and all other religions are exploded errors, things belonging to the past, and to be replaced by more positive knowledge. To them the study of the religions of the world could only have a pathological interest, and their hearts could never warm at the sparks of truth that light up, like stars, the dark yet glorious night of the ancient world. They tell us that the world has passed through the phases of religious and metaphysical errors, in order to arrive at the safe haven of positive knowledge of facts. But if they would but study positive facts, if they would but read, patiently and thoughtfully, the history of the world, as it is, not as it might have been: they would see that, as in geology, so in the history of human thought, theoretic uniformity does not exist, and that the past is never altogether lost. The oldest formations of thought crop out everywhere, and if we dig but deep enough, we shall find that even the sandy desert in which we are asked to live, rests everywhere on the firm foundation of that primeval, yet indestructible granite of the human soul,—religious faith.

There are other philosophers again who would fain narrow the limits of the Divine government of the world to the history of the Jewish and of the Christian nations, who would grudge the very name of religion to the ancient creeds of the world, and to whom the name of natural religion has almost become a term of reproach. To them, too, I should like to say that if they would but study positive facts, if they would but read their own Bible, they would find that the greatness of Divine Love cannot be measured by human standards, and that God has never forsaken a single human soul that has not first forsaken Him. 'He hath made of one blood all nations of men, for to dwell on all the face of the earth; and hath determined the times before appointed, and the bounds of their habitation: that they should seek the Lord, if haply they might feel after Him, and find Him, though He be not far from every one of us.' If they would but dig deep enough, they too would find that what they contemptuously call natural religion is in reality the greatest gift that God has bestowed on the children of man, and that without it, revealed religion itself would have no firm foundation, no living roots in the heart of man.

If by the essays here collected I should succeed in attracting more general attention towards an independent, yet reverent study of the ancient religions of the world, and in dispelling some of the prejudices with which so many have regarded the yearnings after truth embodied in the sacred writings of the Brahmans, the Zoroastrians, and the

Buddhists, in the mythology of the Greeks and
Romans, nay, even in the wild traditions and degraded customs of Polynesian savages, I shall consider myself amply rewarded for the labour which
they have cost me. That they are not free from
errors, in spite of a careful revision to which they
have been submitted before I published them in
this collection, I am fully aware, and I shall be
grateful to any one who will point them out, little
concerned whether it is done in a seemly or unseemly
manner, as long as some new truth is elicited, or
some old error effectually exploded. Though I have
thought it right in preparing these essays for publication, to alter what I could no longer defend as true,
and also, though rarely, to add some new facts that
seemed essential for the purpose of establishing what
I wished to prove, yet in the main they have been
left as they were originally published. I regret
that, in consequence, certain statements of facts and
opinions are repeated in different articles in almost
the same words ; but it will easily be seen that this
could not have been avoided without either breaking
the continuity of an argument, or rewriting large
portions of certain essays. If what is contained in
these repetitions is true and right, I may appeal to
a high authority 'that in this country true things
and right things require to be repeated a great many
times.' If otherwise, the very repetition will provoke criticism and ensure refutation. I have added
to all the articles the dates when they were written,

these dates ranging over the last fifteen years, and
I must beg my readers to bear these dates in mind
when judging both of the form and the matter of
these contributions towards a better knowledge of
the creeds and prayers, the legends and customs of
the ancient world.

M. M.

PARKS END, OXFORD:
October, 1867.

CONTENTS OF FIRST VOLUME.

———·———

I.

LECTURE ON THE VEDAS

SACRED BOOKS OF THE BRAHMANS,[1]

DELIVERED AT THE

PHILOSOPHICAL INSTITUTION, LEEDS, MARCH, 1865.

I HAVE brought with me one volume of my
edition of the Veda, and I should not wonder if
it were the first copy of the work which has ever
reached this busy town of Leeds. Nay, I confess
I have some misgivings that I may have undertaken a hopeless task, and I begin to doubt whether
I shall succeed in explaining to you the interest
which I feel for this ancient collection of sacred
hymns, an interest which has never failed me while
devoting to the publication of this voluminous work
the best twenty years of my life. Many times have
I been asked, But what is the Veda? Why should

---

[1] Some of the points touched upon in this Lecture have been
more fully treated in my 'History of Ancient Sanskrit Literature.'
As the second edition of this work has been out of print for several
years, I have here quoted a few passages from it in full.

VOL. I.   B

it be published? What are we likely to learn from
a book composed nearly four thousand years ago,
and intended from the beginning for an uncultivated
race of mere heathens and savages,—a book which
the natives of India have never published themselves,
although, to the present day, they profess to regard
it as the highest authority for their religion, morals,
and philosophy? Are we, the people of England or
of Europe, in the nineteenth century, likely to gain
any new light on religious, moral, or philosophical
questions from the old songs of the Brahmans? And
is it so very certain that the whole book is not a
modern forgery, without any substantial claims to
that high antiquity which is ascribed to it by the
Hindus, so that all the labour bestowed upon it
would not only be labour lost, but throw dis-
credit on our powers of discrimination, and make
us a laughing-stock among the shrewd natives of
India? These and similar questions I have had to
answer many times when asked by others, and some
of them when asked by myself, before embarking on
so hazardous an undertaking as the publication of
the Rig-veda and its ancient commentary. And, I
believe, I am not mistaken in supposing that many
of those who to-night have honoured me with their
presence may have entertained similar doubts and
misgivings when invited to listen to a Lecture ' On
the Vedas or the Sacred Books of the Brahmans.'

I shall endeavour, therefore, as far as this is possible within the limits of one Lecture, to answer some
of these questions, and to remove some of these doubts,
by explaining to you, first, what the Veda really is,
and, secondly, what importance it possesses, not only
to the·people of India, but to ourselves in Europe,—

and here again, not only to the student of Oriental
languages, but to every student of history, religion,
or philosophy; to every man who has once felt the
charm of tracing that mighty stream of human
thought on which we ourselves are floating onward,
back to its distant mountain-sources; to every one
who has a heart for whatever has once filled the hearts
of millions of human beings with their noblest hopes,
and fears, and aspirations;—to every student of mankind in the fullest sense of that full and weighty word.
Whoever claims that noble title must not forget,
whether he examines the highest achievements of
mankind in our own age, or the miserable failures of
former ages, what man is, and in whose image and
after whose likeness man was made. Whether listening
to the shrieks of the Shaman sorcerers of Tatary, or
to the odes of Pindar, or to the sacred songs of Paul
Gerhard: whether looking at the pagodas of China,
or the Parthenon of Athens, or the cathedral of
Cologne: whether reading the sacred books of the
Buddhists, of the Jews, or of those who worship God
in spirit and in truth, we ought to be able to say,
like the Emperor Maximilian, 'Homo sum, humani
nihil a me alienum puto,' or, translating his
words somewhat freely, 'I am a man, nothing per-
taining to man I deem foreign to myself.' Yes, we
must learn to read in the history of the whole human
race something of our own history; and as in looking
back on the story of our own life, we all dwell with
a peculiar delight on the earliest chapters of our
childhood, and try to find there the key to many of
the riddles of our later life, it is but natural that
the historian, too, should ponder with most intense
interest over the few relics that have been preserved

to him of the childhood of the human race. These
relics are few indeed, and therefore very precious, and
this I may venture to say, at the outset and without
fear of contradiction, that there exists no literary relic
that carries us back to a more primitive, or, if you like,
more childlike state in the history of man[2] than the
Veda. As the language of the Veda, the Sanskrit, is
the most ancient type of the English of the present
day, (Sanskrit and English are but varieties of one and
the same language,) so its thoughts and feelings contain in reality the first roots and germs of that intellectual growth which by an unbroken chain connects
our own generation with the ancestors of the Aryan
race,—with those very people who at the rising and
setting of the sun listened with trembling hearts
to the songs of the Veda, that told them of bright
powers above, and of a life to come after the sun of
their own lives had set in the clouds of the evening.
Those men were the true ancestors of our race ; and
the Veda is the oldest book we have in which to
study the first beginnings of our language, and of all
that is embodied in language. We are by nature
Aryan, Indo-European, not Semitic: our spiritual
kith and kin are to be found in India, Persia, Greece,
Italy, Germany; not in Mesopotamia, Egypt, or
Palestine. This is a fact that ought to be clearly
perceived, and constantly kept in view, in order to
understand the importance which the Veda has for
us, after the lapse of more than three thousand years,

---

[2] 'In the sciences of law and society, old means not old in chronology, but in structure: that is most archaic which lies nearest
to the beginning of human progress considered as a development,
and that is most modern which is farthest removed from that
beginning.'—J. F. McLennan, 'Primitive Marriage,' p. 8.

and after ever so many changes in our language,
thought, and religion.

Whatever the intrinsic value of the Veda, if it
simply contained the names of kings, the description
of battles, the dates of famines, it would still be, by
its age alone, the most venerable of books.   Do we
ever find much beyond such matters in Egyptian
hieroglyphics, or in Cuneiform inscriptions?   In fact,
what does the ancient history of the world before
Cyrus, before 500 B. C., consist of, but meagre lists of
Egyptian, Babylonian, Assyrian dynasties?   What do
the tablets of Karnak, the palaces of Nineveh, and
the cylinders of Babylon tell us about the thoughts
of men?   All is dead and barren, nowhere a sigh, nowhere a jest, nowhere a glimpse of humanity.   There
has been but one oasis in that vast desert of ancient
Asiatic history, the history of the Jews.   Another
such oasis is the Veda.   Here, too, we come to a
stratum of ancient thought, of ancient feelings, hopes,
joys, and fears,—of ancient religion.   There is perhaps
too little of kings and battles in the Veda, and
scarcely anything of the chronological framework of
history.   But poets surely are better than kings,
hymns and prayers are more worth listening to than
the agonies of butchered armies, and guesses at truth
more valuable than unmeaning titles of Egyptian or
Babylonian despots.   It will be difficult to settle
whether the Veda is ' the oldest of books,' and whether
some of the portions of the Old Testament may not
be traced back to the same or even an earlier date
than the oldest hymns of the Veda.   But, in the
Aryan world, the Veda is certainly the oldest book,
and its preservation amounts almost to a marvel.

It is nearly twenty years ago since my attention

was first drawn to the Veda, while attending, in
the years 1846 and 1847, the lectures of Eugène
Burnouf at the Collège de France. I was then
looking out, like most young men at that time of
life, for some great work, and without weighing
long the difficulties which had hitherto prevented
the publication of the Veda, I determined to devote
all my time to the collection of the materials necessary for such an undertaking. I had read the
principal works of the later Sanskrit literature, but
had found little there that seemed to be more than
curious. But to publish the Veda, a work that had
never before been published in India or in Europe,
that occupied in the history of Sanskrit literature
the same position which the Old Testament occupies
in the history of the Jews, the New Testament in
the history of modern Europe, the Koran in the
history of Mohammedanism,—a work which fills a
gap in the history of the human mind, and promises
to bring us nearer than any other work to the first
beginnings of Aryan language and Aryan thought,—
this seemed to me an undertaking not altogether
unworthy a man's life. What added to the charm
of it was that it had once before been undertaken
by Frederick Rosen, a young German scholar,
who died in England before he had finished the
first book, and that after his death no one seemed
willing to carry on his work. What I had to do,
first of all, was to copy not only the text, but the
commentary of the Rig-veda, a work which when
finished will fill six of these large volumes. The
author or rather the compiler of this commentary,
Sâyana Âkârya, lived about 1400 after Christ, that
is to say, about as many centuries after, as the poets

of the Veda lived before, the beginning of our era.
Yet through the 3000 years which separate the
original poetry of the Veda from the latest commentary, there runs an almost continuous stream
of tradition, and it is from it, rather than from
his own brain, that Sâyana draws his explanations
of the sacred texts. Numerous MSS., more or less
complete, more or less inaccurate, of Sâyana's classical
work, existed in the then Royal Library at Paris,
in the Library of the East-India House, then in
Leadenhall Street, and in the Bodleian Library at
Oxford. But to copy and collate these MSS. was
by no means all. A number of other works were
constantly quoted in Sâyana's commentary, and
these quotations had all to be verified. It was
necessary first to copy these works, and to make
indexes to all of them, in order to be able to find
any passage that might be referred to in the larger
commentary. Many of these works have since been
published in Germany and France, but they were
not to be procured twenty years ago. The work,
of course, proceeded but slowly, and many times
I doubted whether I should be able to carry it
through. Lastly came the difficulty,—and by no
means the smallest,—who was to publish a work
that would occupy about six thousand pages in
quarto, all in Sanskrit, and of which probably not
a hundred copies would ever be sold. Well, I came
to England in order to collect more materials at the
East-India House and at the Bodleian Library, and
thanks to the exertions of my generous friend Baron
Bunsen, and of the late Professor Wilson, the Board
of Directors of the East-India Company decided to
defray the expenses of a work which, as they stated

in their letter, 'is in a peculiar manner deserving of the patronage of the East-India Company, connected as it is with the early religion, history, and language of the great body of their Indian subjects.' It thus became necessary for me to take up my abode in England, which has since become my second home. The first volume was published in 1849, the second in 1853, the third in 1856, the fourth in 1862. The materials for the remaining volumes are ready, so that, if I can but make leisure, there is little doubt that before long the whole work will be complete.

Now, first, as to the name. Veda means originally knowing or knowledge, and this name is given by the Brahmans not to one work, but to the whole body of their most ancient sacred literature. Veda is the same word which appears in the Greek οἶδα, I know, and in the English wise, wisdom, to wit[3]. The name of Veda is commonly given to four collections of hymns, which are respectively known by the names of Rig-veda, Yagur-veda, Sâma-veda, and Atharva-veda; but for our own purposes, namely for tracing the earliest growth of religious ideas in India, the only important, the only real Veda, is the Rig-veda.

---

[3] Sanskrit	Greek	Gothic	Anglo-Saxon	German
véda	οἶδα	vait	wât	ich weiss
véttha	οἶσθα	vaist	wâst	du weisst
véda	οἶδε	vait	wât	er weiss
vidvá	—	vitu	—	—
vidáthuh	ἴστον	vituts	—	—
vidútuh	ἴστον	—	—	—
vidmá	ἴσμεν	vitum	witon	wir wissen
vidá	ἴστε	vituth	wite	ihr wisset
vidúh	ἴσασι	vitun	witan	sie wissen.

The other so-called Vedas, which deserve the name of Veda no more than the Talmud deserves the name of Bible, contain chiefly extracts from the Rig-veda, together with sacrificial formulas, charms, and incantations, many of them, no doubt, extremely curious, but never likely to interest any one except the Sanskrit scholar by profession.

The Yagur-veda and Sâma-veda may be described as prayer-books, arranged according to the order of certain sacrifices, and intended to be used by certain classes of priests.

Four classes of priests were required in India at the most solemn sacrifices:

1. The officiating priests, manual labourers, and acolytes; who have chiefly to prepare the sacrificial ground, to dress the altar, slay the victims, and pour out the libations.
2. The choristers, who chant the sacred hymns.
3. The reciters or readers, who repeat certain hymns.
4. The overseers or bishops, who watch and superintend the proceedings of the other priests, and ought to be familiar with all the Vedas.

The formulas and verses to be muttered by the first class are contained in the Yagur-veda-sanhitâ.

The hymns to be sung by the second class are in the Sâma-veda-sanhitâ.

The Atharva-veda is said to be intended for the Brahman or overseer, who is to watch the proceedings of the sacrifice, and to remedy any mistake that may occur[4].

Fortunately, the hymns to be recited by the third

---

[4] 'History of Ancient Sanskrit Literature,' p. 449.

class were not arranged in a sacrificial prayer-book,
but were preserved in an old collection of hymns,
containing all that had been saved of ancient, sacred,
and popular poetry, more like the Psalms than like
a ritual; a collection made for its own sake, and not
for the sake of any sacrificial performances.

I shall, therefore, confine my remarks to the Rig-
veda, which in the eyes of the historical student is
the Veda *par excellence*. Now Rig-veda means the
Veda of hymns of praise, for *Rich*, which before the
initial soft letter of Veda is changed to *Rig*, is derived
from a root which in Sanskrit means to celebrate.

In the Rig-veda we must distinguish again between the original collection of the hymns or Man-
tras, called the Sanhitâ or the collection, being
entirely metrical and poetical, and a number of prose
works, called Brâhmaṇas and Sûtras, written in
prose, and giving information on the proper use of
the hymns at sacrifices, on their sacred meaning, on
their supposed authors, and similar topics.   These
works, too, go by the name of Rig-veda: but though
very curious in themselves, they are evidently of a
much later period, and of little help to us in tracing
the beginnings of religious life in India.   For that
purpose we must depend entirely on the hymns, such
as we find them in the Sanhitâ or the collection of
the Rig-veda.

Now this collection consists of ten books, and
contains altogether 1028 hymns.   As early as about
600 B.C. we find that in the theological schools of
India every verse, every word, every syllable of the
Veda had been carefully counted.   The number of
verses as computed in treatises of that date, varies
from 10,402 to 10,622; that of the words is 153,826,

that of the syllables 432,000[5]. With these numbers, and with the description given in these early treatises of each hymn, of its metre, its deity, its number of verses, our modern MSS. of the Veda correspond as closely as could be expected.

I say, our modern MSS., for all our MSS. are modern, and very modern. Few Sanskrit MSS. are more than four or five hundred years old, the fact being that in the damp climate of India no paper will last for more than a few centuries. How then, you will naturally ask, can it be proved that the original hymns were composed between 1200 and 1500 before the Christian era, if our MSS. only carry us back to about the same date after the Christian era? It is not very easy to bridge over this gulf of nearly three thousand years, but all I can say is that, after carefully examining every possible objection that can be made against the date of the Vedic hymns, their claim to that high antiquity which is ascribed to them, has not, as far as I can judge, been shaken. I shall try to explain on what kind of evidence these claims rest.

You know that we possess no MS. of the Old Testament in Hebrew older than about the tenth century after the Christian era; yet the Septuagint translation by itself would be sufficient to prove that the Old Testament, such as we now read it, existed in MS. previous, at least, to the third century before our era. By a similar train of argument, the works to which I referred before, in which we find every hymn, every verse, every word and syllable of the Veda

---

[5] 'History of Ancient Sanskrit Literature,' second edition, p. 219 seq.

accurately counted by native scholars about five or six
hundred years before Christ, guarantee the existence
of the Veda, such as we now read it, as far back at least
as five or six hundred years before Christ. Now in
the works of that period, the Veda is already considered, not only as an ancient, but as a sacred book;
and, more than this, its language had ceased to be
generally intelligible. The language of India had
changed since the Veda was composed, and learned
commentaries were necessary in order to explain
to the people, then living, the true purport, nay,
the proper pronunciation, of their sacred hymns.
But more than this. In certain exegetical compositions, which are generally comprised under the
name of Sûtras, and which are contemporary
with, or even anterior to, the treatises on the theological statistics just mentioned, not only are the
ancient hymns represented as invested with sacred
authority, but that other class of writings, the
Brâhmanas, standing half-way between the hymns
and the Sûtras, have likewise been raised to the
dignity of a revealed literature. These Brâhmanas,
you will remember, are prose treatises, written in
illustration of the ancient sacrifices and of the hymns
employed at them. Such treatises would only spring
up when some kind of explanation began to be
wanted both for the ceremonial and for the hymns to
be recited at certain sacrifices, and we find, in consequence, that in many cases the authors of the Brâhmanas had already lost the power of understanding
the text of the ancient hymns in its natural and
grammatical meaning, and that they suggested the
most absurd explanations of the various sacrificial
acts, most of which, we may charitably suppose,

had originally some rational purpose. Thus it becomes evident that the period during which the
hymns were composed must have been separated by
some centuries, at least, from the period that gave
birth to the Brâhma*n*as, in order to allow time for
the hymns growing unintelligible and becoming invested with a sacred character. Secondly, the period
during which the Brâhma*n*as were composed must
be separated by some centuries from the authors
of the Sûtras, in order to allow time for further
changes in the language, and more particularly for
the growth of a new theology, which ascribed to
the Brâhma*n*as the same exceptional and revealed
character which the Brâhma*n*as themselves ascribed
to the hymns. So that we want previously to 600
B. C., when every syllable of the Veda was counted,
at least two strata of intellectual and literary growth,
of two or three centuries each; and are thus brought
to 1100 or 1200 B. C. as the earliest time when we
may suppose the collection of the Vedic hymns to
have been finished. This collection of hymns again
contains, by its own showing, ancient and modern
hymns, the hymns of the sons together with the
hymns of their fathers and earlier ancestors; so that
we cannot well assign a date more recent than 1200
to 1500 before our era, for the original composition
of those simple hymns which up to the present day
are regarded by the Brahmans with the same feelings
with which a Mohammedan regards the Koran, a Jew
the Old Testament, a Christian his Gospel.

That the Veda is not quite a modern forgery
can be proved, however, by more tangible evidence.
Iliouen-thsang, a Buddhist pilgrim, who travelled
from China to India in the years 629–645, and who,

in his diary translated from Chinese into French by
M. Stanislas Julien, gives the names of the four
Vedas, mentions some grammatical forms peculiar to
the Vedic Sanskrit, and states that at his time young
Brahmans spent all their time, from the seventh to
the thirtieth year of their age, in learning these
sacred texts. At the time when Hiouen-thsang was
travelling in India, Buddhism was clearly on the
decline. But Buddhism was originally a reaction
against Brahmanism, and chiefly against the exclusive
privileges which the Brahmans claimed, and which
from the beginning were represented by them as
based on their revealed writings, the Vedas, and
hence beyond the reach of human attacks. Buddhism,
whatever the date of its founder, became the state
religion of India under Asoka, the Constantine of
India, in the middle of the third century B. C. This
Asoka was the third king of a new dynasty founded
by Kandragupta, the well-known contemporary of
Alexander and Seleucus, about 315 B. C. The
preceding dynasty was that of the Nandas, and it
is under this dynasty that the traditions of the
Brahmans place a number of distinguished scholars
whose treatises on the Veda we still possess, such
as Saunaka, Kâtyâyana, Âsvalâyana, and others.
Their works, and others written with a similar object
and in the same style, carry us back to about 600
B. C. This period of literature, which is called the
Sûtra period, was preceded, as we saw, by another
class of writings, the Brâhmanas, composed in a
very prolix and tedious style, and containing lengthy
lucubrations on the sacrifices and on the duties of
the different classes of priests. Each of the three
or four Vedas, or each of the three or four classes of

priests, has its own Brâhmaṇas and its own Sûtras;
and as the Brâhmaṇas are presupposed by the Sûtras,
while no Sûtra is ever quoted by the Brâhmaṇas, it
is clear that the period of the Brâhmaṇa literature
must have preceded the period of the Sûtra literature.
There are, however, old and new Brâhmaṇas, and
there are in the Brâhmaṇas themselves long lists of
teachers who handed down old Brâhmaṇas or composed new ones, so that it seems impossible to accommodate the whole of that literature in less than two
centuries, from about 800 to 600 B. C. Before,
however, a single Brâhmaṇa could have been composed, it was not only necessary that there should
have been one collection of ancient hymns, like that
contained in the ten books of the Rig-veda, but the
three or four classes of priests must have been
established, the officiating priests and the choristers
must have had their special prayer-books, nay, these
prayer-books must have undergone certain changes,
because the Brâhmaṇas presuppose different texts,
called sâkhâs, of each of these prayer-books, which
are called the Yagur-veda-sanhitâ, the Sâma-veda-
sanhitâ, and the Atharva-veda-sanhitâ. The work of
collecting the prayers for the different classes of priests,
and of adding new hymns and formulas for purely
sacrificial purposes, belonged probably to the tenth
century B. C., and three generations more would, at
least, be required to account for the various readings
adopted in the prayer-books by different sects, and
invested with a kind of sacred authority, long before
the composition of even the earliest among the Brâhmaṇas. If, therefore, the years from about 1000
to 800 B. C. are assigned to this collecting age, the
time before 1000 B. C. must be set apart for the free

and natural growth of what was then national and
religious, but not yet sacred and sacrificial poetry.
How far back this period extends it is impossible
to tell; it is enough if the hymns of the Rig-veda
can be traced to a period anterior to 1000 B. C.

Much in the chronological arrangement of the
three periods of Vedic literature that are supposed
to have followed the period of the original growth of
the hymns, must of necessity be hypothetical, and has
been put forward rather to invite than to silence
criticism.   In order to discover truth, we must be
truthful ourselves, and must welcome those who
point out our errors as heartily as those who approve
and confirm our discoveries.   What seems, however,
to speak strongly in favour of the historical character
of the three periods of Vedic literature is the uniformity of style which marks the productions of each.
In modern literature we find, at one and the same
time, different styles of prose and poetry cultivated
by one and the same author.   A Goethe writes
tragedy, comedy, satire, lyrical poetry, and scientific
prose; but we find nothing like this in primitive
literature.   The individual is there much less prominent, and the poet's character disappears in the
general character of the layer of literature to which
he belongs.   It is the discovery of such large layers
of literature following each other in regular succession
which inspires the critical historian with confidence
in the truly historical character of the successive
literary productions of ancient India.   As in Greece
there is an epic age of literature, where we should
look in vain for prose or dramatic poetry; as in that
country we never meet with real elegiac poetry before
the end of the eighth century, nor with iambics

before the same date; as even in more modern times rhymed heroic poetry appears in England with the Norman conquest, and in Germany the Minnesänger rise and set with the Swabian dynasty—so, only in a much more decided manner, we see in the ancient and spontaneous literature of India, an age of poets followed by an age of collectors and imitators, that age to be succeeded by an age of theological prose writers, and this last by an age of writers of scientific manuals. New wants produced new supplies, and nothing sprang up or was allowed to live, in prose or poetry, except what was really wanted. If the works of poets, collectors, imitators, theologians, and teachers were all mixed up together—if the Brâhmaṇas quoted the Sûtras, and the hymns alluded to the Brâhmaṇas —an historical restoration of the Vedic literature of India would be almost an impossibility. We should suspect artificial influences, and look with small con- fidence on the historical character of such a literary agglomerate. But he who would question the anti- quity of the Veda must explain how the layers of literature were formed that are super-imposed over the original stratum of the poetry of the Rishis; he who would suspect a literary forgery must show how, when, and for what purpose the 1000 hymns of the Rig-veda could have been forged, and have become the basis of the religious, moral, political, and literary life of the ancient inhabitants of India.

The idea of revelation, and I mean more parti- cularly book-revelation, is not a modern idea, nor is it an idea peculiar to Christianity. Though we look for it in vain in the literature of Greece and Rome, we find the literature of India saturated with this idea from beginning to end. In no

country, I believe, has the theory of revelation
been so minutely elaborated as in India. The name
for revelation in Sanskrit is *Sr*uti, which means
hearing; and this title distinguishes the Vedic
hymns and, at a later time, the Brâhma*n*as also,
from all other works, which, however sacred and
authoritative to the Hindu mind, are admitted to
have been composed by human authors. The Laws
of Manu, for instance, according to the Brahmanic
theology, are not revelation; they are not *S*ruti,
but only Sm*r*iti, which means recollection or
tradition. If these laws or any other work of
authority can be proved on any point to be at
variance with a single passage of the Veda, their
authority is at once overruled. According to the
orthodox views of Indian theologians, not a single
line of the Veda was the work of human authors.
The whole Veda is in some way or other the work
of the Deity; and even those who received the
revelation, or, as they express it, those who saw
it, were not supposed to be ordinary mortals, but
beings raised above the level of common humanity,
and less liable therefore to error in the reception
of revealed truth. The views entertained of revelation by the orthodox theologians of India are far
more minute and elaborate than those of the most
extreme advocates of verbal inspiration in Europe.
The human element, called paurusheyatva in
Sanskrit, is driven out of every corner or hiding-
place, and as the Veda is held to have existed in
the mind of the Deity before the beginning of
time, every allusion to historical events, of which
there are not a few, is explained away with a zeal
and ingenuity worthy of a better cause.

But let me state at once that there is nothing in
the hymns themselves to warrant such extravagant
theories. In many a hymn the author says plainly
that he or his friends made it to please the
gods; that he made it, as a carpenter makes a
chariot (Rv. I. 130, 6 ; V. 2, 11), or like a beautiful
vesture (Rv. V. 29, 15); that he fashioned it in his
heart and kept it in his mind (Rv. I. 171, 2); that
he expects, as his reward, the favour of the god
whom he celebrates (Rv. IV. 6, 21). But though
the poets of the Veda know nothing of the
artificial theories of verbal inspiration, they were
not altogether unconscious of higher influences:
nay, they speak of their hymns as god-given
('devattam,' Rv. III. 37, 4). One poet says (Rv.
VI. 47, 10): 'O god (Indra) have mercy, give me
my daily bread! Sharpen my mind, like the edge
of iron. Whatever I now may utter, longing for
thee, do thou accept it; make me possessed of
God!' Another utters for the first time the famous
hymn, the Gâyatrî, which now for more than
three thousand years has been the daily prayer of
every Brahman, and is still repeated every morning
by millions of pious worshippers: 'Let us meditate
on the adorable light of the divine Creator: may
he rouse our minds[6].' This consciousness of higher
influences, or of divine help in those who uttered
for the first time the simple words of prayer, praise,
and thanksgiving, is very different, however, from

---

[6] 'Tat Savitur varenyam bhargo devasya dhîmahi, dhiyo yo nah
prakodayât.'— Colebrooke, 'Miscellaneous Essays,' i. 30. Many
passages bearing on this subject have been collected by Dr. Muir
in the third volume of his 'Sanskrit Texts,' p. 114 seq.

the artificial theories of verbal inspiration which we
find in the later theological writings; it is indeed
but another expression of that deep-felt dependence
on the Deity, of that surrender and denial of all
that seems to be self, which was felt more or less
by every nation, but by none, I believe, more
strongly, more constantly, than by the Indian. 'It
is He that has made it'—viz. the prayer in which
the soul of the poet has thrown off her burden—
is but a variation of, 'It is He that has made us,'
which is the key-note of all religion, whether ancient
or modern, whether natural or revealed.

I must say no more to-night of, what the Veda is,
for I am very anxious to explain to you, as far as it
is possible, what I consider to be the real importance
of the Veda to the student of history, to the student
of religion, to the student of mankind.

In the study of mankind there can hardly be a
subject more deeply interesting than the study of
the different forms of religion; and much as I
value the Science of Language for the aid which
it lends us in unravelling some of the most complicated tissues of the human intellect, I confess
that to my mind there is no study more absorbing
than that of the Religions of the World:—the study,
if I may so call it, of the various languages in which
man has spoken to his Maker, and of that language
in which his Maker 'at sundry times and in divers
manners' spake to man.

To my mind the great epochs in the world's
history are marked, not by the foundation or the
destruction of empires, by the migrations of races,
or by French revolutions. All this is outward
history, made up of events that seem gigantic and

overpowering to those only who cannot see beyond
and beneath.   The real history of man is the history
of religion: the wonderful ways by which the different families of the human race advanced towards
a truer knowledge and a deeper love of God.   This
is the foundation that underlies all profane history:
it is the light, the soul, and life of history, and without it all history would indeed be profane.

On this subject there are some excellent works in
English, such as Mr. Maurice's ' Lectures on the Religions of the World,' or Mr. Hardwick's ' Christ and
other Masters;' in German I need only mention Hegel's
' Philosophy of Religion,' out of many other learned
treatises on the different systems of religion in the East
and the West.   But in all these works religions are
treated very much as languages were treated during the
last century.   They are rudely classed, either according
to the different localities in which they prevailed, just
as in Adelung's ' Mithridates ' you find the languages
of the world classified as European, African, American,
Asiatic, &c.; or according to their age, as formerly
languages used to be divided into ancient and
modern; or according to their respective dignity,
as languages used to be treated as sacred or profane,
as classical or illiterate.   Now you know that the
Science of Language has sanctioned a totally different system of classification; and that the Comparative Philologist ignores altogether the division
of languages according to their locality, or according to their age, or according to their classical or
illiterate character.   Languages are now classified
genealogically, i. e. according to their real relationship; and the most important languages of Asia,
Europe, and Africa, that is to say, of that part of

the world on which what we call the history of
man has been acted, have been grouped together
into three great divisions, the Aryan or Indo-
European Family, the Semitic Family, and the
Turanian Class. According to that division you
are aware that English together with all the
Teutonic languages of the Continent, Celtic,
Slavonic, Greek, Latin, with its modern offshoots,
such as French and Italian, Persian, and Sanskrit,
are so many varieties of one common type of speech:
that Sanskrit, the ancient language of the Veda, is
no more distinct from the Greek of Homer, or from
the Gothic of Ulfilas, or from the Anglo-Saxon of
Alfred, than French is from Italian. All these languages together form one family, one whole, in which
every member shares certain features in common
with all the rest, and is at the same time distinguished from the rest by certain features peculiarly
its own. The same applies to the Semitic Family,
which comprises, as its most important members,
the Hebrew of the Old Testament, the Arabic of
the Koran, and the ancient languages on the monuments of Phenicia and Carthage, of Babylon and
Assyria. These languages, again, form a compact
family, and differ entirely from the other family,
which we called Aryan or Indo-European. The third
group of languages, for we can hardly call it a family,
comprises most of the remaining languages of Asia,
and counts among its principal members the Tun-
gusic, Mongolic, Turkic, Samoyedic, and Finnic, together with the languages of Siam, the Malay Islands,
Tibet, and Southern India. Lastly, the Chinese language stands by itself, as monosyllabic, the only remnant of the earliest formation of human speech.

Now I believe that the same division which has introduced a new and natural order into the history of languages, and has enabled us to understand the growth of human speech in a manner never dreamt of in former days, will be found applicable to a scientific study of religions. I shall say nothing to-night of the Semitic or Turanian or Chinese religions, but confine my remarks to the religions of the Aryan family. These religions, though more important in the ancient history of the world, as the religions of the Greeks and Romans, of our own Teutonic ancestors, and of the Celtic and Slavonic races, are nevertheless of great importance even at the present day. For although there are no longer any worshippers of Zeus, or Jupiter, of Wodan, Esus[7], or Perkunas[8], the two religions of Aryan origin which still survive, Brahmanism and Buddhism, claim together a decided majority among the inhabitants of the globe. Out of the whole population of the world,

> 31.2 per cent are Buddhists,
> 13.4 per cent are Brahmanists,
> ‾‾‾‾
> 44.6

which together gives us 44 per cent for what may be called living Aryan religions. Of the remaining 56 per cent, 15.7 are Mohammedans, 8.7 per cent non-descript Heathens, 30.7 per cent Christians, and only 0.3 per cent Jews.

---

[7] Mommsen, 'Inscriptiones Helveticae,' 40. Becker, 'Die in-schriftlichen Überreste der Keltischen Sprache,' in ' Beiträge zur Vergleichenden Sprachforschung,' vol. iii. p. 341. Lucan, Phars. 1, 445, ' horrensque feris altaribus Hesus.'

[8] Cf. G. Bühler, 'Über Parjanya,' in Benfey's 'Orient und Occident,' vol. i. p. 214. In the Old Irish, arg, a drop, has been pointed out as derived from the same root as parganya.

Now, as a scientific study of the Aryan languages became possible only after the discovery of Sanskrit, a scientific study of the Aryan religion dates really from the discovery of the Veda. The study of Sanskrit brought to light the original documents of three religions, the Sacred Books of the Brahmans, the Sacred Books of the Magians, the followers of Zoroaster, and the Sacred Books of the Buddhists. Fifty years ago, these three collections of sacred writings were all but unknown, their very existence was doubted, and there was not a single scholar who could have translated a line of the Veda, a line of the Zend-Avesta, or a line of the Buddhist Tripitaka. At present large portions of these, the canonical writings of the most ancient and most important religions of the Aryan race, are published and deciphered, and we begin to see a natural progress, and almost a logical necessity, in the growth of these three systems of worship. The oldest, most primitive, most simple form of Aryan faith finds its expression in the Veda. The Zend-Avesta represents in its language, as well as in its thoughts, a branching off from that more primitive stem; a more or less conscious opposition to the worship of the gods of nature, as adored in the Veda, and a striving after a more spiritual, supreme, moral deity, such as Zoroaster proclaimed under the name of Ahura mazda, or Ormuzd. Buddhism, lastly, marks a decided schism, a decided antagonism against the established religion of the Brahmans, a denial of the true divinity of the Vedic gods, and a proclamation of new philosophical and social doctrines.

Without the Veda, therefore, neither the reforms of Zoroaster nor the new teaching of Buddha would

have been intelligible: we should not know what was
behind them, or what forces impelled Zoroaster and
Buddha to the founding of new religions; how much
they received, how much they destroyed, how much
they created. Take but one word in the religious
phraseology of these three systems. In the Veda
the gods are called Deva. This word in Sanskrit
means bright,—brightness or light being one of the
most general attributes shared by the various manifestations of the Deity, invoked in the Veda, as Sun,
or Sky, or Fire, or Dawn, or Storm. We can see, in
fact, how in the minds of the poets of the Veda, deva,
from meaning bright, came gradually to mean divine.
In the Zend-Avesta the same word daêva means
evil spirit. Many of the Vedic gods, with Indra at
their head, have been degraded to the position of
daêvas, in order to make room for Ahura mazda,
the Wise Spirit, as the supreme deity of the Zoroastrians. In his confession of faith the follower of
Zoroaster declares: 'I cease to be a worshipper of
the daêvas.' In Buddhism, again, we find these
ancient Devas, Indra and the rest, as merely legendary
beings, carried about at shows, as servants of Buddha,
as goblins or fabulous heroes; but no longer either
worshipped or even feared by those with whom the
name of Deva had lost every trace of its original
meaning. Thus this one word Deva marks the
mutual relations of these three religions. But more
than this. The same word deva is the Latin deus,
thus pointing to that common source of language
and religion, far beyond the heights of the Vedic
Olympus, from which the Romans, as well as the
Hindus, draw the names of their deities, and the elements of their language as well as of their religion.

The Veda, by its language and its thoughts, supplies that distant background in the history of all the religions of the Aryan race, which was missed indeed by every careful observer, but which formerly could be supplied by guess-work only. How the Persians came to worship Ormuzd, how the Buddhists came to protest against temples and sacrifices, how Zeus and the Olympian gods came to be what they are in the mind of Homer, or how such beings as Jupiter and Mars came to be worshipped by the Italian peasant:—all these questions, which used to yield material for endless and baseless speculations, can now be answered by a simple reference to the hymns of the Veda. The religion of the Veda is not the source of all the other religions of the Aryan world, nor is Sanskrit the mother of all the Aryan languages. Sanskrit, as compared to Greek and Latin, is an elder sister, not a parent: Sanskrit is the earliest deposit of Aryan speech, as the Veda is the earliest deposit of Aryan faith. But the religion and incipient mythology of the Veda possess the same simplicity and transparency which distinguish the grammar of Sanskrit from Greek, Latin, or German grammar. We can watch in the Veda ideas and their names growing, which in Persia, Greece, and Rome we meet with only as full-grown or as fast decaying. We get one step nearer to that distant source of religious thought and language which has fed the different national streams of Persia, Greece, Rome, and Germany; and we begin to see clearly, what ought never to have been doubted, that there is no religion without God, or, as St. Augustine expressed it, that 'there is no false religion which does not contain some elements of truth.'

I do not wish by what I have said to raise any
exaggerated expectations as to the worth of these
ancient hymns of the Veda, and the character of
that religion which they indicate rather than fully
describe. The historical importance of the Veda can
hardly be exaggerated, but its intrinsic merit, and
particularly the beauty or elevation of its sentiments,
have by many been rated far too high. Large numbers of the Vedic hymns are childish in the extreme:
tedious, low, common-place. The gods are constantly
invoked to protect their worshippers, to grant them
food, large flocks, large families, and a long life; for
all which benefits they are to be rewarded by the
praises and sacrifices offered day after day, or at certain seasons of the year. But hidden in this rubbish
there are precious stones. Only in order to appreciate
them justly, we must try to divest ourselves of the
common notions about Polytheism, so repugnant not
only to our feelings, but to our understanding. No
doubt, if we must employ technical terms, the religion
of the Veda is Polytheism, not Monotheism. Deities
are invoked by different names, some clear and intelligible, such as Agni, fire; Sûrya, the sun;
Ushas, dawn; Maruts, the storms; Prithivî, the
earth; Âp, the waters; Nadî, the rivers: others
such as Varuna, Mitra, Indra, which have become
proper names, and disclose but dimly their original
application to the great aspects of nature, the
sky, the sun, the day. But whenever one of these
individual gods is invoked, they are not conceived
as limited by the powers of others, as superior or
inferior in rank. Each god is to the mind of the
supplicant as good as all gods. He is felt, at the
time, as a real divinity,—as supreme and absolute,—

without a suspicion of those limitations which, to our mind, a plurality of gods must entail on every single god. All the rest disappear for a moment from the vision of the poet, and he only who is to fulfil their desires stands in full light before the eyes of the worshippers. In one hymn, ascribed to Manu, the poet says: 'Among you, O gods, there is none that is small, none that is young; you are all great indeed.' And this is indeed the key-note of the ancient Aryan worship. Yet it would be easy to find in the numerous hymns of the Veda, passages in which almost every important deity is represented as supreme and absolute. Thus in one hymn, Agni (fire) is called 'the ruler of the universe,' 'the lord of men,' 'the wise king, the father, the brother, the son, the friend of man;' nay, all the powers and names of the other gods are distinctly ascribed to Agni. But though Agni is thus highly exalted, nothing is said to disparage the divine character of the other gods. In another hymn another god, Indra, is said to be greater than all: 'The gods,' it is said, 'do not reach thee, Indra, nor men; thou overcomest all creatures in strength.' Another god, Soma, is called the king of the world, the king of heaven and earth, the conqueror of all. And what more could human language achieve, in trying to express the idea of a divine and supreme power, than what another poet says of another god, Varuna: 'Thou art lord of all, of heaven and earth; thou art the king of all, of those who are gods, and of those who are men?'

This surely is not what is commonly understood by Polytheism. Yet it would be equally wrong to call it Monotheism. If we must have a name for it, I should call it Kathenotheism. The con-

sciousness that all the deities are but different names
of one and the same godhead breaks forth indeed
here and there in the Veda. But it is far from being
general. One poet, for instance, says (Rv. I. 164, 46):
' They call him Indra, Mitra, Varuna, Agni; then he
is the beautiful-winged heavenly Garutmat : that
which is One the wise call it in divers manners:
they call it Agni, Yama, Mâtarisvan.' And again, Rv.
X. 114, 5: ' Wise poets make the beautiful-winged,
though he is one, manifold by words.'

I shall read you a few Vedic verses, in which the
religious sentiment predominates, and in which we
perceive a yearning after truth, and after the true
God, untrammeled as yet by any names or any traditions (Rv. X. 121)[9]:

1. In the beginning there arose the golden Child—
He was the one born lord of all that is. He stublished
the earth, and this sky;—Who is the God to whom
we shall offer our sacrifice?

2. He who gives life, He who gives strength;
whose command all the bright gods revere; whose
shadow is immortality, whose shadow is death;—
Who is the God to whom we shall offer our sacrifice?

3. He who through His power is the one king
of the breathing and awakening world;—He who
governs all, man and beast;—Who is the God to
whom we shall offer our sacrifice?

4. He whose greatness these snowy mountains,
whose greatness the sea proclaims, with the distant
river—He whose these regions are, as it were His
two arms;—Who is the God to whom we shall offer
our sacrifice?

<hr>

[9] 'History of Ancient Sanskrit Literature,' p. 569.

5. He through whom the sky is bright and the earth firm—He through whom the heaven was stablished,—nay, the highest heaven,—He who measured out the light in the air;—Who is the God to whom we shall offer our sacrifice?

6. He to whom heaven and earth, standing firm by His will, look up, trembling inwardly—He over whom the rising sun shines forth;—Who is the God to whom we shall offer our sacrifice?

7. Wherever the mighty water-clouds went, where they placed the seed and lit the fire, thence arose He who is the sole life of the bright gods;—Who is the God to whom we shall offer our sacrifice?

8. He who by His might looked even over the water-clouds, the clouds which gave strength and lit the sacrifice; He who alone is God above all gods;—Who is the God to whom we shall offer our sacrifice?

9. May He not destroy us—He the creator of the earth; or He, the righteous, who created the heaven; He also created the bright and mighty waters;—Who is the God to whom we shall offer our sacrifice[10]?

The following may serve as specimens of hymns addressed to individual deities whose names have become the centres of religious thought and legendary traditions; deities, in fact, like Jupiter, Apollo, Mars, or Minerva, no longer mere germs, but fully developed forms of early thought and language:

---

[10] A last verse is added, which entirely spoils the poetical beauty and the whole character of the hymn. Its later origin seems to have struck even native critics, for the author of the Pada text did not receive it. 'O Pragâpati, no other than thou hast embraced all these created things; may what we desired when we called on thee, be granted to us, may we be lords of riches.'

HYMN TO INDRA (Rv. I. 53)[11].

1. Keep silence well[12]! we offer praises to the great Indra in the house of the sacrificer. Does he find treasure for those who are like sleepers? Mean praise is not valued among the munificent.

2. Thou art the giver of horses, Indra, thou art the giver of cows, the giver of corn, the strong lord of wealth: the old guide of man, disappointing no desires, a friend to friends:—to him we address this song.

3. O powerful Indra, achiever of many works, most brilliant god—all this wealth around here is known to be thine alone: take from it, conqueror! bring it hither! Do not stint the desire of the worshipper who longs for thee!

4. On these days thou art gracious, and on these

---

[11] I subjoin for some of the hymns here translated, the translation of the late Professor Wilson, in order to show what kind of difference there is between the traditional rendering of the Vedic hymns, as adopted by him, and their interpretation according to the rules of modern scholarship:

1. We ever offer fitting praise to the mighty Indra, in the dwelling of the worshipper, by which he (the deity) has quickly acquired riches, as (a thief) hastily carries (off the property) of the sleeping. Praise ill expressed is not valued among the munificent.

2. Thou, Indra, art the giver of horses, of cattle, of barley, the master and protector of wealth, the foremost in liberality, (the being) of many days; thou disappointest not desires (addressed to thee); thou art a friend to our friends: such an Indra we praise.

3. Wise and resplendent Indra, the achiever of great deeds, the riches that are spread around are known to be thine: having collected them, victor (over thy enemies), bring them to us: disappoint not the expectation of the worshipper who trusts in thee.

4. Propitiated by these offerings, by these libations, dispel

[12] Favete linguis.

·nights [13], keeping off the enemy from our cows and from our stud.   Tearing [14] the fiend night after night with the help of Indra, let us rejoice in food, freed from haters.

5. Let us rejoice, Indra, in treasure and food, in wealth of manifold delight and splendour.   Let us rejoice in the blessing of the gods, which gives us the strength of offspring, gives us cows first and horses.

6. These draughts inspired thee, O lord of the brave! these were vigour, these libations, in battles, when for the sake of the poet, the sacrificer, thou struckest down irresistibly ten thousands of enemies.

7. From battle to battle [15] thou advancest bravely, from town to town thou destroyest all this with might, when thou, Indra, with Nâmi as thy friend, struckest down from afar the deceiver Namuki.

---

poverty with cattle and horses: may we, subduing our adversary, and relieved from enemies by Indra, (pleased) by our libations, enjoy together abundant food.

5. Indra, may we become possessed of riches, and of food; and with energies agreeable to many, and shining around, may we prosper through thy divine favour, the source of prowess, of cattle, and of horses.

6. Those who were thy allies, (the Maruts,) brought thee joy: protector of the pious, those libations and oblations (that were offered thee on slaying Vritra), yielded thee delight, when thou, unimpeded by foes, didst destroy the ten thousand obstacles opposed to him who praised thee and offered thee libations.

7. Humiliator (of adversaries), thou goest from battle to battle, and destroyest by thy might city after city: with thy foe-prostrating associate, (the thunderbolt,) thou, Indra, didst slay afar off the deceiver named Namuki.

[13] Cf. Rv. I. 112, 25, 'dyúbhir aktúbhih,' by day and by night; also Rv. III. 31, 16. M. M., 'Todtenbestattung,' p. v.

[14] Professor Benfey reads durayantah, but all MSS. that I know, without exception, read darayantah.

[15] For a different translation see Roth, in 'Deutsche Monatsschrift,' p. 89.

8. Thou hast slain Karñaga and Parñaya with the brightest spear of Atithigva. Without a helper thou didst demolish the hundred cities of Vañgrida, which were besieged by *Ri*gisvan.

9. Thou hast felled down with the chariot-wheel these twenty kings of men, who had attacked the friendless Su*s*ravas[16], and gloriously the sixty thousand and ninety-nine forts.

10. Thou, Indra, hast succoured Su*s*ravas with thy succours, Tûrvayâ*na* with thy protections. Thou hast made Kutsa, Atithigva, and Âyu subject to this mighty youthful king.

11. We who in future, protected by the gods, wish to be thy most blessed friends, we shall praise thee, blessed by thee with offspring, and enjoying henceforth a longer life.

The next hymn is one of many addressed to Agni as the god of fire, not only the fire as a powerful element, but likewise the fire of the hearth and the altar, the guardian of the house, the minister of the sacrifice, the messenger between gods and men:

8. Thou hast slain Karñiga and Par*n*aya with thy bright gleaming spear, in the cause of Atithigva: unaided, thou didst demolish the hundred cities of Va*ñ*grida, when besieged by *Ri*gisvan.

9. Thou, renowned Indra, overthrewest by thy not-to-be-overtaken chariot-wheel, the twenty kings of men, who had come against Su*s*ravas, unaided, and their sixty thousand and ninety and nine followers.

10. Thou, Indra, hast preserved Su*s*ravas by thy succour, Tûrva-yâ*na* by thy assistance: thou hast made Kutsa, Atithigva, and Âyu subject to the mighty though youthful Su*s*ravas.

11. Protected by the gods, we remain, Indra, at the close of the sacrifice, thy most fortunate friends: we praise thee, as enjoying through thee excellent offspring, and a long and prosperous life.

[16] See Spiegel, 'Erân,' p. 269, on Khai Khosru=Su*s*ravas.

Hymn to Agni (Rv. II. 6).

1. Agni, accept this log which I offer to thee, accept this my service; listen well to these my songs.

2. With this log, O Agni, may we worship thee, thou son of strength, conqueror of horses! and with this hymn, thou high-born!

3. May we thy servants serve thee with songs, O granter of riches, thou who lovest songs and delightest in riches.

4. Thou lord of wealth and giver of wealth, be thou wise and powerful; drive away from us the enemies!

5. He gives us rain from heaven, he gives us inviolable strength, he gives us food a thousandfold.

6. Youngest of the gods, their messenger, their invoker, most deserving of worship, come, at our praise, to him who worships thee and longs for thy help.

7. For thou, O sage, goest wisely between these two creations (heaven and earth, gods and men), like a friendly messenger between two hamlets.

8. Thou art wise, and thou hast been pleased; perform thou, intelligent Agni, the sacrifice without interruption, sit down on this sacred grass!

The following hymn, partly laudatory, partly deprecatory, is addressed to the Maruts or Rudras, the Storm-gods:

Hymn to the Maruts (Rv. I. 39)[17].

1. When you thus from afar cast forward your measure, like a blast of fire, through whose wisdom is

---

[17] Professor Wilson translates as follows:

1. When, Maruts, who make (all things) tremble, you direct your awful (vigour) downwards from afar, as light (descends from heaven),

it, through whose design? To whom do you go, to whom, ye shakers (of the earth)?

2. May your weapons be firm to attack, strong also to withstand! May yours be the more glorious strength, not that of the deceitful mortal!

3. When you overthrow what is firm, O ye men, and whirl about what is heavy, ye pass through the trees of the earth, through the clefts of the rocks.

4. No real foe of yours is known in heaven, nor in earth, ye devourers of enemies! May strength be yours, together with your race, O Rudras, to defy even now.

5. They make the rocks to tremble, they tear asunder the kings of the forest. Come on, Maruts, like madmen, ye gods, with your whole tribe.

6. You have harnessed the spotted deer to your chariots, a red deer draws as leader. Even the earth listened at your approach, and men were frightened.

---

by whose worship, by whose praise (are you attracted)? To what (place of sacrifice), to whom, indeed, do you repair?

2. Strong be your weapons for driving away (your) foes, firm in resisting them: yours be the strength that merits praise, not (the strength) of a treacherous mortal.

3. Directing Maruts, when you demolish what is stable, when you scatter what is ponderous, then you make your way through the forest (trees) of earth and the defiles of the mountains.

4. Destroyers of foes, no adversary of yours is known above the heavens, nor (is any) upon earth: may your collective strength be quickly exerted, sons of Rudra, to humble (your enemies).

5. They make the mountains tremble, they drive apart the forest trees. Go, divine Maruts, whither you will, with all your progeny, like those intoxicated.

6. You have harnessed the spotted deer to your chariot; the red deer yoked between them, (aids to) drag the car: the firmament listens for your coming, and men are alarmed.

7. O Rudras, we quickly desire your help for our race. Come now to us with help, as of yore, thus for the sake of the frightened Kanva.

8. Whatever fiend, roused by you or roused by mortals, attacks us, tear him from us by your power, by your strength, by your aid.

9. For you, worshipful and wise, have wholly protected Kanva. Come to us, Maruts, with your whole help, as quickly as lightnings come after the rain.

10. Bounteous givers, ye possess whole strength, whole power, ye shakers (of the earth). Send, O Maruts, against the proud enemy of the poets, an enemy, like an arrow.

The following is a simple prayer addressed to the Dawn:

Hymn to Ushas (Rv. VII. 77).

1. She shines upon us, like a young wife, rousing every living being to go to his work. When the fire had to be kindled by men, she made the light by striking down darkness.

2. She rose up, spreading far and wide, and moving everywhere. She grew in brightness, wearing her brilliant garment. The mother of the cows, (the

---

7. Rudras, we have recourse to your assistance for the sake of our progeny: come quickly to the timid Kanva, as you formerly came, for our protection.

8. Should any adversary, instigated by you, or by man, assail us, withhold from him food and strength and your assistance.

9. Praketasas, who are to be unreservedly worshipped, uphold (the sacrificer) Kanva: come to us, Maruts, with undivided protective assistances, as the lightnings (bring) the rain.

10. Bounteous givers, you enjoy unimpaired vigour: shakers (of the earth), you possess undiminished strength: Maruts, let loose your anger, like an arrow, upon the wrathful enemy of the Rishis.

mornings) the leader of the days, she shone gold-coloured, lovely to behold.

3. She, the fortunate, who brings the eye of the gods, who leads the white and lovely steed (of the sun), the Dawn was seen revealed by her rays, with brilliant treasures, following every one.

4. Thou who art a blessing where thou art near, drive far away the unfriendly; make the pasture wide, give us safety! Scatter the enemy, bring riches! Raise up wealth to the worshipper, thou mighty Dawn.

5. Shine for us with thy best rays, thou bright Dawn, thou who lengthenest our life, thou the love of all, who givest us food, who givest us wealth in cows, horses, and chariots.

6. Thou daughter of the sky, thou high-born Dawn, whom the Vasish*th*as magnify with songs, give us riches high and wide: all ye gods protect us always with your blessings.

I must confine myself to shorter extracts, in order to be able to show to you that all the principal elements of real religion are present in the Veda. I remind you again that the Veda contains a great deal of what is childish and foolish, though very little of what is bad and objectionable. Some of its poets ascribe to the gods sentiments and passions unworthy of the deity, such as anger, revenge, delight in material sacrifices; they likewise represent human nature on a low level of selfishness and worldliness. Many hymns are utterly unmeaning and insipid, and we must search patiently before we meet, here and there, with sentiments that come from the depth of the soul, and with prayers in which we could join our-

selves.   Yet there are such passages, and they are
the really important passages, as marking the highest
points to which the religious life of the ancient poets
of India had reached; and it is to these that I shall
now call your attention.

First of all, the religion of the Veda knows of no
idols.   The worship of idols in India is a secondary
formation, a later degradation of the more primitive
worship of ideal gods.

The gods of the Veda are conceived as immortal:
passages in which the birth of certain gods is mentioned have a physical meaning: they refer to the
birth of the day, the rising of the sun, the return of
the year.

The gods are supposed to dwell in heaven, though
several of them, as, for instance, Agni, the god of fire,
are represented as living among men, or as approach-
ing the sacrifice, and listening to the praises of their
worshippers.

Heaven and earth are believed to have been made or
to have been established by certain gods.   Elaborate
theories of creation, which abound in the later works,
the Brâhmanas, are not to be found in the hymns.
What we find are such passages as :

' Agni held the earth, he stablished the heaven by
truthful words' (Rv. I. 67, 3).

' Varuna stemmed asunder the wide firmaments;
he lifted on high the bright and glorious heaven; he
stretched out apart the starry sky and the earth'
(Rv. VII. 86, 1).

More frequently, however, the poets confess their
ignorance of the beginning of all things, and one of
them exclaims :

' Who has seen the first-born? Where was the life,

the blood, the soul of the world? Who went to ask this from any that knew it?' (Rv. I. 164, 4)[18].

Or again, Rv. X. 81, 4: 'What was the forest, what was the tree out of which they shaped heaven and earth? Wise men, ask this indeed in your mind, on what he stood when he held the worlds?

I now come to a more important subject. We find in the Veda, what few would have expected to find there, the two ideas, so contradictory to the human understanding, and yet so easily reconciled in every human heart: God has established the eternal laws of right and wrong, he punishes sin and rewards virtue, and yet the same God is willing to forgive; just, yet merciful; a judge, and yet a father. Consider, for instance, the following lines, Rv. I. 41, 4: 'His path is easy and without thorns, who does what is right.'

And again, Rv. I. 41, 9: 'Let man fear Him who holds the four (dice), before he throws them down (i. e. God who holds the destinies of men in his hand); let no man delight in evil words!'

And then consider the following hymns, and imagine the feelings which alone could have prompted them:

HYMN TO VARUNA (Rv. VII. 89).

1. Let me not yet, O Varuna, enter into the house of clay; have mercy, almighty, have mercy!

2. If I go along trembling, like a cloud driven by the wind; have mercy, almighty, have mercy!

3. Through want of strength, thou strong and bright god, have I gone wrong; have mercy, almighty, have mercy!

---

[18] 'History of Ancient Sanskrit Literature,' p. 20, note.

4. Thirst came upon the worshipper, though he stood in the midst of the waters; have mercy, almighty, have mercy!

5. Whenever we men, O Varuna, commit an offence before the heavenly host, whenever we break the law through thoughtlessness; punish us not, O god, for that offence.

And again, Rv. VII. 86:

1. Wise and mighty are the works of him who stemmed asunder the wide firmaments (heaven and earth). He lifted on high the bright and glorious heaven; he stretched out apart the starry sky and the earth.

2. Do I say this to my own self? How can I get unto Varuna? Will he accept my offering without displeasure? When shall I, with a quiet mind, see him propitiated?

3. I ask, O Varuna, wishing to know this my sin. I go to ask the wise. The sages all tell me the same: Varuna it is who is angry with thee.

4. Was it an old sin, O Varuna, that thou wishest to destroy thy friend, who always praises thee? Tell me, thou unconquerable lord, and I will quickly turn to thee with praise, freed from sin.

5. Absolve us from the sins of our fathers, and from those which we committed with our own bodies. Release Vasishtha, O king, like a thief who has feasted on stolen oxen; release him like a calf from the rope.

6. It was not our own doing, O Varuna, it was necessity (or temptation), an intoxicating draught, passion, dice, thoughtlessness. The old is there to mislead the young; even sleep brings unrighteousness.

7. Let me without sin give satisfaction to the

angry god, like a slave to his bounteous lord. The lord god enlightened the foolish; he, the wisest, leads his worshipper to wealth.

8. O lord Varuna, may this song go well to thy heart! May we prosper in keeping and acquiring! Protect us, O gods, always with your blessings!

The consciousness of sin is a prominent feature in the religion of the Veda, so is likewise the belief that the gods are able to take away from man the heavy burden of his sins. And when we read such passages as 'Varuna is merciful even to him who has committed sin' (Rv. VII. 87, 7), we should surely not allow the strange name of Varuna to jar on our ears, but should remember that it is but one of the many names which men invented in their helplessness to express their ideas of the Deity, however partial and imperfect.

The next hymn, which is taken from the Atharvaveda (IV. 16), will show how near the language of the ancient poets of India may approach to the language of the Bible [19]:

1. The great lord of these worlds sees as if he were near. If a man thinks he is walking by stealth, the gods know it all.

2. If a man stands or walks or hides, if he goes to lie down or to get up, what two people sitting together whisper, King Varuna knows it, he is there as the third.

3. This earth, too, belongs to Varuna, the king, and this wide sky with its ends far apart. The two

---

[19] This hymn was first pointed out by Professor Roth in a dissertation on the Atharva-veda (Tübingen, 1856), and it has since been translated and annotated by Dr. Muir, in his article on the 'Vedic Theogony and Cosmogony,' p. 31.

seas (the sky and the ocean) are Varuna's loins; he
is also contained in this small drop of water.

4. He who should flee far beyond the sky, even
he would not be rid of Varuna, the king.   His spies
proceed from heaven towards this world; with thousand eyes they overlook this earth.

5. King Varuna sees all this, what is between
heaven and earth, and what is beyond.   He has
counted the twinklings of the eyes of men.   As a
player throws the dice, he settles all things.

6. May all thy fatal nooses, which stand spread out
seven by seven and threefold, catch the man who tells
a lie, may they pass by him who tells the truth.

Another idea which we find in the Veda is that of
faith: not only in the sense of trust in the gods, in
their power, their protection, their kindness, but in
that of belief in their existence.   The Latin word
credo, I believe, is the same as the Sanskrit sraddhâ, and this sraddhâ occurs in the Veda:

Rv. I. 102, 2. 'Sun and moon go on in regular
succession, that we may see, Indra, and believe.'

Rv. I. 104, 6. 'Destroy not our future offspring,
O Indra, for we have believed in thy great power.'

Rv. I. 55, 5. 'When Indra hurls again and again his
thunderbolt, then they believe in the brilliant god[20].'

---

[20] During violent thunderstorms the natives of New Holland are
so afraid of War-ru-gu-ra, the evil spirit, that they seek shelter
even in caves haunted by Ingnas, subordinate demons, which at
other times they would enter on no account.   There, in silent terror, they prostrate themselves with their faces to the ground, wait-
ing until the spirit, having expended his fury, shall retire to Uta
(hell) without having discovered their hiding-place.—'Transactions
of Ethnological Society,' vol. iii. p. 229.   Oldfield, 'The Aborigines
of Australia.'

A similar sentiment, namely, that men only
believe in the gods when they see their signs and
wonders in the sky, is expressed by another poet
(Rv. VIII. 21, 14):

'Thou, Indra, never findest a rich man to be thy
friend; wine-swillers despise thee.   But when thou
thunderest, when thou gatherest (the clouds), then
thou art called, like a father.'

And with this belief in god, there is also coupled
that doubt, that true scepticism, if we may so call
it, which is meant to give to faith its real strength.
We find passages even in these early hymns where
the poet asks himself, whether there is really such
a god as Indra,—a question immediately succeeded
by an answer, as if given to the poet by Indra
himself.   Thus we read Rv. VIII. 100, 3:

'If you wish for strength, offer to Indra a hymn
of praise: a true hymn, if Indra truly exist; for
some one says, Indra does not exist!   Who has
seen him?   Whom shall we praise?'

Then Indra answers through the poet:

'Here I am, O worshipper, behold me here! in
might I surpass all things.'

Similar visions occur elsewhere, where the poet,
after inviting a god to a sacrifice, or imploring his
pardon for his offences, suddenly exclaims that he
has seen the god, and that he feels that his prayer is
granted.   For instance:

HYMN TO VARUNA (Rv. I. 25).

1. However we break thy laws from day to day,
men as we are, O god, Varuna,

2. Do not deliver us unto death, nor to the blow
of the furious; nor to the wrath of the spiteful!

3. To propitiate thee, O Varuna, we unbend thy mind with songs, as the charioteer a weary steed.

4. Away from me they flee dispirited, intent only on gaining wealth; as birds to their nests.

5. When shall we bring hither the man, who is victory to the warriors; when shall we bring Varuna, the wide-seeing, to be propitiated?

[6. They (Mitra and Varuna) take this in common; gracious, they never fail the faithful giver.]

7. He who knows the place of the birds that fly through the sky, who on the waters knows the ships;—

8. He, the upholder of order, who knows the twelve months with the offspring of each, and knows the month that is engendered afterwards;—

9. He who knows the track of the wind, of the wide, the bright, the mighty; and knows those who reside on high;—

10. He, the upholder of order, Varuna, sits down among his people; he, the wise, sits there to govern.

11. From thence perceiving all wondrous things, he sees what has been and what will be done.

12. May he, the wise Áditya, make our paths straight all our days; may he prolong our lives!

13. Varuna, wearing golden mail, has put on his shining cloak; the spies sat down around him.

14. The god whom the scoffers do not provoke, nor the tormentors of men, nor the plotters of mischief;—

15. He, who gives to men glory, and not half glory, who gives it even to our own selves;—

16. Yearning for him, the far-seeing, my thoughts move onwards, as kine move to their pastures.

17. Let us speak together again, because my honey has been brought: that thou mayst eat what thou likest, like a friend.

18. Did I see the god who is to be seen by all, did I see the chariot above the earth ? He must have accepted my prayers.

19. O hear this my calling, Varuna, be gracious now; longing for help, I have called upon thee.

20. Thou, O wise god, art lord of all, of heaven and earth: listen on thy way.

21. That I may live, take from me the upper rope, loose the middle, and remove the lowest!

In conclusion, let me tell you that there is in the Veda no trace of metempsychosis or that transmigration of souls from human to animal bodies which is generally supposed to be a distinguishing feature of Indian religion. Instead of this, we find what is really the sine quâ non of all real religion, a belief in immortality, and in personal immortality. Without a belief in personal immortality, religion surely is like an arch resting on one pillar, like a bridge ending in an abyss. We cannot wonder at the great difficulties felt and expressed by bishop Warburton and other eminent divines, with regard to the supposed total absence of the doctrine of immortality or personal immortality in the Old Testament; and it is equally startling that the Sadducees who sat in the same council with the high-priest, openly denied the resurrection[21]. However, though not expressly asserted anywhere, a belief in personal immortality is taken for granted in several passages of the Old Testament, and we can hardly think of Abraham or Moses as without a belief in life and immortality. But while this difficulty, so keenly felt with regard to the Jewish religion, ought to

---

[21] Acts xxii. 30, xxiii. 6.

make us careful in the judgments which we form of
other religions, and teach us the wisdom of charitable
interpretation, it is all the more important to mark
that in the Veda passages occur where immortality
of the soul, personal immortality and personal respon-
sibility after death, are clearly proclaimed.   Thus we
read :

'He who gives alms goes to the highest place in
heaven; he goes to the gods' (Rv. I. 125, 56).

Another poet, after rebuking those who are rich
and do not communicate, says:

'The kind mortal is greater than the great in
heaven!'

Even the idea, so frequent in the later literature of
the Brahmans, that immortality is secured by a son,
seems implied, unless our translation deceives us,
in one passage of the Veda, VII. 56, 24:—'Asmé
(íti) vira*h* maruta*h* sushmí astu *g*ánânâm yá*h* ásura*h*
vi dhartá, apá*h* yéna su-kshitáye tárema, ádha svâm
óka*h* abhí vah syâma.'   'O Maruts, may there be to us
a strong son, who is a living ruler of men: through
whom we may cross the waters on our way to the
happy abode;   then   may   we   come   to   your   own
house!'

One poet prays that he may see again his father
and mother after death (Rv. I. 24, 1); and the fathers
(Pit*r*is) are invoked almost like gods, oblations are
offered to them, and they are believed to enjoy, in
company with the gods, a life of never ending felicity
(Rv. X. 15, 16).

We find this prayer addressed to Soma (Rv. IX.113,7):
'Where there is eternal light, in the world where
the sun is placed, in that immortal imperishable
world place me, O Soma!

' Where king Vaivasvata reigns, where the secret
place of heaven is, where these mighty waters are,
there make me immortal!

' Where life is free, in the third heaven of heavens,
where the worlds are radiant, there make me immortal!

' Where wishes and desires are, where the bowl of
the bright Soma is, where there is food and rejoicing,
there make me immortal!

' Where there is happiness and delight, where joy
and pleasure reside, where the desires of our desire
are attained, there make me immortal[22]!'

Whether the old Rishis believed likewise in a
place of punishment for the wicked, is more doubtful,
though vague allusions to it occur in the Rig-veda, and
more distinct descriptions are found in the Atharva-
veda.   In one verse it is said that the dead is rewarded for his good deeds, that he leaves or casts off all
evil, and glorified takes his new body (Rv. X. 14,8)[23].
The dogs of Yama, the king of the departed, present
some terrible aspects, and Yama is asked to protect
the departed from them (Rv. X. 14, 11).   Again, a
pit (karta) is mentioned into which the lawless

---

[22] Professor Roth, after quoting several passages from the Veda
in which a belief in immortality is expressed, remarks with great
truth : 'We here find, not without astonishment, beautiful conceptions on immortality expressed in unadorned language with childlike conviction.   If it were necessary, we might here find the most
powerful weapons against the view which has lately been revived,
and proclaimed as new, that Persia was the only birthplace of the idea
of immortality, and that even the nations of Europe had derived it
from that quarter.   As if the religious spirit of every gifted race was
not able to arrive at it by its own strength.'—(' Journal of the
German Oriental Society,' vol. iv. p. 427.)   See Dr. Muir's article
on Yama, in the ' Journal of the Royal Asiatic Society,' p. 10.

[23] M. M., Die Todtenbestattung bei den Brahmanen, ' Zeitschrift
der Deutschen Morgenländischen Gesellschaft,' vol. ix. p. xii.

are said to be hurled down (Rv. IX. 73, 8), and into
which Indra casts those who offer no sacrifices (Rv. I.
121, 13). One poet prays that the Âdityas may preserve him from the destroying wolf, and from falling
into the pit (Rv. II, 29, 6). In one passage we read
that ' those who break the commandments of Varuna
and who speak lies are born for that deep place ' (Rv.
IV. 5, 5)[24].

Surely the discovery of a religion like this, as
unexpected as the discovery of the jaw-bone of Abbe-
ville, deserves to arrest our thoughts for a moment,
even in the haste and hurry of this busy life. No
doubt for the daily wants of life, the old division of
religions into true and false is quite sufficient; as for
practical purposes we distinguish only between our own
mother-tongue on the one side, and all other foreign
languages on the other. But, from a higher point of
view, it would not be right to ignore the new evidence
that has come to light; and as the study of geology
has given us a truer insight into the stratification of
the earth, it is but natural to expect that a thoughtful
study of the original works of three of the most important religions of the world, Brahmanism, Magism,
and Buddhism, will modify our views as to the
growth or history of religion, as to the hidden layers
of religious thought beneath the soil on which we
stand. Such inquiries should be undertaken without
prejudice and without fear: the evidence is placed
before us; our duty is to sift it critically, to weigh it
honestly, and to wait for the results.

Three of these results, to which, I believe, a comparative study of religions is sure to lead, I may
state before I conclude this Lecture.

---

[24] Dr. Muir, article on Yama, p. 18.

1. We shall learn that religions in their most ancient form, or in the minds of their authors, are generally free from many of the blemishes that attach to them in later times.

2. We shall learn that there is hardly one religion which does not contain some truth, some important truth; truth sufficient to enable those who seek the Lord and feel after Him, to find Him in their hour of need.

3. We shall learn to appreciate better than ever what we have in our own religion. No one who has not examined patiently and honestly the other religions of the world, can know what Christianity really is, or can join with such truth and sincerity in the words of St. Paul: 'I am not ashamed of the Gospel of Christ.'

II.

CHRIST AND OTHER MASTERS[1].

IN so comprehensive a work as Mr. Hardwick's
'Christ and other Masters,' the number of facts
stated, of topics discussed, of questions raised, is so
considerable that in reviewing it we can select only
one or two points for special consideration. Mr.
Hardwick intends to give in his work, of which the
third volume has just been published, a complete
panorama of ancient religion. After having discussed
in the first volume what he calls the religious tendencies of our age, he enters upon an examination of
the difficult problem of the unity of the human race,
and proceeds to draw, in a separate chapter, the
characteristic features of religion under the Old
Testament. Having thus cleared his way, and established some of the principles according to which
the religions of the world should be judged, Mr.
Hardwick devotes the whole of the second volume
to the religions of India. We find there, first of all,

---

[1] 'Christ and other Masters.' An Historical Inquiry into some of
the chief Parallelisms and Contrasts between Christianity and the
Religious Systems of the Ancient World, with special reference to
prevailing Difficulties and Objections. By Charles Hardwick, M.A.,
Christian Advocate in the University of Cambridge. Parts I, II, III.
Cambridge, 1858.

a short but very clear account of the religion of the
Veda, as far as it is known at present. We then
come to a more matter-of-fact representation of Brahmanism, or the religion of the Hindus, as represented
in the so-called Laws of Manu, and in the ancient
portions of the two epic poems, the Râmâyana and
Mahâbhârata. The next chapter is devoted to the
various systems of Indian philosophy, which all
partake more or less of a religious character, and
form a natural transition to the first subjective
system of faith in India, the religion of Buddha.
Mr. Hardwick afterwards discusses, in two separate
chapters, the apparent and the real correspondences
between Hinduism and revealed religion, and throws
out some hints how we may best account for the
partial glimpses of truth which exist in the Vedas,
the canonical books of Buddhism, and the later
Purânas. All these questions are handled with such
ability, and discussed with so much elegance and
eloquence, that the reader becomes hardly aware of
the great difficulties of the subject, and carries away,
if not quite a complete and correct, at least a very
lucid, picture of the religious life of ancient India.
The third volume, which was published in the beginning of this year, is again extremely interesting,
and full of the most varied descriptions. The religions of China are given first, beginning with an
account of the national traditions, as collected and
fixed by Confucius. Then follows the religious
system of Laotse, or the Tao-ism of China, and lastly
Buddhism again, only under that modified form which
it assumed when introduced from India into China.
After this sketch of the religious life of China,
the most ancient centre of Eastern civilisation,

Mr. Hardwick suddenly transports us to the New
World, and introduces us to the worship of the wild
tribes of America, and to the ruins of the ancient temples in which the civilised races of that continent,
especially the Mexicans, once bowed themselves down
before their god or gods.   Lastly, we have to embark
on the South Sea, and to visit the various islands
which form a chain between the west coast of
America and the east coast of Africa, stretching over
half of the globe, and inhabited by the descendants
of the once united race of the Malayo-Polynesians.

The account which Mr. Hardwick can afford to give
of the various systems of religion in so short a com-
pass as he has fixed for himself, must necessarily be
very general; and his remarks on the merits and
defects peculiar to each, which were more ample in
the second volume, have dwindled down to much
smaller dimensions in the third.   He declares distinctly that he does not write for missionaries.   'It
is not my leading object,' he says, 'to conciliate the
more thoughtful minds of heathendom in favour of
the Christian faith.   However laudable that task
may be, however fitly it may occupy the highest and
the keenest intellect of persons who desire to further
the advance of truth and holiness among our heathen
fellow-subjects, there are difficulties nearer home which
may in fairness be regarded as possessing prior claims
on the attention of a Christian Advocate.'

We confess that we regret that Mr. Hardwick should
have taken this line.   If, in writing his criticism on
the ancient or modern systems of Pagan religion, he
had placed himself face to face with a poor helpless
creature, such as the missionaries have to deal with
—a man brought up in the faith of his fathers,

accustomed to call his god or gods by names sacred
to him from his first childhood—a man who had
derived much real help and consolation from his
belief in these gods—who had abstained from com-
mitting crime, because he was afraid of the anger of
a Divine Being—who had performed severe penance,
because he hoped to appease the anger of the gods—
who had given, not only the tenth part of all he
valued most, but the half, nay, the whole of his
property, as a free offering to his priests, that they
might pray for him or absolve him from his sin—if,
in discussing any of the ancient or modern systems
of pagan religion, Mr. Hardwick had tried to address
his arguments to such a person, we believe he would
himself have felt a more human, real, and hearty
interest in his subject. He would more earnestly have
endeavoured to find out the good elements in every
form of religious belief. No sensible missionary
could bring himself to tell a man who has done all
that he could do, and more than many who have
received the true light of the Gospel, that he was
excluded from all hope of salvation, and by his very
birth and colour handed over irretrievably to eternal
damnation. It is possible to put a charitable interpretation on many doctrines of ancient heathenism,
and the practical missionary is constantly obliged to
do so. Let us only consider what these doctrines
are. They are not theories devised by men who
wish to keep out the truth of Christianity, but
sacred traditions which millions of human beings
are born and brought up to believe in, as we are
born and brought up to believe in Christianity. It
is the only spiritual food which God in his wisdom
has placed within their reach. But if we once begin

to think of modern heathenism, and how certain
tenets of Laotse resemble the doctrines of Comte or
Spinoza, our equanimity, our historical justice, our
Christian charity, are gone. We become advocates
wrangling for victory—we are no longer tranquil
observers, compassionate friends and teachers. Mr.
Hardwick sometimes addresses himself to men like
Laotse or Buddha, who are now dead and gone more
than two thousand years, in a tone of offended orthodoxy, which may or may not be right in modern controversy, but which entirely disregards the fact that it has
pleased God to let these men and millions of human
beings be born on earth without a chance of ever
hearing of the existence of the Gospel. We cannot
penetrate into the secrets of the Divine wisdom, but
we are bound to believe that God has His purpose
in all things, and that He will know how to judge
those to whom so little has been given. Christianity
does not require of us that we should criticise, with
our own small wisdom, that Divine policy which
has governed the whole world from the very beginning. We pity a man who is born blind—we are
not angry with him ; and Mr. Hardwick, in his
arguments against the tenets of Buddha or Laotse,
seems to us to treat these men too much in the
spirit of a policeman who tells a poor blind beggar
that he is only shamming blindness. However, if,
as a Christian Advocate, Mr. Hardwick found it
impossible to entertain, or at least express, any
sympathy with the Pagan world, even the cold
judgment of the historian would have been better
than the excited pleading of a partisan. Surely it
is not necessary, in order to prove that our religion
is the only true religion, that we should insist

on the utter falseness of all other forms of belief. We need not be frightened if we discover traces of truth, traces even of Christian truth, among the sages and lawgivers of other nations. St. Augustine was not frightened by this discovery, and every thoughtful Christian will feel cheered by the words of that pious philosopher, when he boldly declares, that there is no religion which, among its many errors, does not contain some real and divine truth. It shows a want of faith in God, and in His in-scrutable wisdom in the government of the world, if we think we ought to condemn all ancient forms of faith, except the religion of the Jews. A true spirit of Christianity will rather lead us to shut our eyes against many things which are revolting to us in the religion of the Chinese, or the wild Americans, or the civilised Hindus, and to try to discover, as well as we can, how even in these degraded forms of worship a spark of light lies hidden somewhere— a spark which may lighten and warm the heart of the Gentiles, 'who by patient continuance in well-doing, seek for glory, and honour, and immortality.' There is an undercurrent of thought in Mr. Hard-wick's book which breaks out again and again, and which has certainly prevented him from discovering many a deep lesson which may be learnt in the study of ancient religions. He uses harsh language, because he is thinking, not of the helpless Chinese, or the dreaming Hindu whose tenets he controverts, but of modern philosophers; and he is evidently glad of every opportunity where he can show to the latter that their systems are mere *rechauffés* of ancient heathenism. Thus he says, in his introduction to the third volume:

'I may also be allowed to add, that, in the present

chapters, the more thoughtful reader will not fail to recognise the proper tendency of certain current speculations, which are recommended to us on the ground that they accord entirely with the last discoveries of science, and embody the deliberate verdicts of the oracle within us. Notwithstanding all that has been urged in their behalf, those theories are little more than a return to long-exploded errors, a resuscitation of extinct volcanoes; or at best, they merely offer to introduce among us an array of civilising agencies, which, after trial in other countries, have been all found wanting. The governing class of China, for example, have long been familiar with the metaphysics of Spinoza. They have also carried out the social principles of M. Comte upon the largest possible scale. For ages they have been what people of the present day are wishing to become in Europe, with this difference only, that the heathen legislator who had lost all faith in God attempted to redress the wrongs and elevate the moral status of his subjects by the study of political science, or devising some new scheme of general sociology; while the positive philosopher of the present day, who has relapsed into the same positions, is in every case rejecting a religious system which has proved itself the mightiest of all civilisers, and the constant champion of the rights and dignity of men. He offers in the stead of Christianity a specious phase of paganism, by which the nineteenth century after Christ may be assimilated to the golden age of Mencius and Confucius; or, in other words, may consummate its religious freedom, and attain the highest pinnacle of human progress, by reverting to a state of childhood and of moral imbecility.'

Few serious-minded persons will like the temper of
this paragraph. The history of ancient religion is too
important, too sacred a subject to be used as a masked
battery against modern infidelity. Nor should a Christian Advocate ever condescend to defend his cause by
arguments such as a pleader who is somewhat sceptical as to the merits of his case, may be allowed to
use, but which produce on the mind of the Judge the
very opposite effect of that which they are intended
to produce. If we want to understand the religions
of antiquity, we must try, as well as we can, to enter
into the religious, moral, and political atmosphere of
the ancient world. We must do what the historian
does. We must become ancients ourselves, otherwise
we shall never understand the motives and meaning
of their faith. Take one instance. There are some
nations who have always regarded death with the .
utmost horror. Their whole religion may be said to
be a fight against death, and the chief object of
their prayers seems to be a long life on earth. The
Persian clings to life with intense tenacity, and the
same feeling exists among the Jews. Other nations,
on the contrary, regard death in a different light.
Death is to them a passage from one life to another.
No misgiving has ever entered their minds as to a
possible extinction of existence, and at the first call of
the priest—nay, sometimes from a mere selfish yearning after a better life—they are ready to put an end
to their existence on earth. Feelings of this kind
can hardly be called convictions arrived at by the
individual. They are national peculiarities, and they
exercise an irresistible sway over all who belong to
the same nation. The loyal devotion which the
Slavonic nations feel for their sovereign will make

the most brutalized Russian peasant step into the
place where his comrade has just been struck down,
without a thought of his wife, or his mother, or his
children, whom he is never to see again. He does not
do this because, by his own reflection, he has arrived
at the conclusion that he is bound to sacrifice himself
for his emperor or for his country—he does it because
he knows that every one would do the same; and the
only feeling of satisfaction in which he would allow
himself to indulge is, that he was doing his duty. If,
then, we wish to understand the religions of the ancient
nations of the world, we must take into account their
national character.   Nations who value life so little
as the Hindus, and some of the American and Malay
nations, could not feel the same horror of human
sacrifices, for instance, which would be felt by a Jew;
and the voluntary death of the widow would inspire
her nearest relations with no other feeling but that of
compassion and regret at seeing a young bride follow
her husband into a distant land.   She herself would
feel that, in following her husband into death, she
was only doing what every other widow would do—
she was only doing her duty.   In India, where men in
the prime of life throw themselves under the car of
Jaggernâth, to be crushed to death by the idol they
believe in—where the plaintiff who cannot get redress
starves himself to death at the door of his judge—
where the philosopher who thinks he has learnt all
which this world can teach him, and who longs for
absorption into the Deity, quietly steps into the
Ganges, in order to arrive at the other shore of existence—in such a country, however much we may
condemn these practices, we must be on our guard
and not judge the strange religions of such strange

creatures according to our own more sober code of
morality. Let a man once be impressed with a
belief that this life is but a prison, and that he has
but to break through its walls in order to breathe
the fresh and pure air of a higher life—let him once
consider it cowardice to shrink from this act, and a
proof of courage and of a firm faith in God to rush
back to that eternal source from whence he came—
and let these views be countenanced by a whole
nation, sanctioned by priests, and hallowed by poets,
and however we may blame and loathe the custom of
human sacrifices and religious suicides, we shall be
bound to confess that to such a man, and to a whole
nation of such men, the most cruel rites will have a
very different meaning from what they would have
to us. They are not mere cruelty and brutality.
They contain a religious element, and presuppose a
belief in immortality, and an indifference with regard
to worldly pleasures, which, if directed in a different
channel, might produce martyrs and heroes. Here,
at least, there is no danger of modern heresy aping
ancient paganism; and we feel at liberty to express
our sympathy and compassion, even with the most
degraded of our brethren. The Fijians, for instance,
commit almost every species of atrocity; but we can
still discover, as Wilkes remarked in his 'Exploring
Expedition,' that the source of many of their abhor-
rent practices is a belief in a future state, guided
by no just notions of religious or moral obligations.
They immolate themselves; they think it right to
destroy their best friends, to free them from the
miseries of this life; they actually consider it a duty,
and perhaps a painful duty, that the son should
strangle his parents, if requested to do so. Some of

the Fijians, when interrupted by Europeans in the act
of strangling their mother, simply replied that she
was their mother, and they were her children, and
, they ought to put her to death.   On reaching the
grave the mother sat down, when they all, including
children, grandchildren, relations, and friends, took
an affectionate leave of her.   A rope, made of twisted
tapa, was then passed twice around her neck by her
sons, who took hold of it and strangled her—after
which she was put into her grave, with the usual
ceremonies.   They returned to feast and mourn, after
which she was entirely forgotten, as though she had
not existed.   No doubt these are revolting rites; but
the phase of human thought which they disclose is
far from being simply revolting.   There is in these
immolations, even in their most degraded form, a
grain of that superhuman faith which we admire in
the temptation of Abraham; and we feel that the
time will come, nay, that it is coming, when the
voice of the Angel of the Lord will reach those
distant islands, and give a higher and better purpose
to the wild ravings of their religion.

It is among these tribes that the missionary, if he
can speak a language which they understand, gains
the most rapid influence.   But he must first learn
himself to understand the nature of these savages,
and to translate the wild yells of their devotion into
articulate language.   There is, perhaps, no race of
men so low and degraded as the Papuas.   It has
frequently been asserted they had no religion at all.
And yet these same Papuas, if they want to know
whether what they are going to undertake is right
or wrong, squat before their karwar, clasp the
hands over the forehead, and bow repeatedly, at the

same time stating their intentions. If they are seized with any nervous feeling during this process, it is considered as a bad sign, and the project is abandoned for a time—if otherwise, the idol is supposed to approve. Here we have but to translate what they in their helpless language call 'nervous feeling' by our word 'conscience,' and we shall not only understand what they really mean, but confess, perhaps, that it would be well for us if in our own hearts the karwar occupied the same prominent place which it occupies in the cottage of every Papua.

March, 1858.

III

THE VEDA AND ZEND-AVESTA.

THE VEDA.

THE main stream of the Aryan nations has always flowed towards the north-west. No historian can tell us by what impulse these adventurous Nomads were driven on through Asia towards the isles and shores of Europe. The first start of this world-wide migration belongs to a period far beyond the reach of documentary history; to times when the soil of Europe had not been trodden by either Celts, Germans, Slavonians, Romans, or Greeks. But whatever it was, the impulse was as irresistible as the spell which, in our own times, sends the Celtic tribes towards the prairies or the regions of gold across the Atlantic. It requires a strong will, or a great amount of inertness, to be able to withstand the impetus of such national, or rather ethnical, movements. Few will stay behind when all are going. But to let one's friends depart, and then to set out ourselves—to take a road which, lead where it may, can never lead us to join those again who speak our language and worship our gods—is a course which only men of strong individuality and

great self-dependence are capable of pursuing. It
was the course adopted by the southern branch of
the Aryan family, the Brahmanic Aryas of India
and the Zoroastrians of Iran.

At the first dawn of traditional history we see
these Aryan tribes migrating across the snow of the
Himâlaya southward towards the 'Seven Rivers'
(the Indus, the five rivers of the Penjâb, and the
Sarasvati), and ever since India has been called
their home. That before this time they had been
living in more northern regions, within the same
precincts with the ancestors of the Greeks, the
Italians, Slavonians, Germans, and Celts, is a fact
as firmly established as that the Normans of William
the Conqueror were the Northmen of Scandinavia.
The evidence of language is irrefragable, and it is
the only evidence worth listening to with regard to
ante-historical periods. It would have been next
to impossible to discover any traces of relationship
between the swarthy natives of India and their
conquerors whether Alexander or Clive, but for
the testimony borne by language. What other
evidence could have reached back to times when
Greece was not yet peopled by Greeks, nor India
by Hindus? Yet these are the times of which we
are speaking. What authority would have been
strong enough to persuade the Grecian army, that
their gods and their hero ancestors were the same
as those of king Porus, or to convince the English
soldier that the same blood might be running in
his veins and in the veins of the dark Bengalese?
And yet there is not an English jury now-a-days,
which, after examining the hoary documents of language, would reject the claim of a common descent

and a spiritual relationship between Hindu, Greek,
and Teuton. Many words still live in India and in
England that have witnessed the first separation of
the northern and southern Aryans, and these are
witnesses not to be shaken by any cross-examination.
The terms for God, for house, for father, mother, son,
daughter, for dog and cow, for heart and tears, for
axe and tree, identical in all the Indo-European
idioms, are like the watchwords of soldiers. We challenge the seeming stranger; and whether he answer
with the lips of a Greek, a German, or an Indian,
we recognise him as one of ourselves. Though the
historian may shake his head, though the physiologist may doubt, and the poet scorn the idea, all
must yield before the facts furnished by language.
There was a time when the ancestors of the Celts,
the Germans, the Slavonians, the Greeks and Italians,
the Persians and Hindus, were living together beneath the same roof, separate from the ancestors of
the Semitic and Turanian races.

It is more difficult to prove that the Hindu was
the last to leave this common home, that he saw his
brothers all depart towards the setting sun, and that
then, turning towards the south and the east, he
started alone in search of a new world. But as in
his language and in his grammar he has preserved
something of what seems peculiar to each of the
northern dialects singly, as he agrees with the Greek
and the German where the Greek and the German
differ from all the rest, and as no other language
has carried off so large a share of the common
Aryan heirloom—whether roots, grammar, words,
mythes, or legends—it is natural to suppose that,
though perhaps the eldest brother, the Hindu was

the last to leave the central home of the Aryan family.

The Aryan nations who pursued a north-westerly direction, stand before us in history as the principal nations of north-western Asia and Europe. They have been the prominent actors in the great drama of history, and have carried to their fullest growth all the elements of active life with which our nature is endowed. They have perfected society and morals, and we learn from their literature and works of art the elements of science, the laws of art, and the principles of philosophy. In continual struggle with each other and with Semitic and Turanian races, these Aryan nations have become the rulers of history, and it seems to be their mission to link all parts of the world together by the chains of civilisation, commerce, and religion. In a word, they represent the Aryan man in his historical character.

But while most of the members of the Aryan family followed this glorious path, the southern tribes were slowly migrating towards the mountains which gird the north of India. After crossing the narrow passes of the Hindukush or the Himálaya, they conquered or drove before them, as it seems without much effort, the aboriginal inhabitants of the Trans-Himalayan countries. They took for their guides the principal rivers of Northern India, and were led by them to new homes in their beautiful and fertile valleys. It seems as if the great mountains in the north had afterwards closed for centuries their Cyclopean gates against new immigrations, while, at the same time, the waves of the Indian Ocean kept watch over the southern borders of the peninsula. None of the great conquerors of

antiquity,—Sesostris, Semiramis, Nebuchadnezzar, or
Cyrus,—disturbed the peaceful seats of these Aryan
settlers.   Left to themselves in a world of their own,
without a past, and without a future before them,
they had nothing but themselves to ponder on.
Struggles there must have been in India also.   Old
dynasties were destroyed, whole families annihilated, and new empires founded.   Yet the inward
life of the Hindu was not changed by these convul-
sions.   His mind was like the lotus leaf after a
shower of rain has passed over it; his character
remained the same, passive, meditative, quiet, and
thoughtful.   A people of this peculiar stamp was
never destined to act a prominent part in the history
of the world; nay, the exhausting atmosphere of
transcendental ideas in which they lived could not
but exercise a detrimental influence on the active
and moral character of the Indians.   Social and
political virtues were little cultivated, and the ideas
of the useful and the beautiful hardly known to
them.   With all this, however, they had, what the
Greek was as little capable of imagining, as they
were of realising the elements of Grecian life.   They
shut their eyes to this world of outward seeming and
activity, to open them full on the world of thought
and rest.   The ancient Hindus were a nation of
philosophers, such as could nowhere have existed
except in India, and even there in early times alone.
It is with the Hindu mind as if a seed were placed
in a hothouse.   It will grow rapidly, its colours will
be gorgeous, its perfume rich, its fruits precocious
and abundant.   But never will it be like the oak
growing in wind and weather, and striking its roots
into real earth, and stretching its branches into real

air beneath the stars and the sun of heaven. Both
are experiments, the hothouse flower and the Hindu
mind; and as experiments, whether physiological or
psychological, both deserve to be studied.

We may divide the whole Aryan family into two
branches, the northern and the southern. The
northern nations, Celts, Greeks, Romans, Germans,
and Slavonians, have each one act allotted to them
on the stage of history. They have each a national
character to support. Not so the southern tribes.
They are absorbed in the struggles of thought, their
past is the problem of creation, their future the
problem of existence; and the present, which ought
to be the solution of both, seems never to have
attracted their attention, or called forth their energies. There never was a nation believing so firmly
in another world, and so little concerned about this.
Their condition on earth is to them a problem; their
real and eternal life a simple fact. Though this is
said chiefly with reference to them before they were
brought in contact with foreign conquerors, traces
of this character are still visible in the Hindus, as
described by the companions of Alexander, nay, even
in the Hindus of the present day. The only sphere
in which the Indian mind finds itself at liberty to
act, to create, and to worship, is the sphere of
religion and philosophy; and nowhere have religious
and metaphysical ideas struck root so deep in the
mind of a nation as in India. The shape which these
ideas took amongst the different classes of society,
and at different periods of civilisation, naturally
varies from coarse superstition to sublime spiritual-
ism. But, taken as a whole, history supplies no
second instance where the inward life of the soul

has so completely absorbed all the other faculties of a people.

It was natural, therefore, that the literary works of such a nation, when first discovered in Sanskrit MSS. by Wilkins, Sir W. Jones, and others, should have attracted the attention of all interested in the history of the human race. A new page in man's biography was laid open, and a literature as large as that of Greece or Rome was to be studied. The Laws of Manu, the two epic poems, the Râmâyana and Mahâbhârata, the six complete systems of philosophy, works on astronomy and medicine, plays, stories, fables, elegies, and lyrical effusions, were read with intense interest, on account of their age not less than their novelty.

Still this interest was confined to a small number of students, and in a few cases only could Indian literature attract the eyes of men who, from the summit of universal history, survey the highest peaks of human excellence. Herder, Schlegel, Humboldt, and Goethe, discovered what was really important in Sanskrit literature. They saw what was genuine and original, in spite of much that seemed artificial. For the artificial, no doubt, has a wide place in Sanskrit literature. Everywhere we find systems, rules and models, castes and schools, but nowhere individuality, no natural growth, and but few signs of strong originality and genius.

There is, however, one period of Sanskrit literature which forms an exception, and which will maintain its place in the history of mankind, when the name of Kalidâsa and Sakuntalâ will have been long forgotten. It is the most ancient period, the period of the Veda. There is, perhaps, a higher degree of

interest attaching to works of higher antiquity; but
in the Veda we have more than mere antiquity. We
have ancient thought expressed in ancient language.
Without insisting on the fact that even chronolo-
gically the Veda is the first book of the Aryan
nations, we have in it, at all events, a period in the
intellectual life of man to which there is no parallel
in any other part of the world. In the hymns of the
Veda we see man left to himself to solve the riddle
of this world. We see him crawling on like a
creature of the earth with all the desires and weaknesses of his animal nature. Food, wealth, and
power, a large family and a long life, are the theme
of his daily prayers. But he begins to lift up his
eyes. He stares at the tent of heaven, and asks who
supports it? He opens his ears to the winds, and
asks them whence and whither? He is awakened
from darkness and slumber by the light of the sun,
and him whom his eyes cannot behold, and who
seems to grant him the daily pittance of his existence, he calls ' his life, his breath, his brilliant Lord
and Protector.' He gives names to all the powers of
nature, and after he has called the fire Agni, the
sun-light Indra, the storms Maruts, and the dawn
Ushas, they all seem to grow naturally into beings
like himself, nay, greater than himself. He invokes
them, he praises them, he worships them. But still
with all these gods around him, beneath him, and
above him, the early poet seems ill at rest within
himself. There too, in his own breast, he has discovered a power that wants a name, a power nearer
to him than all the gods of nature, a power that is
never mute when he prays, never absent when he
fears and trembles. It seems to inspire his prayers,

and yet to listen to them; it seems to live in him,
and yet to support him and all around him. The
only name he can find for this mysterious power is
Bráhman; for bráhman meant originally force,
will, wish, and the propulsive power of creation.
But this impersonal bráhman, too, as soon as it is
named, grows into something strange and divine.
It ends by being one of many gods, one of the great
triad, worshipped to the present day. And still the
thought within him has no real name; that power
which is nothing but itself, which supports the gods,
the heavens, and every living being, floats before his
mind, conceived but not expressed. At last he calls
it Âtman; for âtman, originally breath or spirit,
comes to mean Self and Self alone—Self whether
divine or human, Self whether creating or suffering,
Self whether one or all, but always Self, independent
and free. 'Who has seen the first-born,' says the
poet, 'when he who has no bones (i. e. form) bore him
that had bones? Where was the life, the blood, the
Self of the world? Who went to ask this from any
that knew it?' (Rv. I. 164, 4). This idea of a divine
Self once expressed, everything else must acknowledge its supremacy, 'Self is the Lord of all things,
Self is the King of all things. As all the spokes
of a wheel are contained in the nave and the circumference, all things are contained in this Self; all
selves are contained in this Self[1]. Bráhman itself is
but Self[2].'

This Âtman also grew; but it grew, as it were,
without attributes. The sun is called the Self of all

[1] Brihad-âranyaka, IV. 5, 15, ed. Roer, p. 487.
[2] Ibid. p. 478. Khândogya-upanishad, VIII. 3, 3–4.

that moves and rests (Rv. I. 115, 1), and still more frequently self becomes a mere pronoun. But Âtman remained always free from mythe and worship, differing in this from the Bráhman (neuter), who has his temples in India even now, and is worshipped as Bráhman (masculine), together with Vishnu and Siva, and other popular gods. The idea of the Âtman or Self, like a pure crystal, was too transparent for poetry, and therefore was handed over to philosophy, which afterwards polished, and turned, and watched it as the medium through which all is seen, and in which all is reflected and known. But philosophy is later than the Veda, and it is of the Vaidik period only I have here to speak [3].

---

[3] In writing the above, I was thinking rather of the mental process that was necessary for the production of such words as brahman, âtman, and others, than of their idiomatic use in the ancient literature of India. It might be objected, for instance, that bráhman, neut. in the sense of creative power or the principal cause of all things, does not occur in the Rig-veda. This is true. But it occurs in that sense in the Atharva-veda, and in several of the Bráhmanas. There we read of ' the oldest or greatest Bráhman which rules everything that has been or will be.' Heaven is said to belong to Bráhman alone (Atharva-veda X. 8, 1). In the Bráhmanas, this Bráhman is called the first-born, the self-existing, the best of the gods, and heaven and earth are said to have been established by it. Even the vital spirits are identified with it (Satapatha-bráhmana VIII. 4, 9, 3).

In other passages, again, this same Bráhman is represented as existing in man (Atharva-veda X. 7, 17), and in this very passage we can watch the transition from the neutral Bráhman into Bráhman, conceived of as a masculine:

Ye purushe bráhma viduh te viduh parameshthinam,

Yo veda parameshthinam, yas ka veda praǵâpatim,

Gyeshtham ye bráhmanam vidus, te skambham anu samviduh.

In the Veda, then, we can study a theogony of
which that of Hesiod is but the last chapter. We
can study man's natural growth, and the results to
which it may lead under the most favourable conditions. All was given him that nature can bestow.
We see him blest with the choicest gifts of the earth,
under a glowing and transparent sky, surrounded by
all the grandeur and all the riches of nature, with a
language 'capable of giving soul to the objects of
sense, and body to the abstractions of metaphysics.' We have a right to expect much from him,
only we must not expect in his youthful poems
the philosophy of the nineteenth century, or the

'They who know Bráhman in man, they know the Highest,
   He who knows the Highest, and he who knows Prajápati (the
      lord of creatures),
And they who know the oldest Bráhmana, they know the Ground.'

The word Bráhmana which is here used, is a derivative form of
Bráhman; but what is most important in these lines is the mixing
of neuter and masculine words, of impersonal and personal deities.
This process is brought to perfection by changing Bráhman, the
neuter, even grammatically into Bráhman, a masculine,—a change
which has taken place in the Áranyakas, where we find Bráhman
used as the name of a male deity. It is this Bráhman, with the
accent on the first, not, as has been supposed, brahmán, the priest,
that appears again in the later literature as one of the divine triad,
Bráhman, Vishnu, Siva.

The word bráhman, as a neuter, is used in the Rig-Veda in the
sense of prayer also, originally what bursts forth from the soul, and,
in one sense, what is revealed. Hence in later times bráhman is
used collectively for the Veda, the sacred word.

Another word, with the accent on the last syllable, is brahmán,
the man who prays, who utters prayers, the priest, and gradually
the Brahman by profession. In this sense it is frequently used
in the Rig-veda (I. 108, 7), but not yet in the sense of Brahman
by birth or caste.

beauties of Pindar, or, with some again, the truths
of Christianity. Few understand children, still fewer
understand antiquity. If we look in the Veda for high
poetical diction, for striking comparisons, for bold
combinations, we shall be disappointed. These early
poets thought more for themselves than for others.
They sought rather, in their language, to be true to
their own thought than to please the imagination
of their hearers. With them it was a great work
achieved for the first time to bind thoughts and
words together, to find expressions or to form new
names. As to similes, we must look to the words
themselves, which, if we compare their radical and
their nominal meaning, will be found full of bold
metaphors. No translation in any modern language
can do them justice. As to beauty, we must discover
it in the absence of all effort, and in the simplicity
of their hearts. Prose was, at that time, unknown,
as well as the distinction between prose and poetry.
It was the attempted imitation of those ancient
natural strains of thought which in later times gave
rise to poetry in our sense of the word, that is to
say, to poetry as an art, with its counted syllables,
its numerous epithets, its rhyme and rhythm, and all
the conventional attributes of 'measured thought.'

In the Veda itself, however—even if by Veda we
mean the Rig-veda only (the other three, the Sâman,
Yagush, and Âtharvana, having solely a liturgical
interest, and belonging to an entirely different
sphere)—in the Rig-veda also, we find much that
is artificial, imitated, and therefore modern, if compared with other hymns. It is true that all the
1017 hymns of the Rig-veda were comprised in a
collection which existed as such before one of those

elaborate theological commentaries known under the name of Brâhmana, was written, that is to say, about 800 B.C. But before the date of their collection these must have existed for centuries. In different songs the names of different kings occur, and we see several generations of royal families pass away before us with different generations of poets. Old songs are mentioned, and new songs. Poets whose compositions we possess are spoken of as the seers of olden times; their names in other hymns are surrounded by a legendary halo. In some cases, whole books or chapters may be pointed out as more modern and secondary, in thought and language. But on the whole the Rig-veda is a genuine document, even in its most modern portions not later than the time of Lycurgus; and it exhibits one of the earliest and rudest phases in the history of mankind; disclosing in its full reality a period of which in Greece we have but traditions and names, such as Orpheus and Linus, and bringing us as near the beginnings in language, thought, and mythology as literary documents can ever bring us in the Aryan world.

Though much time and labour have been spent on the Veda, in England and in Germany, the time is not yet come for translating it as a whole. It is possible and interesting to translate it literally, or in accordance with scholastic commentaries, such as we find in India from Yâska in the fifth century B.C. down to Sâyana in the fourteenth century of the Christian era. This is what Professor Wilson has done in his translation of the first book of the Rig-veda; and by strictly adhering to this principle and excluding conjectural renderings even where they offered themselves most naturally, he has imparted to his work a definite character and a lasting value. The grammar of the Veda, though irregular, and still in a rather floating state, has almost been mastered; the etymology and the meaning of many words, unknown in the later Sanskrit, have been discovered. Many hymns, which are mere prayers for food, for cattle, or for a long life, have been translated, and can leave no doubt as to their real intention. But with the exception of these simple petitions, the whole world of Vedic ideas is so entirely beyond our own intellectual horizon, that instead of translating we can as yet only guess and combine. Here it is no longer a mere question of skilful deciphering. We may collect all the passages where an obscure word occurs, we may compare them and look for a meaning which would be appropriate to all; but the difficulty lies in finding a sense which we can appropriate, and transfer by analogy into our own language and thought. We must be able to translate our feelings and ideas into their language at the same time that we translate their poems and prayers into our language. We must not despair even where their words seem meaningless and their ideas barren or wild. What seems at first childish may at a happier moment disclose a sublime simplicity, and even in helpless expressions we may recognise aspirations after some high and noble idea. When the scholar has done his work, the poet and philosopher must take it up and finish it. Let the scholar collect, collate, sift, and reject— let him say what is possible or not according to the laws of the Vedic language—let him study the commentaries, the Sûtras, the Brâhmaṇas, and even later works, in order to exhaust all the sources from which information can be derived. He must not

despise the tradition of the Brahmans, even where
their misconceptions and the causes of their misconceptions are palpable.   To know what a passage
cannot mean is frequently the key to its real meaning; and whatever reasons may be pleaded for
declining a careful perusal of the traditional interpretations of Yâska or Sâyana, they can all be traced
back to an ill-concealed argumentum paupertatis.
Not a corner in the Brâhmanas, the Sûtras, Yâska,
and Sâyana should be left unexplored before we
venture to propose a rendering of our own. Sâyana,
though the most modern, is on the whole the most
sober interpreter.   Most of his etymological absurdities must be placed to Yâska's account, and the
optional renderings which he allows for metaphysical,
theological, or ceremonial purposes, are mostly due
to his regard for the Brâhmanas.   The Brâhmanas,
though nearest in time to the hymns of the Rig-
veda, indulge in the most frivolous and ill-judged
interpretations.   When the ancient Rishi exclaims
with a troubled heart, 'Who is the greatest of the
gods?   Who shall first be praised by our songs?'—
the author of the Brâhmana sees in the interrogative
pronoun 'Who' some divine name, a place is allotted
in the sacrificial invocations to a god 'Who,' and
hymns addressed to him are called 'Whoish' hymns.
To make such misunderstandings possible, we must
assume a considerable interval between the composition of the hymns and the Brâhmanas.   As the
authors of the Brâhmanas were blinded by theology,
the authors of the still later Niruktas were deceived
by etymological fictions, and both conspired to mislead by their authority later and more sensible commentators, such as Sâyana.   Where Sâyana has no

authority to mislead him, his commentary is at all
events rational; but still his scholastic notions would
never allow him to accept the free interpretation
which a comparative study of these venerable documents forces upon the unprejudiced scholar. We
must therefore discover ourselves the real vestiges
of these ancient poets; and if we follow them
cautiously, we shall find that with some effort we
are still able to walk in their footsteps. We shall
feel that we are brought face to face and mind to
mind with men yet intelligible to us, after we have
freed ourselves from our modern conceits. We shall
not succeed always: words, verses, nay, whole hymns
in the Rig-veda, will and must remain to us a dead
letter. But where we can inspire those early relics
of thought and devotion with new life, we shall
have before us more real antiquity than in all the
inscriptions of Egypt or Nineveh; not only old names
and dates, and kingdoms and battles, but old thoughts,
old hopes, old faith, and old errors, the old Man
altogether—old now, but then young and fresh, and
simple and real in his prayers and in his praises.

The thoughtful bent of the Hindu mind is visible
in the Veda also, but his mystic tendencies are not
yet so fully developed. Of philosophy we find but
little, and what we find is still in its germ. The
active side of life is more prominent, and we meet
occasionally with wars of kings, with rivalries of
ministers, with triumphs and defeats, with war-songs
and imprecations. Moral sentiments and worldly
wisdom are not yet absorbed by phantastic intui-
tions. Still the child betrays the passions of the
man, and there are hymns, though few in number,
in the Veda, so full of thought and speculation that

at this early period no poet in any other nation
could have conceived them.   I give but one specimen, the 129th hymn of the tenth book of the
Rig-veda.   It is a hymn which long ago attracted
the attention of that eminent scholar H. T. Colebrooke, and of which, by the kind assistance of a
friend, I am enabled to offer a metrical translation.
In judging it we should bear in mind that it was
not written by a gnostic or by a pantheistic philosopher, but by a poet who felt all these doubts
and problems as his own, without any wish to convince or to startle, only uttering what had been
weighing on his mind, just as later poets would
sing the doubts and sorrows of their heart.

Nor Aught nor Nought existed; yon bright sky
Was not, nor heaven's broad woof outstretched above.
What covered all? what sheltered? what concealed?
Was it the water's fathomless abyss?
There was not death—yet was there nought immortal,
There was no confine betwixt day and night;
The only One breathed breathless by itself,
Other than It there nothing since has been.
Darkness there was, and all at first was veiled
In gloom profound—an ocean without light—
The germ that still lay covered in the husk
Burst forth, one nature, from the fervent heat.
Then first came love upon it, the new spring
Of mind—yea, poets in their hearts discerned,
Pondering, this bond between created things
And uncreated.   Comes this spark from earth
Piercing and all-pervading, or from heaven?
Then seeds were sown, and mighty powers arose—
Nature below, and power and will above—
Who knows the secret? who proclaimed it here,
Whence, whence this manifold creation sprang?
The Gods themselves came later into being—
Who knows from whence this great creation sprang?

He from whom all this great creation came,
Whether his will created or was mute,
The Most High Seer that is in highest heaven,
He knows it—or perchance even He knows not.

The grammar of the Veda (to turn from the contents to the structure of the work) is important in
many respects. The difference between it and the
grammar of the epic poems would be sufficient of
itself to fix the distance between these two periods
of language and literature. Many words have preserved in these early hymns a more primitive form,
and therefore agree more closely with cognate words
in Greek or Latin. Night, for instance, in the later
Sanskrit is nisâ, which is a form peculiarly Sanskritic,
and agrees in its derivation neither with nox nor
with νύξ. The Vaidik nas or nak, night, is as near to
Latin as can be. Thus mouse in the common Sanskrit
is mûshas or mûshikâ, both derivative forms if
compared with the Latin mus, muris. The Vaidik
Sanskrit has preserved the same primitive noun in
the plural mûsh-as = Lat. mures. There are other
words in the Veda which were lost altogether in the
later Sanskrit, while they were preserved in Greek
and Latin. Dyaus, sky, does not occur as a masculine in the ordinary Sanskrit; it occurs in the Veda,
and thus bears witness to the early Aryan worship of
Dyaus, the Greek Zeús. Ushas, dawn, again in the
later Sanskrit is neuter. In the Veda it is feminine;
and even the secondary Vaidik form Ushâsâ is
proved to be of high antiquity by the nearly corresponding Latin form Aurora. Declension and
conjugation are richer in forms and more unsettled
in their usage. It is a curious fact, for instance,
that no subjunctive mood existed in the common

Sanskrit. The Greeks and Romans had it, and even the language of the Avesta showed clear traces of it. There could be no doubt that the Sanskrit also once possessed this mood, and at last it was discovered in the hymns of the Rig-Veda. Discoveries of this kind may seem trifling, but they are as delightful to the grammarian as the appearance of a star, long expected and calculated, is to the astronomer. They prove that there is natural order in language, and that by a careful induction laws can be established which enable us to guess with great probability either at the form or meaning of words where but scanty fragments of the tongue itself have come down to us.

October, 1853.

THE ZEND-AVESTA.

BY means of laws like that of the Correspondence of Letters, discovered by Rask and Grimm, it has been possible to determine the exact form of words in Gothic, in cases where no trace of them occurred in the literary documents of the Gothic nation. Single words which were not to be found in Ulfilas have been recovered by applying certain laws to their corresponding forms in Latin or Old High-German, and thus retranslating them into Gothic. But a much greater conquest was achieved in Persia. Here comparative philology has actually had to create and reanimate all the materials of language on which it was afterwards to work. Little was known of the language of Persia and Media previous to the Shahnameh of Firdusi, composed about 1000 A.D., and it is due entirely to the inductive method of comparative philology that we have now before us contemporaneous documents of three periods of Persian language, deciphered, translated and explained. We have the language of the Zoroastrians, the language of the Achæmenians, and the language of the Sassanians, which represent the history of the Persian tongue in three successive periods—all now rendered intelligible by the aid of comparative philology, while but fifty years ago their very name and existence were questioned.

The labours of Anquetil Duperron, who first translated the Zend-Avesta, were those of a bold adventurer—not of a scholar. Rask was the first who, with the materials collected by Duperron and himself, analysed the language of the Avesta scientifically. He proved—

1. That Zend was not a corrupted Sanskrit, as supposed by W. Erskine, but that it differed from it as Greek, Latin, or Lithuanian differed from one another and from Sanskrit.

2. That the modern Persian was really derived from Zend as Italian was from Latin; and

3. That the Avesta, or the works of Zoroaster, must have been reduced to writing at least previously to Alexander's conquest. The opinion that Zend was an artificial language (an opinion held by men of great eminence in Oriental philology, beginning with Sir W. Jones) is passed over by Rask as not deserving of refutation.

The first edition of the Zend texts, the critical restitution of the MSS., the outlines of a Zend grammar, with the translation and philological anatomy of considerable portions of the Zoroastrian writings, were the work of the late Eugène Burnouf. He was the real founder of Zend philology. It is clear from his works, and from Bopp's valuable remarks in his ' Comparative Grammar,' that Zend in its grammar and dictionary is nearer to Sanskrit than any other Indo-European language. Many Zend words can be retranslated into Sanskrit simply by changing the Zend letters into their corresponding forms in Sanskrit. With regard to the Correspondence of Letters in Grimm's sense of the word, Zend ranges with Sanskrit and the classical languages. It differs from Sanskrit principally in its sibilants, nasals, and aspirates. The Sanskrit s, for instance, is represented by the Zend h, a change analogous to

that of an original s into the Greek aspirate, only
that in Greek this change is not general. Thus the
geographical name hapta hendu, which occurs in
the Avesta, becomes intelligible if we retranslate the
Zend h into the Sanskrit s. For sapta sindhu, or
the Seven Rivers, is the old Vaidik name of India
itself derived from the five rivers . of the Penjâb,
together with the Indus, and the Sarasvati.

Where Sanskrit differs in words or grammatical
peculiarities from the northern members of the Aryan
family, it frequently coincides with Zend. The
numerals are the same in all these languages up to
100. The name for thousand, however, sahasra, is
peculiar to Sanskrit, and does not occur in any of
the Indo-European dialects except in Zend, where it
becomes hazanra. In the same manner the German
and Slavonic languages have a word for thousand
peculiar to themselves; as also in Greek and Latin
we find many common words which we look for in
vain in any of the other Indo-European dialects.
These facts are full of historical meaning; and with
regard to Zend and Sanskrit, they prove that these
two languages continued together long after they
were separated from the common Indo-European
stock.

Still more striking is the similarity between Persia
and India in religion and mythology. Gods unknown
to any Indo-European nation are worshipped under
the same names in Sanskrit and Zend; and the
change of some of the most sacred expressions in
Sanskrit into names of evil spirits in Zend, only
serves to strengthen the conviction that we have
here the usual traces of a schism which separated a
community that had once been united.

Burnouf, who compared the language and religion
of the Avesta principally with the later classical
Sanskrit, inclined at first to the opinion that this
schism took place in Persia, and that the dissenting
Brahmans immigrated afterwards into India. This
is still the prevailing opinion, but it requires to be
modified in accordance with new facts elicited from
the Veda. Zend, if compared with classical Sanskrit,
exhibits in many points of grammar, features of a
more primitive character than Sanskrit. But it can
now be shown, and Burnouf himself admitted it, that
when this is the case, the Vaidik differs on the very
same points from the later Sanskrit, and has preserved the same primitive and irregular form as the
Zend. I still hold, that the name of Zend was originally a corruption of the Sanskrit word *khandas* (i. e.
metrical language, cf. scandere)[1], which is the name

---

[1] The derivation of *khandas* metre, from the same root which
yielded the Latin scandere, seems to me still the most plausible.
An account of the various explanations of this word, proposed by
Eastern and Western scholars, is to be found in Spiegel's 'Grammar
of the Parsi Language' (preface, and p. 205), and in his translation
of the Vendidad (pp. 44 and 293). That initial *kh* in Sanskrit
may represent an original sk. has never, as far as I am aware, been
denied. (Curtius, 'Grundzüge,' p. 60.) The fact that the root
khand, in the sense of stepping or striding, has not been fixed in
Sanskrit as a verbal, but only as a nominal base, is no real objection
either. The same thing has happened over and over again, and has
been remarked as the necessary result of the dialectic growth of language by so ancient a scholar as Yâska. ('Zeitschrift der Deutschen
Morgenländischen Gesellschaft,' vol. viii. p. 373 seq.) That scandere
in Latin, in the sense of scanning is a late word, does not affect the
question at all. What is of real importance is simply this, that the
principal Aryan nations agree in representing metre as a kind of
stepping or striding. Whether this arose from the fact that ancient
poetry was accompanied by dancing or rhythmic choral movements, is a question which does not concern us here. (Carmen

given to the language of the Veda by Pânini and others. When we read in Pânini's grammar that certain forms occur in *khandas*, but not in the classical language, we may almost always translate the word *khandas* by Zend, for nearly all these rules apply equally to the language of the Avesta.

In mythology also, the 'nomina and numina' of the Avesta appear at first sight more primitive than in

descindentes tripodaverunt in verba hæc: Enos Lases, etc. Orelli, 'Inscript.' No. 2271.) The fact remains that the people of India, Greece, and Italy agree in calling the component elements of their verses feet or steps (πούς, pes, Sanskrit pad or pâda; padapaûkti, a row of feet, and gagatî, i.e. andante, are names of Sanskrit metres). It is not too much, therefore, to say that they may have considered metre as a kind of stepping or striding, and that they may accordingly have called it 'stride.' If then we find the name for metre in Sanskrit *khandas*, i. e. skandas, and if we find that scando in Latin (from which sca(d)la), as we may gather from ascendo and descendo, meant originally striding, and that skand in Sanskrit means the same as scando in Latin, surely there can be little doubt as to the original intention of the Sanskrit name for metre, viz. *khandas*. Hindu grammarians derive *khandas* either from *khad*, to cover, or from *khad*, to please. Both derivations are possible, as far as the letters are concerned. But are we to accept the dogmatic interpretation of the theologians of the *Khandogas*, who tell us that the metres were called *khandas* because the gods, when afraid of death, covered themselves with the metres? Or of the Vâgasaneyins, who tell us that the *khandas* were so called because they pleased Pragâpati? Such artificial interpretations only show that the Brahmans had no traditional feeling as to the etymological meaning of that word, and that we are at liberty to discover by the ordinary means its original intention. I shall only mention from among much that has been written on the etymology of *khandas*, a most happy remark of Professor Kuhn, who traces the Northern skald, poet, back to the same root as the Sanskrit *khandas*, metre. (Kuhn's 'Zeitschrift,' vol. iii. p. 428.) Legerlotz, ibid. viii. 399. The transition of nd into ld is justified by Sanskrit skandhas=A.S. sculdor, shoulder; and German kind=English child. Grimm, 'Geschichte der Deutschen Sprache,' p. 341.

Manu or the Mahâbhârata. But if regarded from a
Vaidik point of view, this relation shifts at once, and
many of the gods of the Zoroastrians come out once
more as mere reflections and deflections of the primitive and authentic gods of the Veda. It can now be
proved, even by geographical evidence, that the Zoroastrians had been settled in India before they immigrated into Persia. I say the Zoroastrians, for we
have no evidence to bear us out in making the same
assertion of the nations of Persia and Media in
general. That the Zoroastrians and their ancestors
started from India during the Vaidik period can
be proved as distinctly as that the inhabitants of
Massilia started from Greece. The geographical
traditions in the first Fargard of the Vendidad do
not interfere with this opinion. If ancient and
genuine, they would embody a remembrance preserved by the Zoroastrians, but forgotten by the
Vaidik poets—a remembrance of times previous to
their first common descent into the country of the
Seven Rivers. If of later origin, and this is more
likely, they may represent a geographical conception
of the Zoroastrians after they had become acquainted
with a larger sphere of countries and nations, subsequent to their emigration from the land of the
Seven Rivers[2].

These and similar questions of the highest importance for the early history of the Aryan language and
mythology, however, must await their final decision,
until the whole of the Veda and the Avesta shall
have been published. Of this Burnouf was fully

---

[2] The purely mythological character of this geographical chapter
has been proved by M. Michel Bréal, ' Journal Asiatique,' 1862.

aware, and this was the reason why he postponed the publication of his researches into the antiquities of the Iranian nation. The same conviction is shared by Westergaard and Spiegel, who are each engaged on an edition of the Avesta, and who, though they differ on many points, agree in considering the Veda as the safest key to an understanding of the Avesta. Professor Roth, of Tübingen, has well expressed the mutual relation of the Veda and Zend-Avesta under the following simile: 'The Veda,' he writes, 'and the Zend-Avesta are two rivers flowing from one fountain-head: the stream of the Veda is the fuller and purer, and has remained truer to its original character; that of the Zend-Avesta has been in various ways polluted, has altered its course, and cannot, with certainty, be traced back to its source.'

As to the language of the Achæmenians, presented to us in the Persian text of the cuneiform inscriptions, there was no room for doubt, as soon as it became legible at all, that it was the same tongue as that of the Avesta, only in a second stage of its continuous growth. The process of deciphering these bundles of arrows by means of Zend and Sanskrit has been very much like deciphering an Italian inscription without a knowledge of Italian, simply by means of classical and mediæval Latin. It would have been impossible, even with the quick perception and patient combination of a Grotefend, to read more than the proper names and a few titles on the walls of the Persian palaces, without the aid of Zend and Sanskrit; and it seems almost providential, as Lassen remarked, that these inscriptions, which at any previous period would have been, in the eyes of either classical or oriental

scholars, nothing but a quaint conglomerate of nails,
wedges, or arrows, should have been rescued from
the dust of centuries at the very moment when the
discovery and study of Sanskrit and Zend had
enabled the scholars of Europe to grapple successfully with their difficulties.

Upon a closer inspection of the language and
grammar of these mountain records of the Achæmenian dynasty, a curious fact came to light which
seemed to disturb the historical relation between the
language of Zoroaster and the language of Darius.
At first, historians were satisfied with knowing that
the edicts of Darius could be explained by the language of the Avesta, and that the difference between
the two, which could be proved to imply a considerable interval of time, was such as to exclude for ever
the supposed historical identity of Darius Hystaspes
and Gushtasp, the mythical pupil of Zoroaster. The
language of the Avesta, though certainly not the
language of Zarathustra[3], displayed a grammar so
much more luxuriant, and forms so much more
primitive than the inscriptions, that centuries must

---

[3] Spiegel states the results of his last researches into the language
of the different parts of the Avesta in the following words:

'We are now prepared to attempt an arrangement of the
different portions of the Zend-Avesta in the order of their
antiquity. First, we place the second part of the Yasna, as
separated in respect to the language of the Zend-Avesta, yet not
composed by Zoroaster himself, since he is named in the third
person; and indeed everything intimates that neither he nor his
disciple Gushtasp was alive. The second place must unquestion-
ably be assigned to the Vendidad. I do not believe that the book
was originally composed as it now stands: it has suffered both
earlier and later interpolations; still, its present form may be
traced to a considerable antiquity. The antiquity of the work

have elapsed between the two periods represented by these two strata of language. When, however, the forms of these languages were subjected to a more searching analysis, it became evident that the phonetic system of the cuneiform inscriptions was more primitive and regular than even that of the earlier portions of the Avesta. This difficulty, however, admits of a solution; and, like many difficulties of the kind, it tends to confirm, if rightly explained, the very facts and views which at first it seemed to overthrow. The confusion in the phonetic system of the Zend grammar is no doubt owing to the influence of oral tradition. Oral tradition, particularly if confided to the safeguard of a learned priesthood, is able to preserve, during centuries of growth and change, the sacred accents of a dead language; but it is liable at least to the slow and imperceptible influences of a corrupt pronunciation. Nowhere can we see this more clearly than in the Veda, where grammatical forms that had ceased to be intelligible, were carefully preserved, while the original pronun-

is proved by its contents, which distinctly show that the sacred literature was not yet completed.

'The case is different with the writings of the last period, among which I reckon the first part of the Yasna, and the whole of the Yeshts. Among these a theological character is unmistakeable, the separate divinities having their attributes and titles dogmatically fixed.

'Altogether, it is interesting to trace the progress of religion in Parsi writings. It is a significant fact, that in the oldest, that is to say, the second part of the Yasna, nothing is fixed in the doctrine regarding God. In the writings of the second period, that is in the Vendidad, we trace the advance to a theological, and, in its way, mild and scientific system. Out of this, in the last place, there springs the stern and intolerant religion of the Sassanian epoch.'—From the Rev. J. Murray Mitchell's Translation.

ciation of vowels was lost, and the simple structure
of the ancient metres destroyed by the adoption of a
more modern pronunciation. The loss of the Di-
gamma in Homer is another case in point. There are
no facts to prove that the text of the Avesta, in the
shape in which the Parsis of Bombay and Yezd now
possess it, was committed to writing previous to the
Sassanian dynasty (226 A.D.). After that time it
can indeed be traced, and to a great extent be con-
trolled and checked by the Huzvaresh translations
made under that dynasty. Additions to it were
made, as it seems, even after these Huzvaresh translations; but their number is small, and we have no
reason to doubt that the text of the Avesta, in the
days of Arda Viráf, was on the whole exactly the
same as at present. At the time when these translations were made, it is clear from their own evidence
that the language of Zarathustra had already suffered, and that the ideas of the Avesta were no
longer fully understood even by the learned. Before
that time we may infer, indeed, that the doctrine
of Zoroaster had been committed to writing, for
Alexander is said to have destroyed the books of
the Zoroastrians, Hermippus of Alexandria is said to
have read them[4]. But whether on the revival of
the Persian religion and literature, that is to say
500 years after Alexander, the works of Zoroaster
were collected and restored from extant MSS., or
from oral tradition, must remain uncertain, and the
disturbed state of the phonetic system would rather
lead us to suppose a long-continued influence of oral
tradition. What the Zend language might become,

---

[4] 'Lectures on the Science of Language,' First Series, p. 95.

if entrusted to the guardianship of memory alone, unassisted by grammatical study and archæological research, may be seen at the present day, when some of the Parsis, who are unable either to read or write, still mutter hymns and prayers in their temples, which, though to them mere sound, disclose to the experienced ear of an European scholar the time-hallowed accents of Zarathustra's speech.

Thus far the history of the Persian language had been reconstructed by the genius and perseverance of Grotefend, Burnouf, Lassen, and last, not least, by the comprehensive labours of Rawlinson, from the ante-historical epoch of Zoroaster down to the age of Darius and Artaxerxes II. It might have been expected that, after that time, the contemporaneous historians of Greece would have supplied the sequel. Unfortunately the Greeks cared nothing for any language except their own; and little for any other history except as bearing on themselves. The history of the Persian language after the Macedonian conquest and during the Parthian occupation is indeed but a blank page. The next glimpse of an authentic contemporaneous document is the inscription of Ardeshir, the founder of the new national dynasty of the Sassanians. It is written, though, it may be, with dialectic difference, in what was once called Pehlevi, and is now more commonly known as Huzvaresh, this being the proper title of the language of the translations of the Avesta. The legends of Sassanian coins, the bilingual inscriptions of Sassanian emperors, and the translation of the Avesta by Sassanian reformers, represent the Persian language in its third phase. To judge from the specimens given by Anquetil Duperron, it was not to be

wondered at that this dialect, then called Pehlevi,
should have been pronounced an artificial jargon.
Even when more genuine specimens of it became
known, the language seemed so overgrown with
Semitic and barbarous words, that it was expelled
from the Iranian family. Sir W. Jones pronounced
it to be a dialect of Chaldaic. Spiegel, however, who
is now publishing the text of these translations, has
established the fact that the language is truly Aryan,
neither Semitic nor barbarous, but Persian in roots
and grammar. He accounts for the large infusion of
foreign terms by pointing to the mixed elements in
the intellectual and religious life of Persia during
and before that period. There was the Semitic
influence of Babylonia, clearly discernible even in
the characters of the Achæmenian inscriptions; there
was the slow infiltration of Jewish ideas, customs,
and expressions, working sometimes in the palaces of
Persian kings, and always in the bazars of Persian
cities, on high roads and in villages; there was the
irresistible power of the Greek genius, which even
under its rude Macedonian garb emboldened oriental
thinkers to a flight into regions undreamed of in their
philosophy; there were the academies, the libraries,
the works of art of the Seleucidæ; there was Edessa
on the Euphrates, a city where Plato and Aristotle
were studied, where Christian, Jewish, and Buddhist
tenets were discussed, where Ephraem Syrus taught,
and Syriac translations were circulated which have
preserved to us the lost originals of Greek and
Christian writers. The title of the Avesta under its
Semitic form Apestako, was known in Syria as
well as in Persia, and the true name of its author,
Zarathustra, is not yet changed in Syriac into the

modern Zerdusht. While this intellectual stream,
principally flowing through Semitic channels, was
irrigating and inundating the west of Asia, the
Persian language had been left without literary cultivation. Need we wonder, then, that the men, who
at the rising of a new national dynasty (226) became
the reformers, teachers, and prophets of Persia, should
have formed their language and the whole train of
their ideas on a Semitic model. Motley as their
language may appear to a Persian scholar fresh from
the Avesta or from Firdusi, there is hardly a language of modern Europe which, if closely sifted,
would not produce the same impression on a scholar
accustomed only to the pure idiom of Homer, Cicero,
Ulfilas, or Cædmon. Moreover, the s o u l of the Sassanian language—I mean its grammar—is Persian
and nothing but Persian; and though meagre when
compared with the grammar of the Avesta, it is
richer in forms than the later Parsi, the Deri, or the
language of Firdusi. The supposition (once maintained) that Pehlevi was the dialect of the western
provinces of Persia is no longer necessary. As well
might we imagine (it is Spiegel's apposite remark,)
that a Turkish work, because it is full of Arabic
words, could only have been written on the frontiers
of Arabia. We may safely consider the Huzvaresh
of the translations of the Avesta as the language of
the Sassanian court and hierarchy. Works also like
the Bundehesh and Minokhired belong by language
and thought to the same period of mystic incubation,
when India and Egypt, Babylonia and Greece, were
sitting together and gossiping like crazy old women,
chattering with toothless gums and silly brains about
the dreams and joys of their youth, yet unable to

recall one single thought or feeling with that vigour
which once gave it life and truth. It was a period
of religious and metaphysical delirium, when everything became everything, when Mâyâ and Sophia,
Mitra and Christ, Virâf and Isaiah, Belus, Zarvan, and
Kronos were mixed up in one jumbled system of inane
speculation, from which at last the East was delivered
by the positive doctrines of Mohammed, the West by
the pure Christianity of the Teutonic nations.

In order to judge fairly of the merits of the
Huzvaresh as a language, it must be remembered
that we know it only from these speculative works,
and from translations made by men whose very language had become technical and artificial in the
schools. The idiom spoken by the nation was
probably much less infected by this Semitic fashion.
Even the translators sometimes give the Semitic
terms only as a paraphrase or more distinct expression side by side with the Persian. And, if
Spiegel's opinion be right that Parsi, and not Huzvaresh, was the language of the later Sassanian
empire, it furnishes a clear proof that Persian had
recovered itself, had thrown off the Semitic ingredients, and again become a pure and national speech.
This dialect (the Parsi) also, exists in translations
only; and we owe our knowledge of it to Spiegel,
the author of the first Parsi grammar.

This third period in the history of the Persian
language, comprehending the Huzvaresh and Parsi,
ends with the downfall of the Sassanians. The Arab
conquest quenched the last sparks of Persian nationality; and the fire-altars of the Zoroastrians were
never to be lighted again, except in the oasis of Yezd
and on the soil of that country which the Zoroastrians

had quitted as the disinherited sons of Manu. Still
the change did not take place at once. Mohl, in his
magnificent edition of the Shahnameh, has treated
this period admirably, and it is from him that I derive
the following facts. For a time, Persian religion,
customs, traditions, and songs survived in the hands
of the Persian nobility and landed gentry (the
Dihkans) who lived among the people, particularly
in the eastern provinces, remote from the capital and
the seats of foreign dominion, Baghdad, Kufah, and
Mosul. Where should Firdusi have collected the
national strains of ancient epic poetry which he
revived in the Shahnameh (1000 A. D.), if the Persian
peasant and the Persian knight had not preserved
the memory of their old heathen heroes, even under
the vigilant oppression of Mohammedan zealots ?
True, the first collection of epic traditions was made
under the Sassanians. But this work commenced
under Nushirvan, and finished under Yezdegird, the
last of the Sassanians, was destroyed by Omar's command. Firdusi himself tells us how this first collection was made by the Dihkan Danishver. ' There
was a Pehlevan,' he says, ' of the family of the
Dihkans, brave and powerful, wise and illustrious,
who loved to study the ancient times, and to collect
the stories of past ages. He summoned from all the
provinces old men who possessed portions of (i.e. who
knew) an ancient work in which many stories were
written. He asked them about the origin of kings
and illustrious heroes, and how they governed the
world which they left to us in this wretched state.
These old men recited before him, one after the other,
the traditions of the kings and the changes in the
empire. The Dihkan listened, and composed a book

worthy of his fame. This is the monument he left
to mankind, and great and small have celebrated his
name.'

The collector of this first epic poem, under
Yezdegird, is called a Dihkan by Firdusi. Dihkan,
according to the Persian dictionaries, means (1)
farmer, (2) historian; and the reason commonly
assigned for this double meaning is, that the Persian farmers happened to be well read in history.
Quatremère, however, has proved that the Dihkans
were the landed nobility of Persia; that they kept
up a certain independence, even under the sway of
the Mohammedan Khalifs, and exercised in the
country a sort of jurisdiction in spite of the com-
missioners sent from Baghdad, the seat of the
government. Thus Danishver even is called a
Dihkan, although he lived previous to the Arab
conquest. With him, the title was only intended
to show that it was in the country and among the
peasants that he picked up the traditions and songs
about Jemshid, Feridun, and Rustem. Of his work,
however, we know nothing. It was destroyed by
Omar; and, though it survived in an Arabic translation, even this was lost in later times. The work,
therefore, had to be recommenced when in the eastern
provinces of Persia a national, though no longer a
Zoroastrian, feeling began to revive. The governors
of these provinces became independent as soon as
the power of the Khalifs, after its rapid rise, began
to show signs of weakness. Though the Mohammedan religion had taken root, even among the
national party, yet Arabic was no longer countenanced by the governors of the eastern provinces.
Persian was spoken again at their courts, Persian

poets were encouraged, and ancient national traditions, stripped of their religious garb, began to be
collected anew. It is said that Jacob, the son of
Leis (870), the first prince of Persian blood who
declared himself independent of the Khalifs, procured fragments of Danishver's epic, and had it
rearranged and continued. Then followed the
dynasty of the Samanians, who claimed descent from
the Sassanian kings. They, as well as the later
dynasty of the Gaznevides, pursued the same popular
policy. They were strong because they rested on
the support of a national Persian spirit. The national
epic poet of the Samanians was Dakiki, by birth a
Zoroastrian. Firdusi possessed fragments of his
work, and has given a specimen of it in the story
of Gushtasp. The final accomplishment, however, of
an idea, first cherished by Nushirvan, was reserved
for Mahmud the Great, the second king of the
Gaznevide dynasty. By his command collections
of old books were made all over the empire. Men
who knew ancient poems were summoned to the
court. One of them was Ader Berzin, who had
spent his whole life in collecting popular accounts
of the ancient kings of Persia. Another was Serv
Azad, from Merv, who claimed descent from Neriman,
and knew all the tales concerning Sam, Zal, and
Rustem, which had been preserved in his family.
It was from these materials that Firdusi composed
his great epic, the Shahnameh. He himself declares,
in many passages of his poem, that he always followed tradition. 'Traditions,' he says, 'have been
given by me; nothing of what is worth knowing has
been forgotten. All that I shall say, others have
said before me : they plucked before me the fruits

in the garden of knowledge.' He speaks in detail
of his predecessors : he even indicates the sources
from which he derives different episodes, and it is
his constant endeavour to convince his readers that
what he relates are not poetical inventions of his
own. Thus only can we account for the fact, first
pointed out by Burnouf, that many of the heroes in
the Shahnameh still exhibit the traits, sadly distorted, it is true, but still unmistakeable, of Vaidik
deities, which had passed through the Zoroastrian
schism, the Achæmenian reign, the Macedonian occupation, the Parthian wars, the Sassanian revival,
and the Mohammedan conquest, and of which the
Dihkans could still sing and tell, when Firdusi's
poem impressed the last stamp on the language of
Zarathustra. Bopp had discovered already, in his
edition of Nalas (1832), that the Zend Vivanhvat
was the same as the Sanskrit Vivasvat; and
Burnouf, in his 'Observations sur la Grammaire
Comparée de M. Bopp,' had identified a second per-
sonage, the Zend Keresâspa with the Sanskrit
Krisâsva. But the similarity between the Zend
Keresâspa and the Garshasp of the Shahnameh
opened a new and wide prospect to Burnouf, and
afterwards led him on to the most striking and
valuable results. Some of these were published in
his last work on Zend, 'Etudes sur la Langue et les
Textes Zends.' This is a collection of articles published originally in the 'Journal Asiatique' between
1840 and 1846 ; and it is particularly the fourth
essay, 'Le Dieu Homa,' which has opened an entirely
new mine for researches into the ancient state of
religion and tradition common to the Aryans before
their schism. Burnouf showed that three of the
most famous names in the Shahnameh, Jemshid,

Feridun, and Garshasp, can be traced back to three heroes mentioned in the Zend-Avesta as the representatives of the three earliest generations of mankind, Yima Kshaêta, Thraêtaona, and Keresâspa, and that the prototypes of these Zoroastrian heroes could be found again in the Yama-Trita, and Krisâsva of the Veda. He went even beyond this. He showed that, as in Sanskrit, the father of Yama is Vivasvat, the father of Yima in the Avesta is Vivanhvat. He showed that as Thraêtaona in Persia is the son of Âthwya, the patronymic of Trita in the Veda is Âptya. He explained the transition of Thraêtaona into Feridun by pointing to the Pehlevi form of the name, as given by Neriosengh, Fredun. This change of an aspirated dental into an aspirated labial, which by many is considered a flaw in this argument, is of frequent occurrence. We have only to think of φήρ and θήρ, of dhûma and fumus, of modern Greek φέλω and θέλω—nay, Menenius's ' first complaint' would suffice to explain it. Burnouf again identified Zohâk, the King of Persia, slain by Feridun, whom even Firdusi still knows by the name of Ash dahâk, with the Azhi dahâka, the biting serpent, as he translates it, destroyed by Thraêtaona in the Avesta; and with regard to the changes which these names, and the ideas originally expressed by them, had to undergo on the intellectual stage of the Aryan nation, he says: ' Il est sans contredit fort curieux de voir une des divinités indiennes les plus vénérées, donner son nom au premier souverain de la dynastie ario-persanne; c'est un des faits qui attestent le plus évidemment l'intime union des deux branches de la

grande famille qui s'est étendue, bien de siècles avant
notre ère, depuis le Gange jusqu'à l'Euphrate.'

The great achievements of Burnouf in this field of
research have been so often ignored, and what by right
belongs to him has been so confidently ascribed to
others, that a faithful representation of the real state of
the case, as here given, will not appear superfluous.
There is no intention, while giving his due to Burnouf, to detract from the merits of other scholars.
Some more minute coincidences, particularly in the
story of Feridun, have subsequently been added by
Roth, Benfey, and Weber.   The first, particularly,
has devoted two most interesting articles to the
identification of Yama-Yima-Jemshid and Trita-
Thraêtaona-Feridun.   Trita, who has generally been
fixed upon as the Vaidik original of Feridun, because
Traitana, whose name corresponds more accurately,
occurs but once in the Rig-veda, is represented in
India as one of the many divine powers ruling the
firmament, destroying darkness, and sending rain,
or, as the poets of the Veda are fond of expressing
it, rescuing the cows and slaying the demons that
had carried them off.   These cows always move along
the sky, some dark, some bright-coloured.   They
low over their pasture; they are gathered by the
winds; and milked by the bright rays of the sun,
they drop from their heavy udders a fertilising
milk upon the parched and thirsty earth.   But
sometimes, the poet says, they are carried off by
robbers and kept in dark caves near the uttermost
ends of the sky.   Then the earth is without rain;
the pious worshipper offers up his prayer to Indra,
and Indra rises to conquer the cows for him.   He
sends his dog to find the scent of the cattle, and

after she has heard their lowing, she returns, and
the battle commences. Indra hurls his thunderbolt; the Maruts ride at his side; the Rudras
roar; till at last the rock is cleft asunder, the
demon destroyed, and the cows brought back to
their pasture. This is one of the oldest mythes
or sayings current among the Aryan nations. It
appears again in the mythology of Italy, in Greece,
in Germany. In the Avesta, the battle is fought
between Thraêtaona and Azhi dahâka, the destroying
serpent. Traitana takes the place of Indra in this
battle in one song of the Veda; more frequently
it is Trita, but other gods also share in the same
honour. The demon, again, who fights against the
gods is likewise called Ahi, or the serpent, in the
Veda. But the characteristic change that has taken
place between the Veda and Avesta is that the
battle is no longer a conflict of gods and demons for
cows, nor of light and darkness for the dawn. It is
the battle of a pious man against the power of evil.
'Le Zoroastrisme,' as Burnouf says, 'en se détachant
plus franchement de Dieu et de la nature, a cer-
tainement tenu plus de compte de l'homme que
n'a fait le Brahmanisme, et on peut dire qu'il a
regagné en profondeur ce qu'il perdait en étendue.
Il ne m'appartient pas d'indiquer ici ce qu'un système
qui tend à développer les instincts les plus nobles
de notre nature, et qui impose à l'homme, comme
le plus important de ses devoirs, celui de lutter
constamment contre le principe du mal, a pu exercer
d'influence sur les destinées des peuples de l'Asie,
chez lesquels il a été adopté à diverses époques. On
peut cependant déjà dire que le caractère religieux
et martial tout à la fois, qui paraît avec des traits

si héroïques dans la plupart des Jeshts, n'a pas dû
être sans action sur la mâle discipline sous laquelle
ont grandi les commencements de la monarchie de
Cyrus.'

A thousand years after Cyrus (for Zohâk is mentioned by Moses of Khorene in the fifth century)
we find all this forgotten once more, and the vague
rumours about Thraêtaona and Azhi Dahâka are
gathered at last, and arranged and interpreted into
something intelligible to later ages. Zohâk is a
three-headed tyrant on the throne of Persia—three-
headed, because the Vaidik Ahi was three-headed,
only that one of Zohâk's heads has now become
human. Zohak has killed Jemshid of the Pesh-
dadian dynasty: Feridun now conquers Zohâk on
the banks of the Tigris. He then strikes him down
with his cow-headed mace, and is on the point of
killing him, when, as Firdusi says, a supernatural
voice whispered in his ear[5]—

> Slay him not now, his time is not yet come,
> His punishment must be prolonged awhile;
> And as he cannot now survive the wound,
> Bind him with heavy chains—convey him straight
> Upon the mountain, there within a cave,
> Deep, dark, and horrible—with none to soothe
> His sufferings, let the murderer lingering die.
> The work of heaven performing, Feridun
> First purified the world from sin and crime.
> Yet Feridun was not an angel, nor
> Composed of musk and ambergris. By justice
> And generosity he gained his fame.
> Do thou but exercise these princely virtues,
> And thou wilt be renowned as Feridun.

As a last stage in the mythe of the Vaidik Traitana

---

[5] Cf. Atkinson's Shahnameh, p. 48.

we may mention versions like those given by Sir
John Malcolm and others, who see in Zohâk the
representative of an Assyrian invasion lasting during
the thousand years of Zohâk's reign, and who change
Feridun into Arbaces the Mede, the conqueror of
Sardanapalus. We may then look at the whole
with the new light which Burnouf's genius has shed
over it, and watch the retrograde changes of Arbaces
into Feridun, of Feridun into Phredûn, of Phredûn
into Thraêtaona, of Thraêtaona into Traitana,—each a
separate phase in the dissolving view of mythology.

As to the language of Persia, its biography is
at an end with the Shahnameh. What follows
exhibits hardly any signs of either growth or decay.
The language becomes more and more encumbered
with foreign words; but the grammar seems to have
arrived at its lowest ebb, and withstands further
change. From this state of grammatical numbness,
languages recover by a secondary formation, which
grows up slowly and imperceptibly at first in the
speech of the people; till at last the reviving spirit
rises upwards, and sweeps away, like the waters in
spring, the frozen surface of an effete government,
priesthood, literature, and grammar.

October, 1853.

IV

THE AITAREYA-BRÂHMANA[1].

THE Sanskrit text, with an English translation of the Aitareya-brâhmana, just published at Bombay by Dr. Martin Haug, the Superintendent of Sanskrit Studies in the Poona College, constitutes one of the most important additions lately made to our knowledge of the ancient literature of India. The work is published by the Director of Public Instruction, in behalf of Government, and furnishes a new instance of the liberal and judicious spirit in which Mr. Howard bestows his patronage on works of real and permanent utility. The Aitareya-brâhmana, containing the earliest speculations of the Brahmans on the meaning of their sacrificial prayers, and the purport of their ancient religious rites, is a work which could be properly edited nowhere but in India. It is only a small work of about two hundred pages, but it presupposes so thorough a familiarity with all the externals of the religion of the Brahmans, the various offices of their priests, the times and seasons of their sacred rites, the form of their innumerable sacrificial utensils, and the preparation

---

[1] 'The Aitareya-brâhmanam of the Rig-veda,' edited and translated by Martin Haug, Ph.D., Superintendent of Sanskrit Studies in the Poona College. Bombay, 1863. London: Trübner & Co.

of their offerings, that no amount of Sanskrit scholarship, such as can be gained in England, would have
been sufficient to unravel the intricate speculations
concerning the matters which form the bulk of the
Aitareya-brâhmana. The difficulty was not to translate the text word for word, but to gain a clear,
accurate, and living conception of the subjects there
treated. The work was composed by persons, and for
persons, who, in a general way, knew the performance of the Vedic sacrifices as well as we know the
performance of our own sacred rites. If we placed
the English Prayer-book in the hands of a stranger
who had never assisted at an English service, we
should find that, in spite of the simplicity and plain-
ness of its language, it failed to convey to the unini-
tiated a clear idea of what he ought and what he
ought not to do in church. The ancient Indian ceremonial, however, is one of the most artificial and
complicated forms of worship that can well be imagined; and though its details are, no doubt, most
minutely described in the Brâhmanas and the Sûtras,
yet, without having seen the actual site on which
the sacrifices are offered, the altars constructed for
the occasion, the instruments employed by different
priests—the *toul-ensemble*, in fact, of the sacred
rites—the reader seems to deal with words, but with
words only, and is unable to reproduce in his imagination the acts and facts which were intended to be
conveyed by them. Various attempts were made to
induce some of the more learned Brahmans to edit
and translate some of their own rituals, and thus
enable European scholars to gain an idea of the actual
performance of their ancient sacrifices, and to enter
more easily into the spirit of the speculations on the

mysterious meaning of these rituals, which are embodied in the so-called Brâhmaṇas, or 'the sayings of the Brahmans.' But although, thanks to the enlightened exertions of Dr. Ballantyne and his associates in the Sanskrit College of Benares, Brahmans might have been found knowing English quite sufficiently for the purpose of a rough and ready translation from Sanskrit into English, such was their prejudice against divulging the secrets of their craft that none could be persuaded to undertake the ungrateful task. Dr. Haug tells us of another difficulty, which we had hardly suspected,—the great scarcity of Brahmans familiar with the ancient Vedic ritual:

'Seeing the great difficulties, nay, impossibility of attaining to anything like a real understanding of the sacrificial art from all the numerous books I had collected, I made the greatest efforts to obtain oral information from some of those few Brahmans who are known by the name of Srotriyas or Srautis, and who alone are the possessors of the sacrificial mysteries as they descended from the remotest times. The task was no easy one, and no European scholar in this country before me ever succeeded in it. This is not to be wondered at; for the proper knowledge of the ritual is everywhere in India now rapidly dying out, and in many parts, chiefly in those under British rule, it has already died out.'

Dr. Haug succeeded, however, at last in procuring the assistance of a real Doctor of Divinity, who had not only performed the minor Vedic sacrifices, such as the full and new moon offerings, but had officiated at some of the great Soma sacrifices, now very rarely to be seen in any part of India. He was induced, we are sorry to say by very mercenary considerations, to

perform the principal ceremonies in a secluded part
of Dr. Haug's premises. This lasted five days, and
the same assistance was afterwards rendered by the
same worthy and some of his brethren whenever
Dr. Haug was in any doubt as to the proper meaning
of the ceremonial treatises which give the outlines of
the Vedic sacrifices. Dr. Haug was actually allowed
to taste that sacred beverage, the Soma, which gives
health, wealth, wisdom, inspiration, nay immortality,
to those who receive it from the hands of a twice-
born priest. Yet, after describing its preparation, all
that Dr. Haug has to say of it is:

'The sap of the plant now used at Poona appears
whitish, has a very stringent taste, is bitter, but not
sour; it is a very nasty drink, and has some intoxicating effect. I tasted it several times, but it was
impossible for me to drink more than some tea-
spoonfuls.'

After having gone through all these ordeals, Dr.
Haug may well say that his explanations of sacrificial
terms, as given in the notes, can be relied upon as
certain; that they proceed from what he himself
witnessed, and what he was able to learn from men
who had inherited the knowledge from the most
ancient times. He speaks with some severity of those
scholars in Europe who have attempted to explain
the technical terms of the Vedic sacrifices without
the assistance of native priests, and without even
availing themselves carefully of the information they
might have gained from native commentaries.

In the preface to his edition of the Aitareya-
brâhmana, Dr. Haug has thrown out some new ideas
on the chronology of Vedic literature which deserve
careful consideration. Beginning with the hymns of

the Rig-veda, he admits, indeed, that there are in
that collection ancient and modern hymns, but he
doubts whether it will be possible to draw a sharp
line between what has been called the *K*handas
period, representing the free growth of sacred poetry,
and the Mantra period, during which the ancient
hymns were supposed to have been collected and
new ones added, chiefly intended for sacrificial purposes.   Dr. Haug maintains that some hymns of a
decidedly sacrificial character should be ascribed to
the earliest period of Vedic poetry.   He takes, for
instance, the hymn describing the horse sacrifice, and
he concludes from the fact that seven priests only
are mentioned in it by name, and that none of them
belongs to the class of the Udgâtars (singers) and
Brahmans (superintendents), that this hymn was
written before the establishment of these two classes
of priests.   As these priests are mentioned in other
Vedic hymns, he concludes that the hymn describing
the horse sacrifice is of a very early date.   Dr. Haug
strengthens his case by a reference to the Zoroastrian
ceremonial, in which, as he says, the chanters and
superintendents are entirely unknown, whereas the
other two classes, the Hotars (reciters) and Adhvar-
yus (assistants) are mentioned by the same names
as Zaotar and Rathwiskare.   The establishment of
the two new classes of priests would, therefore, seem
to have taken place in India after the Zoroastrians
had separated from the Brahmans; and Dr. Haug
would ascribe the Vedic hymns in which no more
than two classes of priests are mentioned to a period
preceding, others in which the other two classes of
priests are mentioned to a period succeeding, that
ancient schism.   We must confess, though doing full

justice to Dr. Haug's argument, that he seems to us
to stretch what is merely negative evidence beyond
its proper limits. Surely a poet, though acquainted
with all the details of a sacrifice and the titles of all
the priests employed in it, might speak of it in a
more general manner than the author of a manual,
and it would be most dangerous to conclude that
whatever was passed over by him in silence did not
exist at the time when he wrote. Secondly, if there
were more ancient titles of priests, the poet would
most likely use them in preference to others that
had been but lately introduced. Thirdly, even the
ancient priestly titles had originally a more general
meaning before they were restricted to their technical significance, just as in Europe bishop meant
originally an overseer, priest an elder, deacon a
minister. In several hymns, some of these titles—
for instance, that of hotar, invoker—are clearly
used as appellatives, and not as titles. Lastly, one
of the priests mentioned in the hymn on the horse
sacrifice, the Agnimindha, is admitted by Dr. Haug
himself to be the same as the Âgnîdhra; and if we
take this name, like all the others, in its technical
sense, we have to recognise in him one of the four
Brahman priests[2]. We should thus lose the ground
on which Dr. Haug's argument is chiefly based, and

---

[2] By an accident two lines containing the names of the sixteen
priests in my 'History of Ancient Sanskrit Literature' (p. 469) have
been misplaced. Âgnîdhra and Potri ought to range with the Brahmans, Pratihartri and Subrahmanya with the Udgâtris. See Âsval.
Sûtras IV. 1 (p. 286, 'Bibliotheca Indica'); and M. M., Todtenbestattung, p. xlvi. It might be said, however, that the Agnimindha
was meant as one of the Hotrâsamsins, or one of the Seven Priests,
the Sapta Hotris. See Haug, Aitareya-brâhmana, vol. i. p. 58.

should have to admit the existence of Brahman
priests as early at least as the time in which the
hymn on the horse sacrifice was composed. But,
even admitting that allusions to a more or less complete ceremonial[3] could be pointed out in certain
hymns, this might help us no doubt in subdividing
and arranging the poetry of the second or Mantra
period, but it would leave the question, whether allusions to ceremonial technicalities are to be considered
as characteristics of later or earlier hymns, entirely
unaffected.   Dr. Haug, who holds that, in the development of the human race, sacrifice comes earlier
than religious poetry, formulas earlier than prayers,
Leviticus earlier than the Psalms, applies this view
to the chronological arrangement of Vedic literature;
and he is, therefore, naturally inclined to look upon
hymns composed for sacrificial purposes, more particularly upon the invocations and formulas of the
Yagur-veda, and upon the Nivids preserved in the
Brâhmaṇas and Sûtras, as relics of greater antiquity
than the free poetical effusions of the Rishis, which
defy ceremonial rules, ignore the settled rank of priests
and deities, and occasionally allude to subjects more
appropriate for profane than for sacred poetry:

'The first sacrifices [he writes] were no doubt
simple offerings performed without much ceremonial.   A few appropriate solemn words, indicating the
giver, the nature of the offering, the deity to which,
as well as the purpose for which it was offered, were
sufficient.   All this would be embodied in the sacrificial formulas known in later times principally by

---

[3] Many such allusions were collected in my ' History of Ancient
Sanskrit Literature,' p. 486 seq.; some of them have lately been
independently discovered by others.

the name of Ya*g*ush, whilst the older one appears
to have been Yâ*gy*â. The invocation of the deity by
different names, and its invitation to enjoy the meal
prepared, may be equally old. It was justly regarded
as a kind of Ya*g*ush, and called Nigada or Nivid.'

In comparing these sacrificial formulas with the
bulk of the Rig-veda hymns, Dr. Haug comes to the
conclusion that the former are more ancient. He
shows that certain of these formulas and Nivids were
known to the poets of the hymns, as they undoubt-
edly were; but this would only prove that these
poets were acquainted with these as well as with
other portions of the ceremonial. It would only
confirm the view advocated by others, that certain
hymns were clearly written for ceremonial purposes,
though the ceremonial presupposed by these hymns
may in many cases prove more simple and primitive
than the ceremonial laid down in the Brâhmanas
and Sûtras. But if Dr. Haug tells us that the Rishis
tried their poetical talent first in the composition of
Yâ*gy*âs, or verses to be recited while an offering was
thrown into the fire, and that the Yâ*gy*âs were afterwards extended into little songs, we must ask, is
this fact or theory? And if we are told that 'there
can be hardly any doubt that the hymns which we
possess are purely sacrificial, and made only for
sacrificial purposes, and that those which express
more general ideas, or philosophical thoughts, or
confessions of sins, are comparatively late,' we can
only repeat our former question. Dr. Haug, when
proceeding to give his proofs that the purely sacrificial poetry is more ancient than either profane
songs or hymns of a more general religious character,
only produces such collateral evidence as may be

found in the literary history of the Jews and the
Chinese—evidence which is curious, but not con-
vincing.   Among the Aryan nations, it has hitherto
been considered as a general rule that poetry- precedes prose.   Now the Yâgyâs and Nivids are prose,
and though Dr. Haug calls it rhythmical prose, yet,
as compared with the hymns, they are prose; and
though such an argument by itself could by no
means be considered as sufficient to upset any solid
evidence to the contrary, yet it is stronger than the
argument derived from the literature of nations who
are neither of them Aryan in language or thought.

But though we have tried to show the insufficiency
of the arguments advanced by Dr. Haug in support
of his theory, we are by no means prepared to deny
the great antiquity of some of the sacrificial formulas
and invocations, and more particularly of the Nivids
to which he for the first time has called attention.
There probably existed very ancient Nivids or invocations, but are the Nivids which we possess the
identical Nivids alluded to in the hymns?   If so,
why have they no accents, why do they not form
part of the Sanhitâs, why were they not preserved,
discussed, and analysed with the same religious care
as the metrical hymns?   The Nivids which we now
possess may, as Dr. Haug supposes, have inspired
the Rishis with the burden of their hymns; but
they may equally well have been put together by
later compilers from the very hymns of the Rishis.
There is many a hymn in the Sanhitâ of the Rig-
veda which may be called a Nivid, i. e. an invitation
addressed to the gods to come to the sacrifices, and
an enumeration of the principal names of each deity.
Those who believe, on more general grounds, that

all religion began with sacrifice and sacrificial
formulas will naturally look on such hymns and on
the Nivids as relics of a more primitive age: while
others who look upon prayer, praise, and thanksgiving, and the unfettered expression of devotion
and wonderment as the first germs of a religious
worship, will treat the same Nivids as productions
of a later age. We doubt whether this problem
can be argued on general grounds. Admitting that
the Jews began with sacrifice and ended with
psalms, it would by no means follow that the Aryan
nations did the same, nor would the chronological
arrangement of the ancient literature of China help
us much in forming an opinion of the growth of the
Indian mind. We must take each nation by itself,
and try to find out what they themselves hold as
to the relative antiquity of their literary documents.
On general grounds, the problem whether sacrifice or
prayer comes first, may be argued ad infinitum,
just like the problem whether the hen comes first
or the egg. In the special case of the sacred literature of the Brahmans, we must be guided by their
own tradition, which invariably places the poetical
hymns of the Rig-veda before the ceremonial hymns
and formulas of the Yagur-veda and Sâma-veda.
The strongest argument that has as yet been brought
forward against this view is, that the formulas of
the Yagur-veda and the sacrificial texts of the Sâma-
veda contain occasionally more archaic forms of
language than the hymns of the Rig-veda. It was
supposed, therefore, that, although the hymns of
the Rig-veda might have been composed at an
earlier time, the sacrificial hymns and formulas were
the first to be collected and to be preserved in the

schools by means of a strict mnemonic discipline. The hymns of the Rig-veda, some of which have no reference whatever to the Vedic ceremonial, being collected at a later time, might have been stripped, while being handed down by oral tradition, of those grammatical forms which in the course of time had become obsolete, but which, if once recognised and sanctioned in theological seminaries, would have been preserved there with the most religious care.

According to Dr. Haug, the period during which the Vedic hymns were composed extends from 1400 to 2000 B.C. The oldest hymns, however, and the sacrificial formulas he would place between 2000 and 2400 B.C. This period, corresponding to what has been called the *Khandas* and Mantra periods, would be succeeded by the Brâhmana period, and Dr. Haug would place the bulk of the Brâhmanas, all written in prose, between 1400 and 1200 B.C. He does not attribute much weight to the distinction made by the Brahmans themselves between revealed and profane literature, and would place the Sûtras almost contemporaneous with the Brâhmanas. The only fixed point from which he starts in his chronological arrangement is the date implied by the position of the solstitial points mentioned in a little treatise, the *Gyotisha*, a date which has been accurately fixed by the Rev. R. Main at 1186 B.C.[4] Dr. Haug fully admits that such an observation was an absolute necessity for the Brahmans in regulating their calendar:

' The proper time [he writes] of commencing and

_____

[4] See preface to the fourth volume of my edition of the Rig-veda.

ending their sacrifices, principally the so-called Sattras or sacrificial sessions, could not be known
without an accurate knowledge of the time of the
sun's northern and southern progress. The knowledge of the calendar forms such an essential part
of the ritual, that many important conditions of the
latter cannot be carried out without the former.
The sacrifices are allowed to commence only at
certain lucky constellations, and in certain months.
So, for instance, as a rule, no great sacrifice can
commence during the sun's southern progress; for
this is regarded up to the present day as an un-
lucky period by the Brahmans, in which even to
die is believed to be a misfortune. The great sacrifices generally take place in spring in the months
of *K*aitra and Vaisâkha (April and May). The
Sattras, which lasted for one year, were, as one
may learn from a careful perusal of the fourth book
of the Aitareya-brâhmana, nothing but an imitation
of the sun's yearly course. They were divided into
two distinct parts, each consisting of six months
of thirty days each; in the midst of both was the
Vishuvat, i.e. equator or central day cutting the
whole Sattra into two halves. The ceremonies were
in both halves exactly the same, but they were in the
latter half performed in an inverted order.'

This argument of Dr. Haug's seems correct as far
as the date of the establishment of the ceremonial
is concerned, and it is curious that several scholars
who have lately written on the origin of the Vedic
calendar, and the possibility of its foreign origin,
should not have perceived the intimate relation
between that calendar and the whole ceremonial
system of the Brahmans. Dr. Haug is, no doubt,

perfectly right when he claims the invention of
the Nakshatras, or the Lunar Zodiac of the Brahmans, if we may so call it, for India; he may be
right also when he assigns the twelfth century as
the earliest date for the origin of that simple astro-
nomical system on which the calendar of the Vedic
festivals is founded. He calls the theories of others,
who have lately tried to claim the first discovery
of the Nakshatras for China, Babylon, or some other
Asiatic country, absurd, and takes no notice of the
sanguine expectations of certain scholars, who imagine they will soon have discovered the very names
of the Indian Nakshatras in Babylonian inscriptions.
But does it follow that, because the ceremonial
presupposes an observation of the solstitial points in
about the twelfth century, therefore the theological
works in which that ceremonial is explained, com-
mented upon, and furnished with all kinds of mysterious meanings, were composed at that early date?
We see no stringency whatever in this argument of
Dr. Haug's, and we think it will be necessary to look
for other anchors by which to fix the drifting wrecks
of Vedic literature.   .

Dr. Haug's two volumes, containing the text of
the Aitareya-brâhmana, translation, and notes, would
probably never have been published, if they had not
received the patronage of the Bombay Government.
However interesting the Brâhmanas may be to
students of Indian. literature, they are of small
interest to the general reader. The greater portion
of them is simply twaddle, and what is worse,
theological twaddle. No person who is not acquainted beforehand with the place which the
Brâhmanas fill in the history of the Indian mind,

could read more than ten pages without being disgusted. To the historian, however, and to the
philosopher they are of infinite importance—to the
former as a real link between the ancient and modern
literature of India; to the latter as a most important phase in the growth of the human mind, in its
passage from health to disease. Such books, which
no circulating library would touch, are just the books
which Governments, if possible, or Universities and
learned societies, should patronise; and if we congratulate Dr. Haug on having secured the enlightened
patronage of the Bombay Government, we may congratulate Mr. Howard and the Bombay Government
on having, in this instance, secured the services of a
bonâ fide scholar like Dr. Haug.[5]

March, 1864.

----

[5] A few paragraphs in this review, in which allusion was made
to certain charges of what might be called 'literary rattening,'
brought by Dr. Haug against some Sanskrit scholars, and more
particularly against the editor of the 'Indische Studien' at Berlin,
have here been omitted, as no longer of any interest. They may
be seen, however, in the ninth volume of that periodical, where my
review has been reprinted, though, as usual, very incorrectly. It
was not I who first brought these accusations, nor should I have felt
justified in alluding to them, if the evidence placed before me had
not convinced me that there was some foundation for them. I am
willing to admit that the language of Dr. Haug and others may have
been too severe, but few will think that a very loud and boisterous
denial is the best way to show that the strictures were quite unde-
served. If, by alluding to these matters and frankly expressing
my disapproval of them, I have given unnecessary pain, I sincerely
regret it. So much for the past. As to the future, care, I trust,
will be taken,—for the sake of the good fame of German scholarship,
which, though living in England, I have quite as much at heart as
if living in Germany,—not to give even the faintest countenance
to similar suspicions. If my remarks should help in producing that
result, I shall be glad to bow my head in silence under the vials
of wrath that have been poured upon it.

V.

ON THE STUDY

OF THE

ZEND-AVESTA IN INDIA[1].

SANSKRIT scholars resident in India enjoy considerable advantages over those who devote themselves to the study of the ancient literature of the Brahmans in this country, or in France and Germany. Although Sanskrit is no longer spoken by the great mass of the people, there are few large towns in which we do not meet with some more or less learned natives—the pandits, or, as they used to be called, pundits—men who have passed through a regular apprenticeship in Sanskrit grammar, and who generally devote themselves to the study of some special branch of Sanskrit literature, whether law, or logic, or rhetoric, or astronomy, or anything else. These men, who formerly lived on the liberality of the Rajahs and on the superstition of the people, find it more and more difficult to make a living among their own countrymen, and are glad to be

---

[1] 'Essays on the Sacred Language, Writings, and Religion of the Parsees.' By Martin Haug, Dr. Phil. Bombay, 1862.

employed by any civilian or officer who takes an
interest in their ancient lore. Though not scholars
in our sense of the word, and therefore of little use
as teachers of the language, they are extremely useful
to more advanced students, who are able to set them
to do that kind of work for which they are fit, and to
check their labours by judicious supervision.   All our
great Sanskrit scholars, from Sir William Jones to
H. H. Wilson, have fully acknowledged their obligations to their native assistants.   They used to work
in Calcutta, Benares, and Bombay with a pandit at
each elbow, instead of the grammar and the dictionary which European scholars have to consult at
every difficult passage.   Whenever an English Sahib
undertook to edit or translate a Sanskrit text, these
pandits had to copy and to collate MSS., to make a
verbal index, to produce parallel passages from other
writers, and, in many cases, to supply a translation
into Hindustani, Bengali, or into their own peculiar
English.   In fact, if it had not been for the assistance thus fully and freely rendered by native scholars,
Sanskrit scholarship would never have made the rapid
progress which, during less than a century, it has
made, not only in India, but in almost every country
of Europe.

With this example to follow, it is curious that
hardly any attempt should have been made by
English residents, particularly in the Bombay Presidency, to avail themselves of the assistance of the
Parsis for the purpose of mastering the ancient language and literature of the worshippers of Ormuzd.
If it is remembered that, next to Sanskrit, there is no
more ancient language than Zend—and that, next to
the Veda, there is, among the Aryan nations, no more

primitive religious code than the Zend-Avesta, it is
surprising that so little should have been done by
the members of the Indian Civil Service in this important branch of study.   It is well known that such
was the enthusiasm kindled in the heart of Anquetil
Duperron by the sight of a facsimile of a page of
the Zend-Avesta, that in order to secure a passage to
India, he enlisted as a private soldier, and spent six
years (1754–1761) in different parts of Western India,
trying to collect MSS. of the sacred writings of Zoroaster, and to acquire from the Dustoors a knowledge
of their contents.   His example was followed, though
in a less adventurous spirit, by Rask, a learned Dane,
who after collecting at Bombay many valuable MSS.
for the Danish Government, wrote in 1826 his essay
' On the Age and Genuineness of the Zend Language.'
Another Dane, at present one of the most learned Zend
scholars in Europe, Westergaard, likewise proceeded
to India (1841–1843), before he undertook to publish
his edition of the religious books of the Zoroastrians.
(Copenhagen, 1852.)   During all this time, while
French and German scholars, such as Burnouf, Bopp,
and Spiegel, were hard at work in deciphering the
curious remains of the Magian religion, hardly anything was contributed by English students living in
the very heart of Parsiism at Bombay and Poona.

We are all the more pleased, therefore, that a
young German scholar, Dr. Haug—who through the
judicious recommendation of Mr. Howard, Director
of Public Instruction in the Bombay Presidency,
was appointed to a Professorship of Sanskrit in the
Poona College—should have grasped the opportunity, and devoted himself to a thorough study of
the sacred literature of the Parsis.   He went to

India well prepared for his task, and he has not
disappointed the hopes which those who knew him
entertained of him on his departure from Germany.
Unless he had been master of his subject before he
went to Poona, the assistance of the Dustoors would
have been of little avail to him. But knowing all
that could be known in Europe of the Zend language and literature, he knew what questions to
ask, he could check every answer, and he could
learn with his eyes what it is almost impossible to
learn from books—namely, the religious ceremonial
and the ritual observances which form so considerable an element in the Vendidad and Vispered.
The result of his studies is now before us in a
volume of 'Essays on the Sacred Language, Writings, and Religion of the Parsees,' published at
Bombay, 1862. It is a volume of only three hundred and sixty-eight pages, and sells in England
for one guinea. Nevertheless, to the student of
Zend it is one of the cheapest books ever published. It contains four Essays: 1. History of the
Researches into the Sacred Writings and Religion
of the Parsees from the earliest times down to the
present; 2. Outline of a Grammar of the Zend
Language; 3. The Zend-Avesta, or the Scripture of
the Parsees; 4. Origin and Development of the
Zoroastrian Religion. The most important portion
is the Outline of the Zend Grammar; for, though a
mere outline, it is the first systematic grammatical
analysis of that curious language. In other languages, we generally begin by learning the grammar,
and then make our way gradually through the
literature. In Zend the grammatical terminations
had first to be discovered by a careful anatomy of

the literature. The Parsis themselves possessed no
such work. Even their most learned priests are
satisfied with learning the Zend-Avesta by heart,
and with acquiring some idea of its import by means
of a Pehlevi translation, which dates from the Sassanian period, or of a Sanskrit translation of still
later date. Hence the translation of the Zend-Avesta
published by Anquetil Duperron, with the assistance
of Dustoor Dârâb, was by no means trustworthy. It
was, in fact, a French translation of a Persian rendering of a Pehlevi version of the Zend original. It was
Burnouf who, aided by his knowledge of Sanskrit,
and his familiarity with the principles of comparative
grammar, approached, for the first time, the very
words of the Zend original. He had to conquer
every inch of ground for himself, and his ‘Commentaire sur le Yasna’ is, in fact, like the deciphering
of one long inscription, only surpassed in difficulty
by his later decipherments of the cuneiform inscriptions of the Achæmenian monarchs of Persia. Aided
by the labours of Burnouf and others, Dr. Haug has
at last succeeded in putting together the disjecta
membra poetæ, and we have now in his Outline,
not indeed a grammar like that of Pânini for Sanskrit,
yet a sufficient skeleton of what was once a living
language, not inferior, in richness and delicacy, even
to the idiom of the Vedas.

There are, at present, five editions, more or less
complete, of the Zend-Avesta. The first was litho-
graphed under Burnouf's direction, and published at
Paris 1829–1843. The second edition of the text,
transcribed into Roman characters, appeared at Leip-
zig 1850, published by Professor Brockhaus. The
third edition, in Zend characters, was given to the

world by Professor Spiegel, 1851; and about the same
time a fourth edition was undertaken by Professor
Westergaard, at Copenhagen, 1852 to 1854.   There
are one or two editions of the Zend-Avesta, published
in India, with Guzerati translations, which we have
not seen, but which are frequently quoted by native
scholars. A German translation of the Zend-Avesta
was undertaken by Professor Spiegel, far superior in
accuracy to that of Anquetil Duperron, yet in the main
based on the Pehlevi version. Portions of the ancient
text had been minutely analysed and translated by
Dr. Haug, even before his departure for the East.

The Zend-Avesta is not a voluminous work. We
still call it the Zend-Avesta, though we are told ˈthat
its proper title is Avesta Zend, nor does it seem at
all likely that the now familiar ᴘame will ever be surrendered for the more correct one.   Who speaks of
Cassius Dio, though we are told that Dio Cassius is
wrong?   Nor do we feel at all convinced that the
name of Avesta Zend is the original and only
correct name.   According to the Parsis, Avesta
means sacred text, Zend its Pehlevi translation.
But in the Pehlevi translations themselves, the original work of Zoroaster is spoken of as Avesta
Zend.   Why it is so called by the Pehlevi translators, we are nowhere told by themselves, and many
conjectures have, in consequence, been started by
almost every Zend scholar.   Dr. Haug supposes that
the earliest portions of the Zend-Avesta ought to
be called Avesta, the later portions Zend—Zend
meaning, according to him, commentary, explanation,
gloss. Neither the word Avesta nor Zend, however, occurs in the original Zend texts, and though
Avesta seems to be the Sanskrit avasthâ, the

Pehlevi apestak, in the sense of 'authorised text,' the etymology of Zend, as derived from a supposed zanti, Sanskrit *gnati*, knowledge, is not free from serious objections. Avesta Zend was most likely a traditional name, hardly understood even at the time of the Pehlevi translators, who retained it in their writings. It was possibly misinterpreted by them, as many other Zend words have been at their hands, and may have been originally the Sanskrit word *khandas*[2], which is applied by the Brahmans to the sacred hymns of the Veda. Certainty on such a point is impossible; but as it is but fair to give a preference to the conjectures of those who are most familiar with the subject, we quote the following explanation of Dr. Haug:

'The meaning of the term "Zend" varied at different periods. Originally it meant the interpretation of the sacred texts descended from Zarathustra and his disciples by the successors of the prophet. In the course of time, these interpretations being regarded as equally sacred with the original texts, both were then called Avesta. Both having become unintelligible to the majority of the Zoroastrians, in consequence of their language having died out, they required a Zend or explanation again. This new Zend was furnished by the most learned priests of the Sassanian period in the shape of a translation into the vernacular language of Persia (Pehlevi) in those days, which translation being the only source to the priests of the present time whence to derive any knowledge of the old texts, is therefore the only Zend or explanation they know of. . . . . The name

---

[2] See page 84.

Pazend, to be met with frequently in connection with Avesta and Zend, denotes the further explanation of the Zend doctrine. . . . . The Pazend language is the same as the so-called Parsi, i.e. the ancient Persian, as written till about the time of Firdusi, 1000 A.D.'

Whatever we may think of the nomenclature thus advocated by Dr. Haug, we must acknowledge in the fullest manner his great merit in separating for the first time the more ancient from the more modern parts of the Zend-Avesta.   Though the existence of different dialects in the ancient texts was pointed out by Spiegel, and although the metrical portions of the Yasna had been clearly marked by Westergaard, it is nevertheless Haug's great achievement to have extracted these early relics, to have collected them, and to have attempted a complete translation of them, as far as such an attempt could be carried out at the present moment.   His edition of the Gâthâs—for this is the name of the ancient metrical portions—marks an epoch in the history of Zend scholarship, and the importance of the recovery of these genuine relics of Zoroaster's religion has been well brought out by Bunsen in the least known of his books, 'Gott in der Geschichte.'   We by no means think that the translations here offered by Dr. Haug are final.   We hope, on the contrary, that he will go on with the work he has so well begun, and that he will not rest till he has removed every dark speck that still covers the image of Zoroaster's primitive faith.   Many of the passages as translated by him are as clear as daylight, and carry conviction by their very clearness.   Others, however, are obscure, hazy, meaningless.   We feel that they must have been intended for something else, something more definite and

forcible, though we cannot tell what to do with the
words as they stand. Sense, after all, is the great
test of translation. We must feel convinced that
there was good sense in these ancient poems, otherwise mankind would not have taken the trouble to
preserve them; and if we cannot discover good sense
in them, it must be either our fault, or the words as
we now read them were not the words uttered by the
ancient prophets of the world. The following are a
few specimens of Dr. Haug's translations, in which the
reader will easily discover the different hues of certainty
and uncertainty, of sense and mere verbiage:

'1. That I will ask Thee, tell me it right, thou
living God! whether your friend (Sraosha) be willing
to recite his own hymn as prayer to my friend (Fra-
shaostra or Vistâspa), thou Wise! and whether he
should come to us with the good mind, to perform
for us true actions of friendship.

'2. That I will ask Thee, tell me it right, thou
living God! How arose the best present life (this
world)? By what means are the present things (the
world) to be supported? That spirit, the holy (Vohu
mano), O true wise spirit! is the guardian of the
beings to ward off from them every evil; He is the
promoter of all life.

'3. That I will ask Thee, tell me it right, thou
living God! Who was in the beginning the Father
and Creator of truth? Who made the sun and stars?
Who causes the moon to increase and wane if not
Thou? This I wish to know, except what I already
know.

'4. That I will ask Thee, tell me it right, thou
living God! Who is holding the earth and the skies
above it? Who made the waters and the trees of the

field? Who is in the winds and storms that they so
quickly run? Who is the Creator of the good-minded
beings, thou Wise?'

This is a short specimen of the earliest portion of
the Zend-Avesta. The following is an extract from
one of the latest, the so-called Ormuzd Yasht:

' Zarathustra asked Ahuramazda after the most
effectual spell to guard against the influence of evil
spirits. He was answered by the Supreme Spirit,
that the utterance of the different names of Ahuramazda protects best from evil. Thereupon Zarathustra begged Ahuramazda to communicate to him
these names. He then enumerates. twenty. The
first is Ahmi, i.e. "I am;" the fourth, Asha-vahista,
i.e. "the best purity;" the sixth, "I am wisdom;" the
eighth, "I am knowledge;" the twelfth, Ahura, i.e.
"living;" the twentieth, "I am who I am, Mazdao."'

Ahuramazda says then further:

' "If you call me at day or at night by these names,
I shall come to assist and help you; the angel Serosh
will then come, the genii of the waters and the trees."
For the utter defeat of the evil spirits, bad men,
witches, Peris, a series of other names are suggested
to Zarathustra, such as protector, guardian, spirit, the
holiest, the best fire-priest, etc.'

Whether the striking coincidence between one of
the suggested names of Ahuramazda, namely, 'I am
who I am,' and the explanation of the name Jehova,
Exodus iii. 14, 'I am that I am,' is accidental or not,
must depend on the age that can be assigned to the
Ormuzd Yasht. The chronological arrangement,
however, of the various portions of the Zend-Avesta
is as yet merely tentative, and these questions must
remain for future consideration. Dr. Haug points out

other similarities between the doctrines of Zoroaster and the Old and New Testaments. 'The Zoroastrian religion,' he writes, 'exhibits a very close affinity to, or rather identity with, several important doctrines of the Mosaic religion and Christianity, such as the personality and attributes of the devil, and the resurrection of the dead.' Neither of these doctrines, however, would seem to be characteristic of the Old or New Testament, and the resurrection of the dead is certainly to be found by implication only, and is nowhere distinctly asserted, in the religious books of Moses.

There are other points on which we should join issue with Dr. Haug—as, for instance, when, on page 17, he calls the Zend the elder sister of Sanskrit. This seems to us in the very teeth of the evidence so carefully brought together by himself in his Zend grammar. If he means the modern Sanskrit, as distinguished from the Vedic, his statement would be right to some extent; but even thus, it would be easy to show many grammatical forms in the later Sanskrit more primitive than their corresponding forms in Zend. These, however, are minor points compared with the great results of his labours which Dr. Haug has brought together in these four Essays; and we feel certain that all who are interested in the study of ancient language and ancient religion will look forward with the greatest expectations to Dr. Haug's continued investigations of the language, the literature, the ceremonial, and the religion of the descendants of Zoroaster.

December, 1862.

VI.

PROGRESS OF ZEND SCHOLARSHIP[1].

THERE are certain branches of philological research which seem to be constantly changing, shifting, and, we hope, progressing. After the key to the interpretation of ancient inscriptions has been found, it by no means follows that every word can at once be definitely explained, or every sentence correctly construed. Thus it happens that the same hieroglyphic or cuneiform text is rendered differently by different scholars; nay, that the same scholar proposes a new rendering not many years after his first attempt at a translation has been published. And what applies to the decipherment of inscriptions applies with equal force to the translation of ancient texts. A translation of the hymns of the Veda, or of the Zend-Avesta, and, we may add, of the Old Testament too, requires exactly the same process as the deciphering of an inscription. The only safe way of finding the real meaning of words in the sacred texts of the Brahmans, the Zoroastrians, or the Jews, is to compare every passage in which the same word occurs, and to look for a meaning that is equally applicable to all, and can at the same time be

---

[1] 'A Lecture on an Original Speech of Zoroaster.' By Martin Haug. Bombay, 1865.

defended on grammatical and etymological grounds.
This is no doubt a tedious process, nor can it be free
from uncertainty; but it is an uncertainty inherent
in the subject itself, for which it would be unfair to
blame those by whose genius and perseverance so
much light has been shed on the darkest pages of
ancient history. To those who are not acquainted
with the efforts by which Grotefend, Burnouf, Lassen,
and Rawlinson unravelled the inscriptions of Cyrus,
Darius, and Xerxes, it may seem inexplicable, for
instance, how an inscription which at one time was
supposed to confirm the statement, known from Herodotus, that Darius obtained the sovereignty of Persia
by the neighing of his horse, should now yield so
very different a meaning. Herodotus relates that
after the assassination of Smerdis the six conspirators
agreed to confer the royal dignity on him whose
horse should neigh first at sunrise. The horse of
Darius neighed first, and he was accordingly elected
king of Persia. After his election, Herodotus states
that Darius erected a stone monument containing
the figure of a horseman, with the following inscription: 'Darius, the son of Hystaspes, obtained the
kingdom of the Persians by the virtue of his horse
(giving its name), and of Oibareus, his groom.' Lassen translated one of the cuneiform inscriptions,
copied originally by Niebuhr from a huge slab built
in the southern wall of the great platform at Persepolis, in the following manner: 'Auramazdis magnus
est. Is maximus est deorum. Ipse Darium regem
constituit, benevolens imperium obtulit. Ex volun-
tate Auramazdis Darius rex sum. Generosus sum
Darius rex hujus regionis Persicæ; hanc mihi Auramazdis obtulit " hoc pomœrio ope equi (Choaspis)

claræ virtutis."' This translation was published in
1844, and the arguments by which Lassen supported
it, in the sixth volume of the 'Zeitschrift für die
Kunde des Morgenlandes,' may be read with interest
and advantage even now when we know that this
eminent scholar was mistaken in his analysis. The
first step towards a more correct translation was
made by Professor Holtzmann, who in 1845 pointed
out that Smerdis was murdered at Susa, not at Persepolis; and that only six days later Darius was elected
king of Persia, which happened again at Susa, and
not at Persepolis. The monument, therefore, which
Darius erected in the προάστειον, or suburb, in the place
where the fortunate event which led to his elevation
occurred, and the inscription recording the event in
loco, could not well be looked for at Persepolis.
But far more important was the evidence derived
from a more careful analysis of the words of the
inscription itself. Niba, which Lassen translated as
pomœrium, occurs in three other places, where it
certainly cannot mean suburb. It seems to be an
adjective meaning splendid, beautiful. Besides, nibâ
is a nominative singular in the feminine, and so is
the pronoun hyâ which precedes, and the two words
which follow it—uvaspâ and umartiyâ. Professor
Holtzmann translated therefore the same sentence
which Professor Lassen had rendered by 'hoc pomœrio ope equi (Choaspis) claræ virtutis,' by 'quæ
nitida, herbosa, celebris est,' a translation which is
in the main correct, and has been adopted afterwards both by Sir H. Rawlinson and M. Oppert. Sir
H. Rawlinson translates the whole passage as follows:
'This province of Persia which Ormazd has granted
to me, which is illustrious, abounding in good horses,

producing good men.' Thus vanished the horse of
Darius, and the curious confirmation which the cuneiform inscription was at one time supposed to lend to
the Persian legend recorded by Herodotus.

It would be easy to point out many passages of
this kind, and to use them in order to throw dis-
credit on the whole method by which these and
other inscriptions have lately been deciphered. It
would not require any great display of forensic or
parliamentary eloquence, to convince the public at
large, by means of such evidence, that all the labours
of Grotefend, Burnouf, Lassen, and Rawlinson had
been in vain, and to lay down once for all the
general principle that the original meaning of inscriptions written in a dead language, of which the
tradition is once lost, can never be recovered. Fortunately, questions of this kind are not settled by
eloquent pleading or by the votes of majorities, but,
on the contrary, by the independent judgment of
the few who are competent to judge. The fact
that different scholars should differ in their interpretations, or that the same scholar should reject his
former translation, and adopt a new one that possibly
may have to be surrendered again as soon as new
light can be thrown on points hitherto doubtful and
obscure—all this, which in the hands of those who
argue for victory and not for truth, constitutes so
formidable a weapon, and appeals so strongly to the
prejudices of the many, produces very little effect on
the minds of those who understand the reason of
these changes, and to whom each new change represents but a new step in advance in the discovery of
truth.

Nor should the fact be overlooked that, if there

seems to be less change in the translation of the books of the Old Testament for instance, or of Homer, it is due in a great measure to the absence of that critical exactness at which the decipherers of ancient inscriptions and the translators of the Veda and Zend-Avesta aim in rendering each word that comes before them. If we compared the translation of the Septuagint with the authorised version of the Old Testament, we should occasionally find discrepancies nearly as startling as any that can be found in the different translations of the cuneiform inscriptions, or of the Veda and Zend-Avesta. In the Book of Job, the Vulgate translates the exhortation of Job's wife by 'Bless God and die;' the English version by 'Curse God and die;' the Septuagint by 'Say some word to the Lord and die.' Though, at the time when the Seventy translated the Old Testament, Hebrew could hardly be called a dead language, yet there were then many of its words the original meaning of which even the most learned rabbi would have had great difficulty in defining with real accuracy. The meaning of words changes imperceptibly and irresistibly. Even where there is a literature, and a printed literature like that of modern Europe, four or five centuries work such a change that few even of the most learned divines in England would find it easy to read and to understand accurately a theological treatise written in English four hundred years ago. The same happened, and happened to a far greater extent, in ancient languages. Nor was the sacred character attributed to certain writings any safeguard. On the contrary, greater violence is done by successive interpreters to sacred writings than to any other relics of ancient literature. Ideas grow and change, yet each generation tries to find its own ideas reflected in the sacred pages of their early prophets, and, in addition to the ordinary influences which blur and obscure the sharp features of old words, artificial influences are here at work distorting the natural expression of words which have been invested with a sacred authority. Passages in the Veda or Zend-Avesta which do not bear on religious or philosophical doctrines are generally explained simply and naturally, even by the latest of native commentators. But as soon as any word or sentence can be so turned as to support a doctrine, however modern, or a precept however irrational, the simplest phrases are tortured and mangled till at last they are made to yield their assent to ideas the most foreign to the minds of the authors of the Veda and Zend-Avesta.

To those who take an interest in these matters we may recommend a small Essay lately published by the Rev. R. G. S. Browne—the 'Mosaic Cosmogony'—in which the author endeavours to establish a literal translation of the first chapter of Genesis. Touching the first verb that occurs in the Bible, he writes: 'What is the meaning or scope of the Hebrew verb, in our authorised version, rendered by "created"? To English ears and understandings the sound comes naturally, and by long use irresistibly, as the representation of an ex nihilo creation. But, in the teeth of all the Rabbinical and Cabbalistic fancies of Jewish commentators, and with reverential deference to modern criticism on the Hebrew Bible, it is not so. R. D. Kimchi, in his endeavour to ascertain the shades of difference existing between the terms used in the Mosaic cosmogony, has assumed that

our Hebrew verb barâ has the full signification of
ex nihilo creavit.   Our own Castell, a profound
and self-denying scholar, has entertained the same
groundless notion.   And even our illustrious Bryan
Walton was not inaccessible to this oblique ray of
Rabbinical ignis fatuus.'

Mr. Browne then proceeds to quote Gesenius, who
gives as the primary meaning of barâ, he cut, cut
out, carved, planed down, polished; and he refers to
Lee, who characterises it as a silly theory that barâ
meant to create ex nihilo.   In Joshua xvii. 15 and
18, the same verb is used in the sense of cutting
down trees; in Psalm civ. 30 it is translated by
'Thou renewest the face of the earth.'   In Arabic,
too, according to Lane, barâ means properly, though
not always, to create out of pre-existing matter.
All this shows that in the verb barâ, as in the
Sanskrit tvaksh or taksh,[2] there is no trace of the
meaning assigned to it by later scholars, of a creation
out of nothing.   That idea in its definiteness was a
modern 'idea, most likely called forth by the contact
between Jews and Greeks at Alexandria.   It was
probably in contradistinction to the Greek notion of
matter as co-eternal with the Creator, that the Jews,
to whom Jehovah was all in all, asserted, for the
first time deliberately, that God had made all things
out of nothing.   This became afterwards the received
and orthodox view of Jewish and Christian divines,
though the verb barâ, so far from lending any support
to this theory, would rather show that, in the minds
of those whom Moses addressed and whose language
he spoke, it could only have called forth the simple

---

[2] See Jurmann, in Kuhn's 'Zeitschrift,' xi. p. 388.

conception of fashioning or arranging—if, indeed, it
called forth any more definite conception than the
general and vague one conveyed by the ποιεῖν of the
Septuagint.   To find out how the words of the Old
Testament were understood by those to whom they
were originally addressed is a task attempted by
very few interpreters of the Bible.   The great
majority of readers transfer without hesitation the
ideas which they connect with words as used in the
nineteenth century to the mind of Moses or his
contemporaries, forgetting altogether the distance
which divides their language and their thoughts
from the thoughts and language of the wandering
tribes of Israel.

How many words, again, there are in Homer
which have indeed a traditional interpretation, as
given by our dictionaries and commentaries, but the
exact purport of which is completely lost, is best
known to Greek scholars.   It is easy enough to translate πολέμοιο γέφυραι by the bridges of war, but what
Homer really meant by these γέφυραι has never been
explained.   It is extremely doubtful whether bridges,
in our sense of the word, were known at all at the
time of Homer; and even if it could be proved that
Homer used γέφυραι in the sense of a dam, the
etymology, i. e. the earliest history of the word,
would still remain obscure and doubtful.   It is
easy, again, to see that ἱερός in Greek means something like the English sacred.   But how, if it did
so, the same adjective could likewise be applied to a
fish or to a chariot, is a question which, if it is to be
answered at all, can only be answered by an etymological analysis of the word.[3]   To say that sacred

---

[3] On ἱερός, the Sanskrit ishira, lively, see Kuhn's 'Zeitschrift,'
vol. ii. p. 275, vol. iii. p. 134.

may mean marvellous, and therefore big, is saying
nothing, particularly as Homer does not speak of
catching big fish, but of catching fish in general.

. These considerations—which might be carried
much further, but which, we are afraid, have carried
us away too far from our original subject—were
suggested to us while reading a lecture lately
published by Dr. Haug, and originally delivered by
him at Bombay, in 1864, before an almost exclusively Parsi audience. In that lecture Dr. Haug
gives a new translation of ten short paragraphs of
the Zend-Avesta, which he had explained and translated in his ‘Essays on the Sacred Language of the
Parsees,’ published in 1862. To an ordinary reader
the difference between the two translations, published within the space of two years, might certainly
be perplexing, and calculated to shake his faith in
the soundness of a method that can lead to such
varying results. Nor can it be denied that, if
scholars who are engaged in these researches are
bent on representing their last translation as final
and as admitting of no further improvement, the
public has a right to remind them that ‘finality’ is
as dangerous a thing in scholarship as in politics.
Considering the difficulty of translating the pages
of the Zend-Avesta, we can never hope to have
every sentence of it rendered into clear and intelligible English. Those who for the first time reduced the sacred traditions of the Zoroastrians to
writing were separated by more than a thousand
years from the time of their original composition.
After that came all the vicissitudes to which manuscripts are exposed during the process of being
copied by more or less ignorant scribes. The most

ancient MSS. of the Zend-Avesta date from the
beginning of the fourteenth century. It is true
there is an early translation of the Zend-Avesta,
the Pehlevi translation, and a later one in Sanskrit
by Neriosengh. But the Pehlevi translation, which
was made under the auspices of the Sassanian kings
of Persia, served only to show how completely the
literal and grammatical meaning of the Zend-Avesta
was lost even at that time, in the third century after
Christ; while the Sanskrit translation was clearly
made, not from the original, but from the Pehlevi.
It is true, also, that even in more modern times the
Parsis of Bombay were able to give to Anquetil
Duperron and other Europeans what they considered as a translation of the Zend-Avesta in modern
Persian. But a scholar like Burnouf, who endeavoured for the first time to give an account of every
word in the Zend text, to explain each grammatical
termination, to parse every sentence, and to establish the true meaning of each term by an etymological analysis and by a comparison of cognate
words in Sanskrit, was able to derive but scant
assistance from these traditional translations. Professor Spiegel, to whom we owe a complete edition
and translation of the Zend-Avesta, and who has
devoted the whole of his life to the elucidation of
the Zoroastrian religion, attributes a higher value
to the tradition of the Parsis than Dr. Haug. But
he also is obliged to admit that he could ascribe
no greater authority to these traditional translations
and glosses than a Biblical scholar might allow to
Rabbinical commentaries. All scholars are agreed
in fact on this, that whether the tradition be right
or wrong, it requires in either case to be confirmed

by an independent grammatical and etymological
analysis of the original text. Such an analysis is
no doubt as liable to error as the traditional translation itself, but it possesses this advantage, that it
gives reasons for every word that has to be translated, and for every sentence that has to be construed. It is an excellent discipline to the mind
even where the results at which we arrive are
doubtful or erroneous, and it has imparted to these
studies a scientific value and general interest which
they could not otherwise have acquired.

We shall give a few specimens of the translations
proposed by different scholars of one or two verses
of the Zend-Avesta. We cannot here enter into the
grammatical arguments by which each of these translations is supported. We only wish to show what is
the present state of Zend scholarship, and though
we would by no means disguise the fact of its somewhat chaotic character, yet we do not hesitate to
affirm that, in spite of the conflict of the opinions of
different scholars, and in spite of the fluctuation of
systems apparently opposed to each other, progress
may be reported, and a firm hope expressed that
the essential doctrines of one of the earliest forms
of religion may in time be recovered and placed
before us in their original purity and simplicity.
We begin with the Pehlevi translation of a passage
in Yasna, 45:

'Thus the religion is to be proclaimed; now give
an attentive hearing, and now listen, that is, keep
your ear in readiness, make your works and speeches
gentle. Those who have wished from nigh and far
to study the religion, may now do so. For now all
is manifest, that Anhuma (Ormazd) created, that

Anhuma created all these beings; that at the second
time, at the (time of the) future body, Aharman
does not destroy (the life of) the worlds. Aharman
made evil desire and wickedness to spread through
his tongue.'

Professor Spiegel, in 1859, translated the same passage, of which the Pehlevi is a running commentary
rather than a literal rendering, as follows:

' Now I will tell you, lend me your ear, now hear
what you desired, you that came from near and from
afar! It is clear, the wise (spirits) have created all
things; evil doctrine shall not for a second time
destroy the world. The Evil One has made a bad
choice with his tongue.'

Next follows the translation of the passage as
published by Dr. Haug in 1862:

' All ye, who have come from nigh and far, listen
now and hearken to my speech. Now I will tell you
all about that pair of spirits how it is known to
the wise. Neither the ill-speaker (the devil) shall
destroy the second (spiritual) life, nor that man
who, being a liar with his tongue, professes the
false (idolatrous) belief.'

The same scholar, in 1865, translates the same
passage somewhat differently:

' All you that have come from near and far should
now listen and hearken to what I shall proclaim.
Now the wise have manifested this universe as a
duality. Let not the mischief-maker destroy the
second life, since he, the wicked, chose with his
tongue the pernicious doctrine.'

The principal difficulty in this paragraph consists
in the word which Dr. Haug translated by duality,
viz. dûm, and which he identifies with Sanskrit

dvam, i.e. dvandvam, pair. Such a word, as far
as we are aware, does not occur again in the Zend-
Avesta, and hence it is not likely that the uncertainty attaching to its meaning will ever be
removed. Other interpreters take it as a verb in
the second person plural, and hence the decided difference of interpretation.

The sixth paragraph of the same passage is explained by the Pehlevi translator as follows:

' Thus I proclaimed that among all things the
greatest is to worship God. The praise of purity
is (due) to him who has a good knowledge, (to
those) who depend on Ormazd. I hear Spentô-
mainyu (who is) Ormazd; listen to me, to what I
shall speak (unto you). Whose worship is intercourse with the Good Mind; one can know (experience) the divine command to do good through
inquiry after what is good. That which is in the
intellect they teach me as the best, viz. the inborn
(heavenly) wisdom, (that is, that the divine wisdom
is superior to the human).'

Professor Spiegel translates:

' Now I will tell you of all things the greatest.
It is praise with purity of Him who is wise from those
who exist. The holiest heavenly being, Ahuramazda,
may hear it, He for whose praise inquiry is made from
the holy spirit, may He teach me the best by his
intelligence.'

Dr. Haug in 1862:

' Thus I will tell you of the greatest of all
(Sraosha), who is praising the truth, and doing good,
and of all who are gathered round him (to assist him),
by order of the holy spirit (Ahuramazda). The
living Wise may hear me; by means of his goodness

the good mind increases (in the world).   He may lead me with the best of his wisdom.'

Dr. Haug in 1865:

' I will proclaim as the greatest of all things that one should be good, praising only truth.   Ahuramazda will hear those who are bent on furthering (all that is good).   May he whose goodness is communicated by the Good Mind instruct me in his best wisdom.'

To those who are interested in the study of Zend, and wish to judge for themselves of the trustworthiness of these various translations, we can recommend a most useful work lately published in Germany by Dr. F. Justi, ' Handbuch der Zendsprache,' containing a complete dictionary, a grammar, and selections from the Zend-Avesta.

September, 1865.

VII.

GENESIS AND THE ZEND-AVESTA[1].

O THAT scholars could have the benefit of a little legal training, and learn at least the difference between what is probable and what is proven! What an advantage also, if they had occasionally to address a jury of respectable tradespeople, and were forced to acquire the art, or rather not to shrink from the effort, of putting the most intricate and delicate points in the simplest and clearest form of which they admit! What a lesson again it would be to men of independent research, if, after having amassed ever so many bags full of evidence, they had always before their eyes the fear of an impatient judge who wants to hear nothing but what is important and essential, and hates to listen to anything that is not to the

---

[1] ' Érân, das Land zwischen dem Indus und Tigris, Beiträge zur Kenntniss des Landes und seiner Geschichte.' Von Dr. Friedrich Spiegel. Berlin, 1863.

Professor Spiegel has published a reply to my article in the ' Ausland,' 19th March, 1868. His chief argument is, that other scholars, such as Bohlen, Gesenius, Ewald, Delitzsch, Knobel, Windischmann, have held the same or very similar opinions. This is perfectly true, but Dr. Spiegel will forgive me for saying that the opinions of these scholars are, as he says they ought to be, well known even in England, and that we want to know what he has to say on these questions, not what others have thought before him, who were far less competent to form an opinion than the editor and translator of the Avesta.

point, however carefully it may have been worked
out, and however eloquently it may be laid before
him! There is hardly one book published now-a-days
which, if everything in it that is not to the purpose
were left out, could not be reduced to half its size.
If authors could make up their minds to omit everything that is only meant to display their learning, to
exhibit the difficulties they had to overcome, or to
call attention to the ignorance of their predecessors,
many a volume of thirty sheets would collapse into a
pamphlet of fifty pages, though in that form it would
probably produce a much greater effect than in its
more inflated appearance.

Did the writers of the Old Testament borrow
anything from the Egyptians, the Babylonians, the
Persians, or the Indians, is a simple enough question.
It is a question that may be treated quite apart
from any theological theories; for the Old Testament,
whatever view the Jews may take of its origin, may
surely be regarded by the historian as a really historical book, written at a certain time in the history
of the world, in a language then spoken and understood, and proclaiming certain facts and doctrines
meant to be acceptable and intelligible to the Jews,
such as they were at that time, an historical nation,
holding a definite place by the side of their more or
less distant neighbours, whether Egyptians, Assyrians,
Persians, or Indians. It is well known that we have
in the language of the New Testament the clear
vestiges of Greek and Roman influences, and if we
knew nothing of the historical intercourse between
those two nations and the writers of the New Testament, the very expressions used by them—not only
their language, but their thoughts, their allusions,
illustrations, and similes—would enable us to say

that some historical contact had taken place between
the philosophers of Greece, the lawgivers of Rome,
and the people of Judea. Why then should not the
same question be asked with regard to more ancient
times? Why should there be any hesitation in
pointing out in the Old Testament an Egyptian
custom, or a Greek word, or a Persian conception?
If Moses was learned in all the wisdom of the
Egyptians, nothing surely would stamp his writings
as more truly historical than traces of Egyptian
influences that might be discovered in his laws. If
Daniel prospered in the reign of Cyrus the Persian,
every Persian word that could be discovered in
Daniel would be most valuable in the eyes of a
critical historian. The only thing which we may
fairly require in investigations of this kind is that
the facts should be clearly established. The subject
is surely an important one—important historically,
quite apart from any theological consequences that
may be supposed to follow. It is as important to
find out whether the authors of the Old Testament
had come in contact with the language and ideas of
Babylon, Persia, or Egypt, as it is to know that
the Jews, at the time of our Lord's appearance, had
been reached by the rays of Greek and Roman
civilisation—that in fact our Lord, his disciples, and
many of his followers, spoke Greek as well as Hebrew
(i. e. Chaldee), and were no strangers to that sphere
of thought in which the world of the Gentiles, the
Greeks, and Romans had been moving for centuries.

Hints have been thrown out from time to time
by various writers that certain ideas in the Old
Testament might be ascribed to Persian influences,
and be traced back to the Zend-Avesta, the sacred

writings of Zoroaster. Much progress has been made
in the deciphering of these ancient documents, since
Anquetil Duperron brought the first instalment of
MSS. from Bombay, and since the late Eugène Burnouf, in his 'Commentaire sur le Yasna,' succeeded in
establishing the grammar and dictionary of the Zend
language upon a safe basis. Several editions of the
works of Zoroaster have been published in France, Den-
mark, and Germany; and after the labours of Spiegel,
Westergaard, Haug, and others, it might be supposed
that such a question as the influence of Persian ideas
on the writers of the Old Testament might at last be
answered either in the affirmative or in the negative.
We were much pleased, therefore, on finding that Professor Spiegel, the learned editor and translator of the
Avesta, had devoted a chapter of his last work, 'Erân,
das Land zwischen dem Indus und Tigris, ' to the problem in question. We read his chapter, ' Avesta und
die Genesis, oder die Beziehungen der Eranier zu den
Semiten,' with the warmest interest, and when we
had finished it, we put down the book with the very
exclamation with which we began our article.

We do not mean to say anything disrespectful to
Professor Spiegel, a scholar brimfull of learning, and
one of the two or three men who know the Avesta
by heart. He is likewise a good Semitic scholar,
and knows enough of Hebrew to form an independent opinion on the language, style, and general
character of the different books of the Old Testament.
He brings together in his Essay a great deal of
interesting information, and altogether would seem
to be one of the most valuable witnesses to give
evidence on the point in question. Yet suppose him
for a moment in a court of justice where, as in a

patent case, some great issue depends on the question whether certain ideas had first been enunciated by the author of Genesis or the author of the Avesta; suppose him subjected to a cross-examination by a brow-beating lawyer, whose business it is to disbelieve and make others disbelieve every assertion that the witness makes, and we are afraid the learned Professor would break down completely. Now it may be said that this is not the spirit in which learned inquiries should be conducted, that authors have a right to a certain respect, and may reckon on a certain amount of willingness on the part of their readers. Such a plea may, perhaps, be urged when all preliminary questions in a contest have been disposed of, when all the evidence has been proved to lie in one direction, and when even the most obstinate among the gentlemen of the jury feel that the verdict is as good as settled. But in a question like this, where everything is doubtful, or, we should rather say, where all the prepossessions are against the view which Dr. Spiegel upholds, it is absolutely necessary for a new witness to be armed from top to toe, to lay himself open to no attack, to measure his words, and advance step by step in a straight line to the point that has to be reached. A writer like Dr. Spiegel should know that he can expect no mercy; nay, he should himself wish for no mercy, but invite the heaviest artillery against the floating battery which he has launched into the troubled waters of Biblical criticism. If he feels that his case is not strong enough, the wisest plan surely is to wait, to accumulate new strength if possible, or, if no new evidence is forthcoming, to acknowledge openly that there is no case.

M. Bréal—who, in his interesting Essay 'Hercule et Cacus,' has lately treated the same problem, the influence of Persian ideas on the writers of the Old Testament—gives an excellent example of how a case of this kind should be argued. He begins with the apocryphal books, and he shows that the name of an evil spirit like Asmodeus, which occurs in Tobit, could be borrowed from Persia only. It is a name inexplicable in Hebrew, and it represents very closely the Parsi Eshem-dev, the Zend Aêshma daêva, the spirit of concupiscence, mentioned several times in the Avesta (Vendidad, c. 10), as one of the devs, or evil spirits. Now this is the kind of evidence we want for the Old Testament. We can easily discover a French word in English, nor is it difficult to tell a Persian word in Hebrew. Are there any Persian words in Genesis, words of the same kind as Asmodeus in Tobit? No such evidence has been brought forward, and the only words we can think of which, if not Persian, may be considered of Aryan origin, are the names of such rivers as Tigris and Euphrates ; and of countries such as Ophir and Havilah among the descendants of Shem, Javan, Meshech, and others among the descendants of Japhet. These names are probably foreign names, and as such naturally mentioned by the author of Genesis in their foreign form. If there are other words of Aryan or Iranian origin in Genesis, they ought to have occupied the most prominent place in Dr. Spiegel's pleading.

We now proceed, and we are again quite willing to admit that, even without the presence of Persian words, the presence of Persian ideas might be detected by careful analysis. No doubt this is a much

more delicate process, yet, as we can discover Jewish
and Christian ideas in the Koran, there ought to be
no insurmountable difficulty in pointing out any
Persian ingredients in Genesis, however disguised
and assimilated. Only, before we look for such
ideas, it is necessary to show the channel through
which they could possibly have flowed either from
the Avesta into Genesis, or from Genesis into the
Avesta. History shows us clearly how Persian
words and ideas could have found their way into
such late works as Tobit, or even into the book of
Daniel, whether he flourished in the reign of Darius,
or in the reign of Cyrus the Persian. But how did
Persians and Jews come in contact, previously to the
age of Cyrus? Dr. Spiegel says that Zoroaster was
born in Arran. This name is given by mediæval
Mohammedan writers to the plain washed by the
Araxes, and was identified by Anquetil Duperron
with the name Airyana vaêga, which the Zend-
Avesta gives to the first created land of Ormuzd.
The Parsis place this sacred country in the vicinity
of Atropatene, and it is clearly meant as the northern-
most country known to the author or authors of the
Zend-Avesta. We think that Dr. Spiegel is right
in defending the geographical position assigned by
tradition to Airyana vaêga, against modern theories
that would place it more eastward in the plain of
Pamer, nor do we hesitate to admit that the name
(Airyana vaêga, i. e. the seed of the Aryan) might
have been changed into Arran. We likewise acknowledge the force of the arguments by which he shows
that the books now called Zend-Avesta were composed in the Eastern, and not in the Western,
provinces of the Persian monarchy, though we are

hardly prepared to subscribe at once to his conclusion (p. 270) that, because Zoroaster is placed by the
Avesta and by later traditions in Arran, or the
Western provinces, he could not possibly be the
author of the Avesta, a literary production which
would appear to belong exclusively to the Eastern
provinces. The very tradition to which Dr. Spiegel
appeals represents Zoroaster as migrating from Arran
to Balkh, to the court of Gustasp, the son of Lohrasp;
and, as one tradition has as much value as another,
we might well admit that the work of Zoroaster,
as a religious teacher, began in Balkh, and from
thence extended still further East. But admitting
that Arran, the country washed by the Araxes, was
the birthplace of Zoroaster, can we possibly follow
Dr. Spiegel when he says, Arran seems to be identical
with Haran, the starting point of the Hebrew people?[2]
Does he mean the names to be identical? Then how
are the aspirate and the double r to be explained?
how is it to be accounted for that the late mediæval
corruption of Airyana vaêga, namely, Arran, should
appear in Genesis? And if the dissimilarity of the two
names is waived, is it possible in two lines to settle
the much contested situation of Haran, and thus to

---

[2] See Spiegel, 'Eran,' p. 274. 'Der Ausgangspunct des Hebräischen
Volkes, auf den seine Geschichte selbst hinweist, ist Haran, welches
Land mit Arran, d. i., Airyana vaedscha identisch zu sein scheint.'
Professor Spiegel, in answer to my remarks, has declared that by
Haran he did not mean the land of Haran, or more correctly
Charan, where Terah died, (supposed to be the same as the Greek
Κάρραι,) but Haran, the son of Terah, the father of Lot, who died in
the land of his nativity, in Ur of the Chaldees (Genesis xi. 28).
That some of the personal names in Genesis represent towns or
places rather than individuals, is clear enough, but with regard to
Haran, the son of Terah, the case is more than doubtful.

determine the ancient watershed between the Semitic
and Aryan nations ? The Abbé Banier, more than
a hundred years ago, pointed out that Haran, whither
Abraham repaired, was the metropolis of Sabism, and
that Magism was practised in Ur of the Chaldees
('Mythology explained by History,' vol. i. book iii.
cap. 3), but the time for such vague identifications
has surely passed. Dr. Spiegel having, as he believes,
established the most ancient meeting-point between
Abraham and Zoroaster, proceeds to argue that
whatever ideas are shared in common by Genesis
and the Avesta must be referred to that very ancient
period when personal intercourse was still possible
between Abraham and Zoroaster, the prophets of the
Jews and the Iranians. Now, here the counsel for
the defence would remind Dr. Spiegel that Genesis
was not the work of Abraham, nor, according to
Dr. Spiegel's view, was Zoroaster the author of the
Zend-Avesta; and that therefore the neighbourly
intercourse between Zoroaster and Abraham in the
country of Arran had nothing to do with the ideas
shared in common by Genesis and the Avesta. But
even if we admitted, for argument's sake, that as
Dr. Spiegel puts it, the Avesta contains Zoroastrian
and Genesis Abrahamitic ideas, surely there was
ample opportunity for Jewish ideas to find admission
into what we call the Avesta, or for Iranian ideas to
find admission into Genesis, after the date of Abraham and Zoroaster, and before the time when we
find the first MSS. of Genesis and the Avesta. The
Zend MSS. of the Avesta are very modern, so are
the Hebrew MSS. of Genesis, which do not carry us
beyond the tenth century after Christ. The text of
the Avesta, however, can be checked by the Pehlevi

translation, which was made under the Sassanian
dynasty (226–651 A.D.), just as the text of Genesis
can be checked by the Septuagint translation, which
was made in the third century before Christ.   Now,
it is known that about the same time and in the
same place—namely at Alexandria—where the Old
Testament was rendered into Greek, the Avesta also
was translated into the same language, so that we
have at Alexandria in the third century B.C. a well
established historical contact between the believers in
Genesis and the believers in the Avesta, and an easy
opening for that exchange of ideas which, according
to Dr. Spiegel, could have taken place nowhere but
in Arran, and at the time of Abraham and Zoroaster.
It might be objected that this was wrangling for
victory, and not arguing for truth, and that no real
scholar would admit that the Avesta, in its original
form, did not go back to a much earlier date than the
third century before Christ. Yet, when such a general
principle is to be laid down, that all that Genesis
and Avesta share in common must belong to a time
before Abraham had started for Canaan, and Zoroaster
for Balkh, other possible means of later intercourse
should surely not be entirely lost sight of.

For what happens ?   The very first tradition that
is brought forward as one common to both these
ancient works—namely, that of the Four Ages of the
World—is confessedly found in the later writings
only of the Parsis, and cannot be traced back in its
definite shape beyond the time of the Sassanians
(Erân, p. 275)[3]. Indications of it are said to be found

---

[3] Professor Spiegel in his latest essay (1868) writes: 'It is an
error if Müller believes that the division into four ages cannot be

in the earlier writings, but these indications are
extremely vague. But we must advance a step further, and after reading very carefully the three
pages devoted to this subject by Dr. Spiegel, we must
confess we see no similarity whatever on that point
between Genesis and the Avesta. In Genesis, the
Four Ages have never assumed the form of a theory,
as in India, Persia, or perhaps in Greece. If we say
that the period from Adam to Noah is the first, that
from Noah to Abraham the second, that from Abraham to the death of Jacob the third, that beginning
with the exile in Egypt the fourth, we are transfer-
ring our ideas to Genesis, but we cannot say that the
writer of Genesis himself laid a peculiar stress on this
fourfold division. The Parsis, on the contrary, have
a definite system. According to them the world is
to last 12,000 years. During the first period of
3,000 years, the world was created. During the
second period Gayo-maratan, the first man lived
by himself, without suffering from the attacks of
evil. During the third period of 3,000 years the
war between good and evil, between Ormuzd and
Ahriman, began with the utmost fierceness; and it
will gradually abate during the fourth period of
3,000 years, which is still to elapse before the final victory of good. Where here is the similarity between
Genesis and the Avesta? We are referred by Dr.
Spiegel to Dr. Windischmann's ' Zoroastrian Studies,'

---

traced in the ancient writings. The period of 12,000 years is mentioned several times, and it is easy to show that the Avesta conceives
the distribution of that period (into four ages) exactly in the same
manner as the later heroic legend, or *must* so conceive it.' All
depends on chapter and verse in the Zend-Avesta where Dr. Spiegel
can show that the four ages are definitely mentioned.

and to his discovery that there are ten generations
between Adam and Noah, as there are ten generations between Yima and Thraêtaona; that there are
twelve generations between Shem and Isaac, as there
are twelve between Thraêtaona and Manus̆kitra; and
that there are thirteen generations between Isaac
and David, as there are thirteen between Manus̆kitra
and Zarathustra. What has the learned counsel for
the defence to say to this? First, that the name of
Shem is put by mistake for that of Noah. Secondly,
that Yima, who is here identified with Adam, is
never represented in the Avesta as the first man, but
is preceded there by numerous ancestors, and surrounded by numerous subjects, who are not his offspring. Thirdly, that in order to establish in Genesis
three periods of ten, twelve, and thirteen generations,
it is necessary to count Isaac, who clearly belongs to
the third, as a member of the second, so that in reality
the number of generations is the same in one only out
of the three periods, which surely proves nothing. As
to any similarity between the Four Yugas of the Brahmans and the Four Ages of the Parsis, we can only
say that, if it exists, no one has as yet brought it out.
The Greeks, again, who are likewise said to share
the primitive doctrine of the Four Ages, believe really
in five, and not in four, and separate them in a
manner which does not in the least remind us of
Hindu Yugas, Hebrew patriarchs, or the battle between Ormuzd and Ahriman.

We proceed to a second point—the Creation as
related in Genesis and the Avesta. Here we certainly

⁴ Dr. Spiegel says in his defence that the Septuagint and the
Vulgate add one more generation after Arphaxad; but see Bunsen's
remarks on this interpolation in his ' Bibelwerk,' Genesis xi. 12.

find some curious coincidences. The world is created
in six days in Genesis, and in six periods in the Avesta,
which six periods together form one year. In Genesis
the creation ends with the creation of man, so it does
in the Avesta. On all other points Dr. Spiegel admits
the two accounts differ, but they are said to agree
again in the temptation and the fall. As Dr. Spiegel
has not given the details of the temptation and the
fall from the Avesta, we cannot judge of the points
which he considers to be borrowed by the Jews from
the Persians; but if we consult M. Bréal, who has
treated the same subject more fully in his ' Hercule
et Cacus,' we find there no more than this, that the
Dualism of the Avesta, the struggle between Ormuzd
and Ahriman, or the principles of light and darkness,
is to be considered as the distant reflex of the grand
struggle between Indra, the god of the sky, and
Vritra, the demon of night and darkness, which
forms the constant burden of the hymns of the Rig-
veda. In this view there is some truth, but we
doubt whether it fully exhibits the vital principle
of the Zoroastrian religion, which is founded on a
solemn protest against the whole worship of the
powers of nature invoked in the Vedas, and on the
recognition of one supreme power, the God of Light,
in every sense of the word—the spirit Ahura, who
created the world and rules it, and defends it against
the power of evil. That power of evil which in the
most ancient portions of the Avesta has not yet
received the name of Ahriman (i.e. aṅgro mainyus),
may afterwards have assumed some of the epithets
which in an earlier period were bestowed on Vritra
and other enemies of the bright gods, and among
them, it may have assumed the name of serpent.

But does it follow, because the principle of evil in the
Avesta is called serpent, or azhi dahâka, that therefore the serpent mentioned in the third chapter of
Genesis must be borrowed from Persia?   Neither in
the Veda nor in the Avesta does the serpent ever assume that subtil and insinuating form which it wears
in Genesis; and the curse pronounced on it, 'to be
cursed above all cattle, and above every beast of the
field,' is not in keeping with the relation of Vritra to
Indra, or Ahriman to Ormuzd, who face each other
almost as equals.   In later books, such as 1 Chronicles xxi. 1, where Satan is mentioned as provoking
David to number Israel (the very same provocation
which in 2 Samuel xxiv. 1 is ascribed to the anger of
the Lord moving David to number Israel and Judah),
and in all the passages of the New Testament where
the power of evil is spoken of as a person, we may
admit the influence of Persian ideas and Persian expressions, though even here strict proof is by no
means easy.   As to the serpent in Paradise, it is a
conception that might have sprung up among the
Jews as well as among the Brahmans; and the serpent that beguiled Eve seems hardly to invite comparison with the much grander conceptions of the
terrible power of Vritra and Ahriman in the Veda
and Avesta.

Dr. Spiegel next discusses the similarity between
the Garden of Eden and the Paradise of the Zoroastrians, and though he admits that here again he relies
chiefly on the Bundehesh, a work of the Sassanian
period, he maintains that that work may well be
compared to Genesis, because it contains none but
really ancient traditions.   We do not for a moment
deny that this may be so, but in a case like the

present, where everything depends on exact dates,
we decline to listen to such a plea. We value
Dr. Spiegel's translations from the Bundehesh most
highly, and we believe with him (p. 283) that there
is little doubt as to the Pishon being the Indus, and
the Gihon the Jaxartes. The identification, too, of
the Persian river-name Ranha (the Vedic Rasâ) with
the Araxes, the name given by Herodotus (i. 202) to
the Jaxartes, seems very ingenious and well established. But we should still like to know why and
in what language the Indus was first called Pishon,
and the Jaxartes, or, it may be, the Oxus, Gihon.

We next come to the two trees in the garden of
Eden, the tree of knowledge and the tree of life.
Dr. Windischmann has shown that the Iranians, too,
were acquainted with two trees, one called Gao-
kerena, bearing the white Haoma, the other called
the Painless tree. We are told first that these two
trees are the same as the one fig tree out of which
the Indians believe the world to have been created.
Now, first of all, the Indians believed no such thing,
and secondly, there is the same difference between
one and two trees as there is between ·North and
South. But we confess that until we know a good
deal more about these two trees of the Iranians, we
feel no inclination whatever to compare the Painless tree and the tree of knowledge of good and
evil, though perhaps the white Haoma tree might
remind us of the tree of life, considering that Haoma,
as well as the Indian Soma, was supposed to give
immortality to those who drank its juice. We likewise
consider the comparison of the Cherubim who keep
the way of the tree of life and the guardians of the
Soma in the Veda and Avesta, as deserving attention,

and we should like to see the etymological derivation of Cherubim from γρύφες, Greifen, and of
Seraphim from the Sanskrit sarpa, serpents, either
confirmed or refuted.

The Deluge is not mentioned in the sacred writings
of the Zoroastrians, nor in the hymns of the Rig-
veda. It is mentioned, however, in one of the latest
Brâhmaṇas, and the carefully balanced arguments
of Burnouf, who considered the tradition of the
Deluge as borrowed by the Indians from Semitic
neighbours, seem to us to be strengthened, rather
than weakened, by the isolated appearance of the
story of the Deluge in this one passage out of the
whole of the Vedic literature. Nothing, however, has
yet been pointed out to force us to admit a Semitic
origin for the story of the Flood, as told in the
Satapatha-brâhmaṇa, and afterwards repeated in the
Mahâbhârata and the Purâṇas: the number of days
being really the only point on which the two accounts
startle us by their agreement.

That Noah's ark rested upon the mountain of
Ararat, and that Ararat may admit of a Persian etymology, is nothing to the point. The etymology
itself is ingenious, but no more. The same remark
applies to all the rest of Dr. Spiegel's arguments.
Thraêtaona, who has before been compared to Noah,
divided his land among his three sons, and gave Iran
to the youngest, an injustice which exasperated his
brothers, who murdered him. Now it is true that
Noah, too, had three sons, but here the similarity
ends; for that Terah had three sons, and that one
of them only, Abram, took possession of the land of
promise, and that of the two sons of Isaac, the
youngest became the heir, is again of no consequence

for our immediate purpose, though it may remind
Dr. Spiegel and others of the history of Thraêtaona.
We agree with Dr. Spiegel, that Zoroaster's character
resembles most closely the true Semitic notion of a
prophet.   He is considered worthy of personal intercourse with Ormuzd; he receives from Ormuzd every
word, though not, as Dr. Spiegel says, every letter of
the law.   But if Zoroaster was a real character, so
was Abraham, and their being like each other proves
in no way that they lived in the same place, or at the
same time, or that they borrowed aught one from the
other.   What Dr. Spiegel says of the Persian name
of the Deity, Ahura, is very doubtful.   Ahura, he
says, as well as ahu, means lord, and must be traced
back to the root ah, the Sanskrit as, which means to
be, so that Ahura would signify the same as Jahve,
he who is.   The root 'as' no doubt means to be, but
it has that meaning because it originally meant to
breathe.   From it, in its original sense of breathing,
the Hindus formed asu, breath, and asura, the name
of God, whether it meant the breathing one, or the
giver of breath.   This asura became in Zend ahura,
and if it assumed the general meaning of Lord, this
is as much a secondary meaning as the meaning of
demon or evil spirit, which asura assumed in the
later Sanskrit of the Brâhmanas.

   After this, Dr. Spiegel proceeds to sum up his
evidence.   He has no more to say, but he believes
that he has proved the following points: a very early
intercourse between Semitic and Aryan nations; a
common belief shared by both in a paradise situated
near the sources of the Oxus and Jaxartes; the dwelling together of Abraham and Zoroaster in Haran,
Arran, or Airyana vaêga.   Semitic and Aryan nations,

he tells us, still live together in those parts of the world, and so it was from the beginning. As the form of the Jewish traditions comes nearer to the Persian than to the Indian traditions, we are asked to believe that these two races lived in the closest contact before, from this ancient hearth of civilisation, they started towards the West and the East—that is to say, before Abraham migrated to Canaan, and before India was peopled by the Brahmans.

We have given a fair account of Dr. Spiegel's arguments, and we need not say that we should have hailed with equal pleasure any solid facts by which to establish either the dependence of Genesis on the Zend-Avesta, or the dependence of the Zend-Avesta on Genesis. It would be absurd to resist facts where facts exist; nor can we imagine any reason why, if Abraham came into personal contact with Zoroaster, the Jewish patriarch should have learnt nothing from the Iranian prophet, or vice versâ. If such an intercourse could be established, it would but serve to strengthen the historical character of the books of the Old Testament, and would be worth more than all the elaborate theories that have been started on the purely miraculous origin of these books. But though we by no means deny that some more tangible points of resemblance may yet be discovered between the Old Testament and the Zend-Avesta, we must protest against having so interesting and so important a matter handled in such an unbusinesslike manner.

April, 1864.

VIII.

THE MODERN PARSIS[1].

I.

IT is not fair to speak of any religious sect by a
name to which its members object. Yet the
fashion of speaking of the followers of Zoroaster as
Fire-worshippers is so firmly established that it will
probably continue long after the last believers in
Ormuzd have disappeared from the face of the
earth. At the present moment, the number of the
Zoroastrians has dwindled down so much that they
hardly find a place in the religious statistics of the
world. Berghaus in his 'Physical Atlas' gives the
following division of the human race according to
religion:

Buddhists	31.2 per cent.
Christians	30.7 ,,
Mohammedans	15.7 ,,
Brahmanists	13.4 ,,
Heathens	8.7 ,,
Jews	0.3 ,,

He nowhere states the number of the Fire-worshippers, nor does he tell us under what head they

---

[1] 'The Manners and Customs of the Parsees.' By Dadabhai
Naoroji, Esq. Liverpool, 1861.
  'The Parsee Religion.' By Dadabhai Naoroji, Esq. Liverpool, 1861.

are comprised in his general computation. The
difficulties of a religious census are very great, particularly when we have to deal with Eastern nations.
About two hundred years ago, travellers estimated
the Gabars (as they are called in Persia) at eighty
thousand families, or about 400,000 souls. At present the Pársis in Western India amount to about
100,000, to which, if we add 5,500 in Yezd and
Kirman, we get a total of 105,500. The number
of the Jews is commonly estimated at 3,600,000;
and if they represent 0.3 per cent. of mankind, the
Fire-worshippers could not claim at present more
than about 0.01 per cent of the whole population
of the earth. Yet there were periods in the history
of the world when the worship of Ormuzd threatened to rise triumphant on the ruins of the temples
of all other gods. If the battles of Marathon and
Salamis had been lost, and Greece had succumbed
to Persia, the state religion of the empire of Cyrus,
which was the worship of Ormuzd, might have
become the religion of the whole civilised world.
Persia had absorbed the Assyrian and Babylonian
empires; the Jews were either in Persian captivity
or under Persian sway at home; the sacred monuments of Egypt had been mutilated by the hands
of Persian soldiers. The edicts of the great king,
the king of kings, were sent to India, to Greece,
to Scythia, and to Egypt; and if ' by the grace of
Auramazda' Darius had crushed the liberty of
Greece, the purer faith of Zoroaster might easily
have superseded the Olympian fables. Again, under
the Sassanian dynasty (226–651 A.D.) the revived
national faith of the Zoroastrians assumed such
vigour that Shapur II, like another Diocletian, could

aim at the extirpation of the Christian faith. The
sufferings of the persecuted Christians in the East
were as terrible as they had ever been in the West;
nor was it by the weapons of Roman emperors or
by the arguments of Christian divines that the fatal
blow was dealt to the throne of Cyrus and the altars
of Ormuzd. The power of Persia was broken at
last by the Arabs; and it is due to them that the
religion of Ormuzd, once the terror of the world,
is now, and has been for the last thousand years,
a mere curiosity in the eyes of the historian.

The sacred writings of the Zoroastrians, commonly
called the Zend-Avesta, have for about a century
occupied the attention of European scholars, and,
thanks to the adventurous devotion of Anquetil
Duperron, and the careful researches of Rask,
Burnouf, Westergaard, Spiegel, and Haug, we have
gradually been enabled to read and interpret what
remains of the ancient language of the Persian
religion. The problem was not an easy one, and
had it not been for the new light which the science
of language has shed on the laws of human speech,
it would have been as impossible to Burnouf as
it was to Hyde, the celebrated Professor of Hebrew
and Arabic at Oxford, to interpret with grammatical
accuracy the ancient remnants of Zoroaster's doctrine.
How that problem was solved is well known to all
who take an interest in the advancement of modern
scholarship. It was as great an achievement as
the deciphering of the cuneiform edicts of Darius;
and no greater compliment could have been paid
to Burnouf and his fellow-labourers than that
scholars, without inclination to test their method,
and without leisure to follow these indefatigable

pioneers through all the intricate paths of their
researches, should have pronounced the deciphering
of the ancient Zend as well as of the ancient Persian
of the Achæmenian period to be impossible, incredible, and next to miraculous.

While the scholars of Europe are thus engaged
in disinterring the ancient records of the religion
of Zoroaster, it is of interest to learn what has become of that religion in those few settlements where
it is still professed by small communities. Though
every religion is of real and vital interest in its
earliest state only, yet its later development too,
with all its misunderstandings, faults and corruptions, offers many an instructive lesson to the
thoughtful student of history. Here is a religion,
one of the most ancient of the world, once the state
religion of the most powerful empire, driven away
from its native soil, deprived of political influence,
without even the prestige of a powerful or enlightened priesthood, and yet professed by a handful of
exiles—men of wealth, intelligence, and moral worth
in Western India—with an unhesitating fervour such
as is seldom to be found in larger religious communities. It is well worth the earnest endeavour of
the philosopher and the divine to discover, if possible, the spell by which this apparently effete
religion continues to command the attachment of
the enlightened Parsis of India, and makes them
turn a deaf ear to the allurements of the Brahmanic
worship and the earnest appeals of Christian missionaries. We believe that to many of our readers the
two pamphlets, lately published by a distinguished
member of the Parsi community, Mr. Dadabhai
Naoroji, Professor of Guzerati at University College,

London, will open many problems of a more than
passing interest. One is a Paper read before the
Liverpool Philomathic Society, 'On the Manners
and Customs of the Parsees;' the other is a Lecture
delivered before the Liverpool Literary and Philosophical Society, 'On the Parsee Religion.'

In the first of these pamphlets, we are told that
the small community of Parsis in Western India
is at the present moment divided into two parties,
the Conservatives and the Liberals. Both are equally
attached to the faith of their ancestors, but they
differ from each other in their modes of life—the
Conservatives clinging to all that is established and
customary, however absurd and mischievous, the
Liberals desiring to throw off the abuses of former
ages, and to avail themselves, as much as is consistent
with their religion and their Oriental character, of
the advantages of European civilisation. ' If I say,'
writes our informant, ' that the Parsees use tables,
knives and forks, &c., for taking their dinners, it
would be true with regard to one portion, and
entirely untrue with regard to another. In one
house you see in the dining-room the dinner table
furnished with all the English apparatus for its
agreeable purposes; next door, perhaps, you see
the gentleman perfectly satisfied with his primitive
good old mode of squatting on a piece of mat, with
a large brass or copper plate (round, and of the size
of an ordinary tray) before him, containing all the
dishes of his dinner, spread on it in small heaps,
and placed upon a stool about two or three inches
high, with a small tinned copper cup at his side
for his drinks, and his fingers for his knives and
forks. He does this, not because he cannot afford

to have a table, &c., but because he would not have
them in preference to his ancestral mode of life, or,
perhaps, the thought has not occurred to him that he
need have anything of the kind.'

Instead, therefore, of giving a general description
of Parsi life at present, Mr. Dadabhai Naoroji gives
us two distinct accounts—first of the old, secondly
of the new school. He describes the incidents in
the daily life of a Parsi of the old school, from
the moment he gets out of bed to the time of his
going to rest, and the principal ceremonies from
the hour of his birth to the hour of his burial.
Although we can gather from the tenour of his
writings that the author himself belongs to the
Liberals, we must give him credit for the fairness
with which he describes the party to which he is
opposed. There is no sneer, no expression of contempt anywhere, even when, as in the case of the
Nirang, the temptation must have been considerable.
What this Nirang is we may best state in the words
of the writer:

'The Nirang is the urine of cow, ox, or she-goat,
and the rubbing of it over the face and hands is
the second thing a Parsee does after getting out of
bed. Either before applying the Nirang to the face
and hands, or while it remains on the hands after
being applied, he should not touch anything directly
with his hands; but, in order to wash out the Nirang,
he either asks somebody else to pour water on his
hands, or resorts to the device of taking hold of the
pot through the intervention of a piece of cloth, such
as a handkerchief or his Sudrâ, i. e. his blouse. He
first pours water on one hand, then takes the pot in
that hand and washes his other hand, face, and feet.'

Strange as this process of purification may appear, it becomes perfectly disgusting when we are told that women, after childbirth, have not only to undergo this sacred ablution, but have actually to drink a little of the Nirang, and that the same rite is imposed on children at the time of their investiture with the Sudrâ and Kusti, the badges of the Zoroastrian faith. The Liberal party have completely surrendered this objectionable custom, but the old school still keep it up, though their faith, as Dadabhai Naoroji says, in the efficacy of Nirang to drive away Satan may be shaken. 'The Reformers,' our author writes, 'maintain, that there is no authority whatever in the original books of Zurthosht for the observance of this dirty practice, but that it is altogether a later introduction. The old adduce the authority of the works of some of the priests of former days, and say the practice ought to be observed. They quote one passage from the Zend-Avesta corroborative of their opinion which their opponents deny as at all bearing upon the point.' Here, whatever our own feelings may be about the Nirang, truth obliges us to side with the old school, and if our author had consulted the ninth Fasgard of the Vendidad (page 120, line 21, in Brockhaus's edition), he would have seen that both the drinking and the rubbing in of the so-called Gaomaezo—i. e. Nirang—are clearly enjoined by Zoroaster in certain purificatory rights. The custom rests, therefore, not only on the authority of a few priests of former days, but on the ipsissima verba of the Zend-Avesta, the revealed word of Ormuzd; and if, as Dadabhai Naoroji writes, the Reformers of the day will not go beyond abolishing and disavowing the ceremonies and notions that have no authority in the original Zend-Avesta, we are afraid that the washing with Nirang, and even the drinking of it, will have to be maintained. A pious Parsi has to say his prayers sixteen times at least every day—first on getting out of bed, then during the Nirang operation, again when he takes his bath, again when he cleanses his teeth, and when he has finished his morning ablutions. The same prayers are repeated whenever, during the day, a Parsi has to wash his hands. Every meal—and there are three—begins and ends with prayer, besides the grace, and before going to bed the work of the day is closed by a prayer. The most extraordinary thing is that none of the Parsis—not even their priests—understand the ancient language in which these prayers are composed. We must quote the words of our author, who is himself of the priestly caste, and who says:

'All prayers, on every occasion, are said, or rather recited, in the old original Zend language, neither the reciter nor the people around intended to be edified, understanding a word of it. There is no pulpit among the Parsees. On several occasions, as on the occasion of the Ghumbars, the bimestral holidays, the third day's ceremonies for the dead, and other religious or special holidays, there are assemblages in the temple ; prayers are repeated, in which more or less join, but there is no discourse in the vernacular of the people. Ordinarily, every one goes to the fire-temple whenever he likes, or, if it is convenient to him, recites his prayers himself, and as long as he likes, and gives, if so inclined, something to the priests to pray for him.'

In another passage, our author says:

'Far from being the teachers of the true doctrines and duties of their religion, the priests are generally the most bigoted and superstitious, and exercise much injurious influence over the women especially, who, until lately, received no education at all. The priests have, however, now begun to feel their degraded position. Many of them, if they can do so, bring up their sons in any other profession but their own. There are, perhaps, a dozen among the whole body of professional priests who lay claim to a knowledge of the Zend-Avesta : but the only respect in which they are superior to their brethren is, that they have learnt the meanings of the words of the books as they are taught, without knowing the language, either philosophically or grammatically.'

Mr. Dadabhai Naoroji proceeds to give a clear and graphic description of the ceremonies to be observed at the birth and the investiture of children, at the betrothal of children, at marriages and at funerals, and he finally discusses some of the distinguishing features of the national character of the Parsis. The Parsis are monogamists. They do not eat anything cooked by a person of another religion; they object to beef, pork, or ham. Their priesthood is hereditary. None but the son of a priest can be a priest, but it is not obligatory for the son of a priest to take orders. The high-priest is called Dustoor, the others are called Mobed.

The principal points for which the Liberals among the Parsis are, at the present moment, contending, are the abolition of the filthy purifications by means of Nirang, the reduction of the large number of obligatory prayers; the prohibition of early betrothal

and marriage; the suppression of extravagance at
weddings and funerals; the education of women, and
their admission into general society. · A society has
been formed, called 'the Rahanumaee Mazdiashna,'
i. e. the Guide of the Worshippers of God.   Meet-
ings are held, speeches made, tracts distributed.
A counter society, too, has been started, called
'the True Guides;' and we readily believe what
Mr. Dadabhai Naoroji tells us—that, as in Europe,
so in India, the Reformers have found themselves
strengthened by the intolerant bigotry and the
weakness of the arguments of their opponents.   The
Liberals have made considerable progress, but their
work is as yet but half done, and they will never
be able to carry out their religious and social reforms
successfully, without first entering on a critical study
of the Zend-Avesta, to which, as yet, they profess to
appeal as the highest authority in matters of faith,
law, and morality.

    We propose, in another article, to consider the state
of religion among the Parsis of the present day.

    August, 1862.

                       II.

    THE so-called Fire-worshippers certainly do not
worship the fire, and they naturally object to a name
which seems to place them on a level with mere
idolaters.   All they admit is, that in their youth
they are taught to face some luminous object while
worshipping God (p. 7), and that they regard the
fire, like other great natural phenomena, as an emblem of the Divine power (p. 26).   But they assure

us that they never ask assistance or blessings from
an unintelligent material object, nor is it even considered necessary to turn the face to any emblem
whatever in praying to Ormuzd. The most honest,
however, among the Parsis, and those who would
most emphatically protest against the idea of their
ever paying divine honours to the sun or the fire,
admit the existence of some kind of national instinct
—an indescribable awe felt by every Parsi with regard
to light and fire. The fact that the Parsis are the
only Eastern people who entirely abstain from smok-
ing is very significant; and we know that most of
them would rather not blow out a candle, if they
could help it. It is difficult to analyse such a feeling, but it seems, in some respects, similar to that
which many Christians have about the cross. They
do not worship the cross, but they have peculiar feelings of reverence for it, and it is intimately connected
with some of their most sacred rites.

But although most Parsis would be very ready
to tell us what they do not worship, there are but
few who could give a straightforward answer if
asked what they do worship and believe. Their
priests, no doubt, would say that they worship
Ormuzd and believe in Zoroaster, his prophet; and
they would appeal to the Zend-Avesta, as containing
the Word of God, revealed by Ormuzd to Zoroaster.
If more closely pressed, however, they would have
to admit that they cannot understand one word of
the sacred writings in which they profess to believe,
nor could they give any reason why they believe
Zoroaster to have been a true prophet, and not an
impostor. 'As a body,' says Mr. Dadabhai Naoroji,
'the priests are not only ignorant of the duties and

objects of their own profession, but are entirely
uneducated, except that they are able to read and
write, and that, also, often very imperfectly.   They
do not understand a single word of their prayers
and recitations, which are all in the old Zend
language.'

What, then, do the laity know about religion?
What makes the old teaching of Zoroaster so dear
to them that, in spite of all differences of opinion
among themselves, young and old seem equally
determined never to join any other religious community?   Incredible as it may sound, we are told
by the best authority, by an enlightened yet strictly
orthodox Parsi, that there is hardly a man or a
woman who could give an account of the faith that
is in them.   'The whole religious education of a
Parsi child consists in preparing by rote a certain
number of prayers in Zend, without understanding
a word of them; the knowledge of the doctrines of
their religion being left to be picked up from casual
conversation.'   A Parsi, in fact, hardly knows what
his faith is.   The Zend-Avesta is to him a sealed
book; and though there is a Guzerati translation
of it, that translation is not made from the original,
but from a Pehlevi paraphrase, nor is it recognised
by the priests as an authorised version.   Till about
five and twenty years ago, there was no book from
which a Parsi of an inquiring mind could gather
the principles of his religion.   At that time, and,
as it would seem, chiefly in order to counteract the
influence of Christian missionaries, a small Dialogue
was written in Guzerati—a kind of Catechism,
giving, in the form of questions and answers, the
most important tenets of Parsiism.   We shall quote

some passages from this Dialogue, as translated by
Mr. Dadabhai Naoroji.   The subject of it is thus
described:

*A few Questions and Answers to acquaint the
Children of the holy Zarthosti Community with
the Subject of the Mazdiashna Religion, i. e. the
Worship of God.*

Question. Whom do we, of the Zarthosti community, believe in ?

Answer. We believe in only one God, and do not
believe in any besides Him.

Q. Who is that one God?

A. The God who created the heavens, the earth,
the angels, the stars, the sun, the moon, the fire, the
water, or all the four elements, and all things of
the two worlds; that God we believe in.   Him we
worship, him we invoke, him we adore.

Q. Do we not believe in any other God?

A. Whoever believes in any other God but this, is
an infidel, and shall suffer the punishment of hell.

Q. What is the form of our God?

A. Our God has neither face nor form, colour nor
shape, nor fixed place.   There is no other like him.
He is himself singly such a glory that we cannot
praise or describe him; nor our mind comprehend
him.

So far, no one could object to this Catechism, and
it must be clear that the Dualism, which is generally
mentioned as the distinguishing feature of the Persian religion—the belief in two Gods, Ormuzd, the
principle of good, and Ahriman, the principle of
evil—is not countenanced by the modern Parsis.
Whether it exists in the Zend-Avesta is another

question, which, however, cannot be discussed at present [1].

The Catechism continues:

Q. What is our religion?

A. Our religion is ' Worship of God.'

Q. Whence did we receive our religion?

A. God's true prophet—the true Zurthost (Zoroaster) Asphantamân Anoshirwân—brought the religion to us from God.

Here it is curious to observe that not a single question is asked as to the claim of Zoroaster to be considered a true prophet. He is not treated as a divine being, nor even as the son of Ormuzd. Plato, indeed, speaks of Zoroaster as the son of Oromazes (Alc. i. p. 122 a), but this is a mistake, not countenanced, as far as we are aware, by any of the Parsi writings, whether ancient or modern. With the Parsis, Zoroaster is simply a wise man, a prophet favoured by God, and admitted into God's immediate presence ; but all this, on his own showing only, and without any supernatural credentials, except some few miracles recorded of him in books of doubtful authority. This shows, at all events, how little the Parsis have been exposed to controversial discussions; for, as this is so weak a point in their system that it would have invited the attacks of every opponent, we may be sure that the Dustoors would have framed some argument in defence, if such defence had ever been needed.

The next extract from the Catechism treats of the canonical books:

[1] See page 140.

Q. What religion has our prophet brought us from God?

A. The disciples of our prophet have recorded in several books that religion. Many of these books were destroyed during Alexander's conquest; the remainder of the books were preserved with great care and respect by the Sassanian kings. Of these again, the greater portion were destroyed at the Mohammedan conquest by Khalif Omar, so that we have now very few books remaining; viz. the Vandidad, the Yazashné, the Visparad, the Khordeh Avesta, the Vistasp Nusk, and a few Pehlevi books. Resting our faith upon these few books, we now remain devoted to our good Mazdiashna religion. We consider these books as heavenly books, because God sent the tidings of these books to us through the holy Zurthost.

Here, again, we see theological science in its infancy. 'We consider these books as heavenly books because God sent the tidings of these books to us through the holy Zurthost,' is not very powerful logic. It would have been more simple to say, 'We consider them heavenly books because we consider them heavenly books.' However, whether heavenly or not, these few books exist. They form the only basis of the Zoroastrian religion, and the principal source from which it is possible to derive any authentic information as to its origin, its history, and its real character.

That the Parsis are of a tolerant character with regard to such of their doctrines as are not of vital importance, may be seen from the following extract:

Q. Whose descendants are we?

A. Of Gayomars. By his progeny was Persia populated.

Q. Was Gayomars the first man?

A. According to our religion he was so, but the wise men of our community, of the Chinese, the Hindus, and several other nations, dispute the assertion, and say that there was human population on the earth before Gayomars.

The moral precepts which are embodied in this Catechism do the highest credit to the Parsis:

Q. What commands has God sent us through his prophet, the exalted Zurthost?

A. To know God as one; to know the prophet, the exalted Zurthost, as the true prophet; to believe the religion and the Avesta brought by him as true beyond all manner of doubt; to believe in the goodness of God; not to disobey any of the commands of the Mazdiashna religion; to avoid evil deeds; to exert oneself in good deeds; to pray five times in the day; to believe on the reckoning and justice on the fourth morning after death; to hope for heaven and to fear hell; to consider doubtless the day of general destruction and resurrection; to remember always that God has done what he willed, and shall do what he wills; to face some luminous object while worshipping God.

Then follow several paragraphs which are clearly directed against Christian missionaries, and more particularly against the doctrine of vicarious sacrifice and prayer:

' Some deceivers, [the Catechism says,] with the view of acquiring exaltation in this world, have set themselves up as prophets, and, going among the labouring and ignorant people, have persuaded them that, "if you commit sin, I shall intercede for you, I shall plead for you, I shall save you," and thus deceive them; but the wise among the people know the deceit.'

This clearly refers to Christian missionaries, but whether Roman Catholic or Protestant is difficult to say. The answer given by the Parsis is curious and significant:

'If any one commit sin,' they reply, ' under the belief that he shall be saved by somebody, both the deceiver as well as the deceived shall be damned to the day of Rastâ Khez. . . . There is no saviour. In the other world you shall receive the return according to your actions. . . . Your saviour is your deeds, and God himself. He is the pardoner and the giver. If you repent your sins and reform, and if the Great Judge consider you worthy of pardon, or would be merciful to you, He alone can and will save you.'

It would be a mistake to suppose that the whole doctrine of the Parsis is contained in the short Guzerati Catechism, translated by Mr. Dadabhai Naoroji; still less can it be comprised in the fragmentary extracts here given. Their sacred writings, the Yasna, Vispered, and Vendidad, the productions of much earlier ages, contain many ideas, both religious and mythological, which belong to the past, to the childhood of our race, and which no educated Parsi could honestly profess to believe in now. This difficulty of reconciling the more enlightened faith of the present generation with the mytho-

logical phraseology of their old sacred writings is
solved by the Parsis in a very simple manner.
They do not, like Roman Catholics, prohibit the
reading of the Zend-Avesta ; nor do they, like
Protestants, encourage a critical study of their
sacred texts.   They simply ignore the originals of
their sacred writings.   They repeat them in their
prayers without attempting to understand them,
and they acknowledge the insufficiency of every
translation of the Zend-Avesta that has yet been
made, either in Pehlevi, Sanskrit, Guzerati, French,
or German.   Each Parsi has to pick up his religion
as best he may.   Till lately, even the Catechism
did not form a necessary part of a child's religious
education.   Thus the religious belief of the present
Parsi communities is reduced to two or three fundamental doctrines; and these, though professedly
resting on the teaching of Zoroaster, receive their
real sanction from a much higher authority.   A
Parsi believes in one God, to whom he addresses
his prayers.   His morality is comprised in these
words—pure thoughts, pure words, pure deeds.
Believing in the punishment of vice and the reward
of virtue, he trusts for pardon to the mercy of God.
There is a charm, no doubt, in so short a creed ; and
if the whole of Zoroaster's teaching were confined
to this, there would be some truth in what his
followers say of their religion—namely, that ' it is
for all, and not for any particular nation.'

   If now we ask again, how it is that neither
Christians, nor Hindus, nor Mohammedans have had
any considerable success in converting the Parsis,
and why even the more enlightened members of
that small community, though fully aware of the

many weak points of their own theology, and deeply
impressed with the excellence of the Christian religion, morals, and general civilisation, scorn the idea
of ever migrating from the sacred ruins of their
ancient faith, we are able to discover some reasons;
though they are hardly sufficient to account for so
extraordinary a fact.

First, the very compactness of the modern Parsi
creed accounts for the tenacity with which the
exiles of Western India cling to it. A Parsi is
not troubled with many theological problems or
difficulties. Though he professes a general belief
in the sacred writings of Zoroaster, he is not asked
to profess any belief in the stories incidentally mentioned in the Zend-Avesta. If it is said in the Yasna
that Zoroaster was once visited by Homa, who appeared before him in a brilliant supernatural body,
no doctrine is laid down as to the exact nature of
Homa. It is said that Homa was worshipped by
certain ancient sages, Vivanhvat, Áthwya, and Thrita,
and that, as a reward for their worship, great heroes
were born as their sons. The fourth who worshipped
Homa was Pourushaspa, and he was rewarded by the
birth of his son Zoroaster. Now the truth is, that
Homa is the same as the Sanskrit Soma, well known
from the Veda as an intoxicating beverage used at
the great sacrifices, and afterwards raised to the rank
of a deity. The Parsis are fully aware of this, but
they do not seem in the least disturbed by the occurrence of such ' fables and endless genealogies.' They
would not be shocked if they were told, what is a
fact, that most of these old wives' fables have their
origin in the. religion which they most detest, the
religion of the Veda, and that the heroes of the

Zend-Avesta are the same who, with slightly changed names, appear again as Jemshid, Feridun, Gershâsp, &c., in the epic poetry of Firdusi.

Another fact which accounts for the attachment of the Parsis to their religion is its remote antiquity and its former glory. Though age has little to do with truth, the length of time for which any system has lasted seems to offer a vague argument in favour of its strength. It is a feeling which the Parsi shares in common with the Jew and the Brahman, and which even the Christian missionary appeals to when confronting the systems of later prophets.

Thirdly, it is felt by the Parsis that in changing their religion, they would not only relinquish the heirloom of their remote forefathers, but of their own fathers; and it is felt as a dereliction of filial piety to give up what was most precious to those whose memory is most precious and almost sacred to themselves.

If in spite of all this, many people, most competent to judge, look forward with confidence to the conversion of the Parsis, it is because, in the most essential points, they have already, though unconsciously, approached as near as possible to the pure doctrines of Christianity. Let them but read the Zend-Avesta, in which they profess to believe, and they will find that their faith is no longer the faith of the Yasna, the Vendidad, and the Vispered. As historical relics, these works, if critically interpreted, will always retain a prominent place in the great library of the ancient world. As oracles of religious faith, they are defunct, and a mere anachronism in the age in which we live.

On the other hand, let missionaries read their Bible,

and let them preach that Christianity which once
conquered the world—the genuine and unshackled
Gospel of Christ and the Apostles.   Let them respect
native prejudices, and be tolerant with regard to all
that can be tolerated in a Christian community.   Let
them consider that Christianity is not a gift to be
pressed on unwilling minds, but ·the highest of all
privileges which natives can receive at the hands of
their present rulers.   Natives of independent and
honest character cannot afford at present to join the
ranks of converts without losing that true caste which
no man ought to lose—namely, self-respect.   They
are driven to prop up their tottering religions, rather
than profess a faith which seems dictated to them
by their conquerors.   Such feelings ought to be respected.   Finally, let missionaries study the sacred
writings on which the faith of the Parsis is professedly founded.   Let them examine the bulwarks
which they mean to overthrow.   They will find them
less formidable from within than from without.   But
they will also discover that they rest on a foundation
which ought never to be touched—a faith in one
God, the Creator, the Ruler, and the Judge of the
world.

August, 1862.

IX.

BUDDHISM[1].

IF the words of St. Paul, 'Prove all things, hold fast that which is good,' may be supposed to refer to spiritual things, and, more especially, to religious doctrines, it must be confessed that few only, whether theologians or laymen, have ever taken to heart the apostle's command. How many candidates for holy orders are there who could give a straightforward answer if asked to enumerate the principal religions of the world, or to state the names of their founders, and the titles of the works which are still considered by millions of human beings as the sacred authorities for their religious belief? To study such books as the Koran of the Mohammedans, the Zend-Avesta of the Parsis, the King's of the Confucians, the Tao-te-King of the Taoists, the Vedas of the Brahmans, the Tripitaka of the Buddhists, the Sûtras of the Jains, or the Granth of the Sikhs, would be considered by many mere waste of time. Yet St. Paul's command is very clear and simple; and to maintain that it referred to the heresies of his own time only, or to the philosophical systems of the Greeks and Romans, would be to narrow the horizon

---

[1] 'Le Bouddha et sa Religion.' Par J. Barthélemy Saint-Hilaire, Membre de l'Institut. Paris, 1860.

of the apostle's mind, and to destroy the general
applicability of his teaching to all times and to all
countries. Many will ask what possible good could
be derived from the works of men who must have
been either deceived or deceivers, nor would it be
difficult to quote some passages in order to show
the utter absurdity and worthlessness of the religious books of the Hindus and Chinese. But this
was not the spirit in which the apostle of the Gentiles addressed himself to the Epicureans and Stoics,
nor is this the feeling with which a thoughtful Christian and a sincere believer in the divine government of the world is likely to rise from a perusal
of any of the books which he knows to be or to have
been the only source of spiritual light and comfort
to thousands and thousands among the dwellers on
earth.

Many are the advantages to be derived from a
careful study of other religions, but the greatest of
all is that it teaches us to appreciate more truly
what we possess in our own. When do we feel the
blessings of our own country more warmly and
truly than when we return from abroad? It is the
same with regard to religion. Let us see what other
nations have had and still have in the place of religion; let us examine the prayers, the worship, the
theology even of the most highly civilised races,—
the Greeks, the Romans, the Hindus, the Persians,—
and we shall then understand more thoroughly what
blessings are vouchsafed to us in being allowed to
breathe from the first breath of life the pure air of
a land of Christian light and knowledge. We are
too apt to take the greatest blessings as matters of
course, and even religion forms no exception. We

have done so little to gain our religion, we have
suffered so little in the cause of truth, that however
highly we prize our own Christianity, we never prize
it highly enough until we have compared it with the
religions of the rest of the world.

This, however, is not the only advantage; and we
think that M. Barthélemy Saint-Hilaire has formed
too low an estimate of the benefits to be derived from
a thoughtful study of the religions of mankind when
he writes of Buddhism: 'Le seul, mais immense
service que le Bouddhisme puisse nous rendre, c'est
par son triste contraste de nous faire apprécier
mieux encore la valeur inestimable de nos croyances,
en nous montrant tout ce qu'il en coûte à l'humanité
qui ne les partage point.' This is not all. If a
knowledge of other countries and a study of the
manners and customs of foreign nations teach us
to appreciate what we have at home, they likewise
form the best cure of that national conceit and want
of sympathy with which we are too apt to look on
all that is strange and foreign. The feeling which
led the Hellenic races to divide the whole world into
Greeks and Barbarians is so deeply engrained in
human nature that not even Christianity has been
able altogether to remove it. Thus when we cast
our first glance into the labyrinth of the religions
of the world, all seems to us darkness, self-deceit,
and vanity. It sounds like a degradation of the
very name of religion to apply it to the wild
ravings of Hindu Yogins or the blank blasphemies
of Chinese Buddhists. But as we slowly and
patiently wend our way through the dreary prisons,
our own eyes seem to expand, and we perceive a
glimmer of light where all was darkness at first.

We learn to understand the saying of one who more than anybody had a right to speak with authority on this subject, that 'there is no religion which does not contain a spark of truth.' Those who would limit the riches of God's goodness and forbearance and long suffering, and would hand over the largest portion of the human race to inevitable perdition, have never adduced a tittle of evidence from the Gospel or from any other trustworthy source in support of so unhallowed a belief. They have generally appealed to the devilries and orgies of heathen worship; they have quoted the blasphemies of Oriental Sufis and the immoralities sanctioned by the successors of Mohammed; but they have seldom, if ever, endeavoured to discover the true and original character of the strange forms of faith and worship which they call the work of the devil. If the Indians had formed their notions of Christianity from the soldiers of Cortez and Pizarro, or if the Hindus had studied the principles of Christian morality in the lives of Clive and Warren Hastings; or, to take a less extreme case, if a Mohammedan, settled in England, were to test the practical working of Christian charity by the spirit displayed in the journals of our religious parties, their notions of Christianity would be about as correct as the ideas which thousands of educated Christians entertain of the diabolical character of heathen religion. Even Christianity has been depraved into Jesuitism and Mormonism, and if we, as Protestants, claim the right to appeal to the Gospel as the only test by which our faith is to be judged, we must grant a similar privilege to Mohammedans and Buddhists, and to all who possess a written, and, as they

believe, revealed authority for the articles of their
faith.

But though no one is likely to deny the necessity
of studying each religion in its most ancient form
and from its original documents, before we venture
to pronounce our verdict, the difficulties of this
task are such that in them more than in anything
else, must be sought the cause why so few of our
best thinkers and writers have devoted themselves
to a critical and historical study of the religions
of the world. All important religions have sprung
up in the East. Their sacred books are written
in Eastern tongues, and some of them are of such
ancient date that those even who profess to
believe in them, admit that they are unable to
understand them without the help of translations
and commentaries. Until very lately the sacred
books of three of the most important religions,
those of the Brahmans, the Buddhists, and the
Parsis, were totally unknown in Europe. It was
one of the most important results of the study of
Sanskrit, or the ancient language of India, that
through it the key, not only to the sacred books
of the Brahmans, the Vedas, but likewise to those
of the Buddhists and Zoroastrians, was recovered.
And nothing shows more strikingly the rapid progress of Sanskrit scholarship than that even Sir
William Jones, whose name has still, with many, a
more familiar sound than the names of Colebrooke,
Burnouf, and Lassen, should have known nothing of
the Vedas; that he should never have read a line of
the canonical books of the Buddhists, and that he
actually expressed his belief that Buddha was the
same as · the Teutonic deity Wodan or Odin, and

Sâkya, another name of Buddha, the same as Shishac,
king of Egypt. The same distinguished scholar
never perceived the intimate relationship between the
language of the Zend-Avesta and Sanskrit, and he
declared the whole of the Zoroastrian writings to
be modern forgeries.

Even at present we are not yet in possession of
a complete edition, much less of any trustworthy
translation, of the Vedas; we only possess the
originals of a few books of the Buddhist canon;
and though the text of the Zend-Avesta has been
edited in its entirety, its interpretation is beset with
greater difficulties than that of the Vedas or the
Tripitaka. A study of the ancient religions of
China, those of Confucius and Laotse, presupposes
an acquaintance with Chinese, a language which
it takes a life to learn thoroughly; and even the
religion of Mohammed, though more accessible than
any other Eastern religion, cannot be fully examined
except by a master of Arabic. It is less surprising,
therefore, than it might at first appear, that a
comprehensive and scholarlike treatment of the religions of the world should still be a desideratum.
Scholars who have gained a knowledge of the language, and thereby free access to original documents,
find so much work at hand which none but themselves can do, that they grudge the time for collecting and arranging, for the benefit of the public at
large, the results which they have obtained. Nor
need we wonder that critical historians should rather
abstain from the study of the religions of antiquity
than trust to mere translations and second-hand
authorities.

Under these circumstances we feel all the more

thankful if we meet with a writer like M. Barthélemy Saint-Hilaire, who has acquired a knowledge
of Eastern languages sufficient to enable him to
consult original texts and to control the researches
of other scholars, and who at the same time commands that wide view of the history of human
thought which enables him to assign to each system
its proper place, to perceive its most salient features,
and to distinguish between what is really important
and what is not, in the lengthy lucubrations of
ancient poets and prophets. M. Barthélemy Saint-
Hilaire is one of the most accomplished scholars
of France; and his reputation as the translator of
Aristotle has made us almost forget that the Professor of Greek Philosophy at the Collège de France[2]
is the same as the active writer in the 'Globe' of
1827, and the ' National' of 1830; the same who
signed the protest against the July ' ordonnances,'
and who in 1848 was Chief Secretary of the Pro-
visional Government. If such a man takes the
trouble to acquire a knowledge of Sanskrit, and to
attend in the same College where he was professor,
the lectures of his own colleague, the late Eugène
Burnouf, his publications on Hindu philosophy and
religion will naturally attract a large amount of
public interest. The Sanskrit scholar by profession
works and publishes chiefly for the benefit of other
Sanskrit scholars. He is satisfied with bringing to
light the ore which he has extracted by patient
labour from among the dusty MSS. of the East-

---

[2] M. Barthélemy St. Hilaire resigned the chair of Greek literature
at the Collège de France after the *coup d'état* of 1851, declining to take
the oath of allegiance to the existing government.

India House. He seldom takes the trouble to separate the metal from the ore, to purify or to strike it into current coin. He is but too often apt to forget that no lasting addition is ever made to the treasury of human knowledge unless the results of special research are translated into the universal language of science, and rendered available to every person of intellect and education. A division of labour seems most conducive to this end. We want a class of interpreters, men such as M. Barthélemy Saint-Hilaire, who are fully competent to follow and to control the researches of professional students, and who at the same time have not forgotten the language of the world.

In his work on Buddhism, of which a second edition has just appeared, M. Barthélemy Saint-Hilaire has undertaken to give to the world at large the really trustworthy and important results which have been obtained by the laborious researches of Oriental scholars, from the original documents of that interesting and still mysterious religion. It was a task of no ordinary difficulty, for although these researches are of very recent date, and belong to a period of Sanskrit scholarship posterior to Sir W. Jones and Colebrooke, yet such is the amount of evidence brought together by the combined industry of Hodgson, Turnour, Csoma de Körös, Stanislas Julien, Foucaux, Fausböll, Spence Hardy, but above all, of the late Eugène Burnouf, that it required no common patience and discrimination to compose from such materials so accurate, and at the same time so lucid and readable a book on Buddhism as that which we owe to M. Barthélemy Saint-Hilaire. The greater part of it appeared ori-

ginally in the 'Journal. des Savants,' the time-
honoured organ of the French Academy, which
counts on its staff the names of Cousin, Flourens,
Villemain, Biot, Mignet, Littré, &c., and admits as
contributors sixteen only of the most illustrious
members of that illustrious body, *la crème de la
crème.*

Though much had been said and written about
Buddhism,—enough to frighten priests by seeing
themselves anticipated in auricular confession, beads,
and tonsure by the Lamas of Tibet[3], and to discon-
cert philosophers by finding themselves outbid in
positivism and nihilism by the inmates of Chinese
monasteries,—the real beginning of an historical
and critical study of the doctrines of Buddha dates
from the year 1824. In that year Mr. Hodgson
announced the fact that the original documents of
the Buddhist canon had been preserved in Sanskrit
in the monasteries of Nepal. Before that time
our information on Buddhism had been derived
at random from China, Japan, Burmah, Tibet,

---

[3] The late Abbé Huc pointed out the similarities between the
Buddhist and Roman Catholic ceremonials with such *naïveté*, that,
to his surprise, he found his delightful 'Travels in Tibet' placed on
the 'Index.' 'On ne peut s'empêcher d'être frappé,' he writes, 'de
leur rapport avec le Catholicisme. La crosse, la mitre, la dalma-
tique, la chape ou pluvial, que les grands Lamas portent en voyage,
ou lorsqu'ils font quelque cérémonie hors du temple; l'office à
deux chœurs, la psalmodie, les exorcismes, l'encensoir soutenu par
cinq chaines, et pouvant s'ouvrir et se fermer à volonté; les
bénédictions données par les Lamas en étendant la main droite sur
la tête des fidèles; le chapelet, le célibat ecclésiastique, les retraites
spirituelles, le culte des saints, les jeûnes, les processions, les litanies,
l'eau bénite; voilà autant de rapports que les Bouddhistes ont avec
nous.' He might have added tonsure, relics, and the confessional.

Mongolia, and Tatary; and though it was known
that the Buddhist literature in all these countries
professed itself to be derived, directly or indirectly,
from India, and that the technical terms of that
religion, not excepting the very name of Buddha,
had their etymology in Sanskrit only, no hope was
entertained that the originals of these various translations could ever be recovered. Mr. Hodgson,
who settled in Nepal in 1821, as political resident
of the East-India Company, and whose eyes were
always open, not only to the natural history of that
little-explored country, but likewise to its antiquities, its languages, and traditions, was not long
before he discovered that his friends, the priests of
Nepal, possessed a complete literature of their own.
That literature was not written in the spoken
dialects of the country, but in Sanskrit.   Mr.
Hodgson procured a catalogue of all the works,
still in existence, which formed the Buddhist canon.
He afterwards succeeded in procuring copies of these
works, and he was able in 1824 to send about sixty
volumes to the Asiatic Society of Bengal.   As no
member of that society seemed inclined to devote
himself to the study of these MSS., Mr. Hodgson
sent two complete collections of the same MSS. to
the Asiatic Society of London and the Société
Asiatique of Paris. Before alluding to the brilliant
results which the last-named collection produced in
the hands of Eugène Burnouf, we must mention
the labours of other students, which preceded the
publication of Burnouf's researches.

Mr. Hodgson himself gave to the world a number
of valuable essays written on the spot, and afterwards collected under the title of ' Illustrations of

the Literature and Religion of the Buddhists,'
Serampore, 1841. He established the important
fact, in accordance with the traditions of the priests
of Nepal, that some of the Sanskrit documents
which he recovered had existed in the monasteries
of Nepal ever since the second century of our era,
and that the whole of that collection had, five or
six hundred years later, when Buddhism became
definitely established in Tibet, been translated
into the language of that country. As the art
of printing had been introduced from China
into Tibet, there was less difficulty in procuring
complete copies of the Tibetan translation of the
Buddhist canon. The real difficulty was to find a
person acquainted with the language. By a fortunate concurrence of circumstances, however, it so
happened that about the same time when Mr.
Hodgson's discoveries began to attract the attention of Oriental scholars at Calcutta, a Hungarian,
of the name of Alexander Csoma de Körös, arrived
there. He had made his way from Hungary to
Tibet on foot, without any means of his own, and
with the sole object of discovering somewhere in
Central Asia the native home of the Hungarians.
Arrived in Tibet, his enthusiasm found a new vent
in acquiring a language which no European before
his time had mastered, and in exploring the vast
collection of the canonical books of the Buddhists,
preserved in that language. Though he arrived at
Calcutta almost without a penny, he met with a
hearty welcome from the members of the Asiatic
Society, and was enabled with their assistance to
publish the results of his extraordinary researches.
People have complained of the length of the sacred

books of other nations, but there are none that approach in bulk to the sacred canon of the Tibetans.
It consists of two collections, commonly called the
Kanjur and Tanjur. The proper spelling of their
names is Bkah-hgyur, pronounced Kah-gyur, and
Bstan-hgyur, pronounced Tan-gyur. The Kanjur
consists, in its different editions, of 100, 102, or 108
volumes folio. It comprises 1083 distinct works.
The Tanjur consists of 225 volumes folio, each
weighing from four to five pounds in the edition
of Peking. Editions of this colossal code were
printed at Peking, Lhassa, and other places. The
edition of the Kanjur published at Peking, by command of the Emperor Khian-Lung, sold for £600.
A copy of the Kanjur was bartered for 7000 oxen
by the Buriates, and the same tribe paid 1200 silver
roubles for a complete copy of the Kanjur and
Tanjur together[4]. Such a jungle of religious literature—the most excellent hiding-place, we should
think, for Lamas and Dalai-Lamas—was too much
even for a man who could travel on foot from Hungary to Tibet. The Hungarian enthusiast, however,
though he did not translate the whole, gave a most
valuable analysis of this immense bible, in the
twentieth volume of the 'Asiatic Researches,' sufficient to establish the fact that the principal portion
of it was a translation from the same Sanskrit
originals which had been discovered in Nepal by
Mr. Hodgson. Csoma de Körös died soon after he
had given to the world the first fruits of his labours,
—a victim to his heroic devotion to the study of
ancient languages and religions.

---

[4] 'Die Religion des Buddha,' von Köppen, vol. ii. p. 282.

It was another fortunate coincidence that, con-
temporaneously with the discoveries of Hodgson
and Csoma de Körös, another scholar, Schmidt of
St. Petersburg, had so far advanced in the study
of the Mongolian language, as to be able to translate portions of the Mongolian version of the Buddhist canon, and thus forward the elucidation of
some of the problems connected with the religion
of Buddha.

It never rains but it pours. Whereas for years,
nay, for centuries, not a single original document
of the Buddhist religion had been accessible to the
scholars of Europe, we witness, in the small space
of ten years, the recovery of four complete Buddhist
literatures. In addition to the discoveries of Hodgson in Nepal, of Csoma de Körös in Tibet, and of
Schmidt in Mongolia, the Honourable George Turnour suddenly presented to the world the Buddhist
literature of Ceylon, composed in the sacred language of that island, the ancient Pâli. The existence
of that literature had been known before. Since
1826 Sir Alexander Johnston had been engaged in
collecting authentic copies of the Mahâvansa, the
Râgâvali, and the Râgaratnâkari. These copies
were translated at his suggestion from Pâli into
modern Singhalese and thence into English. The
publication was entrusted to Mr. Edward Upham,
and the work appeared in 1833, under the title of
' Sacred and Historical Works of Ceylon,' dedicated
to William IV. Unfortunately, whether through
fraud or through misunderstanding, the priests who
were to have procured an authentic copy of the
Pâli originals and translated them into the vernacular language, appear to have formed a compilation

of their own from various sources. The official
translators by whom this mutilated Singhalese
abridgment was to have been rendered into English,
took still greater liberties; and the 'Sacred and
Historical Books of Ceylon' had hardly been published before Burnouf, then a mere beginner in the
study of Pâli, was able to prove the utter uselessness of that translation. Mr. Turnour, however,
soon made up for this disappointment. He set to
work in a more scholarlike spirit, and after acquiring himself a knowledge of the Pâli language, he
published several important essays on the Buddhist
canon, as preserved in Ceylon. These were followed
by an edition and translation of the Mahâvansa, or
the history of Ceylon, written in the fifth century
after Christ, and giving an account of the island
from the earliest times to the beginning of the
fourth century A.D. Several continuations of that
history are in existence, but Mr. Turnour was prevented by an early death from continuing his
edition beyond the original portion of that chronicle.
The exploration of the Ceylonese literature has since
been taken up again by the Rev. D. J. Gogerly
(died 1862), whose essays are unfortunately scattered
about in Singhalese periodicals and little known in
Europe; and by the Rev. Spence Hardy, for twenty
years Wesleyan Missionary in Ceylon. His two
works, 'Eastern Monachism' and 'Manual of Buddhism,' are full of interesting matter, but as they are
chiefly derived from Singhalese, and even more modern sources, they require to be used with caution[5].

---

[5] The same author has lately published another valuable work,
'The Legends and Theories of the Buddhists.' London, 1866. He
died in 1868.

In the same manner as the Sanskrit originals of
Nepal were translated by Buddhist missionaries
into Tibetan, Mongolian, and, as we shall soon see,
into Chinese and Mandshu[6], the Pâli originals of
Ceylon were carried to Burmah and Siam, and
translated there into the languages of those countries. Hardly anything has as yet been done for
exploring the literature of these two countries,
which open a promising field for any one ambitious
to follow in the footsteps of Hodgson, Csoma, and
Turnour.

A very important collection of Buddhist MSS.
has lately been brought from Ceylon to Europe by
M. Grimblot, and is now deposited in the Imperial
Library at Paris. This collection, to judge from a
report published in 1866 in the 'Journal des Savants'
by M. Barthélemy Saint-Hilaire, consists of no less
than eighty-seven works; and, as some of them are
represented by more than one copy, the total number of MSS. amounts to one hundred and twenty-one.
They fill altogether 14,000 palm leaves, and are written partly in Singhalese, partly in Burmese characters. Next to Ceylon, Burmah and Siam would seem
to be the two countries most likely to yield large
collections of Pâli MSS., and the MSS. which now
exist in Ceylon may, to a considerable extent, be
traced back to these two countries. At the beginning
of the sixteenth century, the Tamil conquerors of
Ceylon are reported to have burnt every Buddhist
book they could discover, in the hope of thus destroying the vitality of that detested religion. Buddhism,
however, though persecuted — or, more probably,

---

[6] 'Mélanges Asiatiques,' vol. ii. p. 373.

because persecuted—remained the national religion of the island, and in the eighteenth century it had recovered its former ascendency. Missions were then sent to Siam to procure authentic copies of the sacred documents; priests properly ordained were imported from Burmah; and several libraries, which contain both the canonical and the profane literature of Buddhism, were founded at Dadala, Ambagapitya, and other places.

The sacred canon of the Buddhists is called the Tripi*t*aka, i.e. the three baskets. The first basket contains all that has reference to morality, or Vinaya; the second contains the Sûtras, i.e. the discourses of Buddha; the third includes all works treating of dogmatic philosophy or metaphysics. The second and third baskets are sometimes comprehended under the general name of Dharma, or law, and it has become usual to apply to the third basket the name of Abhidharma, or by-law. The first and second pi*t*akas contain each five separate works; the third contains seven. M. Grimblot has secured MSS. of nearly every one of these works, and he has likewise brought home copies of the famous commentaries of Buddhaghosha. These commentaries are of great importance ; for although Buddhaghosha lived as late as 430 A. D., he is supposed to have been the translator of more ancient commentaries, brought in 316 B. C. to Ceylon from Magadha by Mahinda, the son of Asoka, translated by him from Pâli into Singhalese, and retranslated by Buddhaghosha into Pâli, the original language both of the canonical books and of their commentaries. Whether historical criticism will allow to the commentaries of Buddhaghosha the authority due to documents of the fourth century before Christ, is a question that has yet to be settled. But even as a collector of earlier traditions and as a writer of the fifth century after Christ, his authority would be considerable with regard to the solution of some of the most important problems of Indian history and chronology. Some scholars who have written on the history of Buddhism have clearly shown too strong an inclination to treat the statements contained in the commentaries of Buddhaghosha as purely historical, forgetting the great interval of time by which he is separated from the events which he relates. No doubt if it could be proved that Buddhaghosha's works were literal translations of the so-called Attakathás or commentaries brought by Mahinda to Ceylon, this would considerably enhance their historical value. But the whole account of these translations rests on tradition, and if we consider the extraordinary precautions taken, according to tradition, by the LXX translators of the Old Testament, and then observe the discrepancies between the chronology of the Septuagint and that of the Hebrew text, we shall be better able to appreciate the risk of trusting to Oriental translations, even to those that pretend to be literal. The idea of a faithful literal translation seems altogether foreign to Oriental minds. Granted that Mahinda translated the original Páli commentaries into Singhalese, there was nothing to restrain him from inserting anything that he thought likely to be useful to his new converts. Granted that Buddhaghosha translated these translations back into Páli, why should he not have incorporated any facts that were then believed and had been handed down by tradition from generation to generation? Was he not at liberty—nay, would he

not have felt it his duty, to explain apparent difficulties, to remove contradictions, and to correct
palpable mistakes? In our time, when even the
contemporaneous evidence of Herodotus, Thucydides,
Livy, or Jornandes is sifted by the most uncompro-
mising scepticism, we must not expect a more merciful
treatment for the annals of Buddhism. Scholars
engaged in special researches are too willing to
acquiesce in evidence, particularly if that evidence
has been discovered by their own efforts and comes
before them with all the charms of novelty. But, in
the broad daylight of historical criticism, the prestige
of such a witness as Buddhaghosha soon dwindles
away, and his statements as to kings and councils
eight hundred years before his time are in truth
worth no more than the stories told of Arthur by
Geoffrey of Monmouth, or the accounts we read in
Livy of the early history of Rome.

One of the most important works of M. Grimblot's
collection, and one that we hope will soon be published, is a history of Buddhism in Ceylon, called the
Dîpavansa. The only work of the same character
which has hitherto been known is the Mahâvansa,
published by the Honourable George Turnour. But
this is professedly based on the Dîpavansa, and is
probably of a much later date. Mahânâma, the
compiler of the Mahâvansa, lived about 500 A. D.
His work was continued by later chroniclers to the
middle of the eighteenth century. Though Mahânâma wrote towards the end of the fifth century
after Christ, his own share of the chronicle seems to
have ended with the year 302 A. D., and a commentary which he wrote on his own chronicle likewise breaks off at that period. The exact date of

the Dipavansa is not yet known; but as it also
breaks off with the death of Mâhasena in 302 A.D.,
we cannot ascribe to it, for the present, any higher
authority than could be commanded by a writer of
the fourth century after Christ.

We now return to Mr. Hodgson. His collections
of Sanskrit MSS. had been sent, as we saw, to the
Asiatic Society of Calcutta from 1824 to 1839, to
the Royal Asiatic Society in London in 1835, and
to the Société Asiatique of Paris in 1837. They
remained dormant at Calcutta and in London. At
Paris, however, these Buddhist MSS. fell into the
hands of Burnouf. Unappalled by their size and
tediousness, he set to work, and was not long before
he discovered their extreme importance. After
seven years of careful study, Burnouf published, in
1844, his 'Introduction à l'Histoire du Buddhisme.'
It is this work which laid the foundation for a systematic study of the religion of Buddha. Though
acknowledging the great value of the researches
made in the Buddhist literatures of Tibet, Mongolia, China, and Ceylon, Burnouf showed that
Buddhism, being of Indian origin, ought to be
studied first of all in the original Sanskrit documents, preserved in Nepal. Though he modestly
called his work an Introduction to the History of
Buddhism, there are few points of importance on
which his industry has not brought together the
most valuable evidence, and his genius shed a novel
and brilliant light. The death of Burnouf in 1851
put an end to a work which, if finished according to
the plan sketched out by the author in the preface,
would have been the most perfect monument of
Oriental scholarship. A volume published after

his death, in 1852, contains a translation of one of
the canonical books of Nepal, with notes and appen-
dices, the latter full of the most valuable information
on some of the more intricate questions of Buddhism.
Though much remained to be done, and though a
very small breach only had been made in the vast
pile of Sanskrit MSS. presented by Mr. Hodgson to
the Asiatic Societies of Paris and London, no one
has been bold enough to continue what Burnouf
left unfinished.. The only important additions to
our knowledge of Buddhism since his death are an
edition of the Lalita-Vistara or the life of Buddha,
prepared by a native, the learned Babu Rajendralal
Mittra; an edition of the Pâli original of the Dhammapadam, by Dr. Fausböll, a Dane; and last, not
least, the excellent translation by M. Stanislas Julien,
of the life and travels of Hiouen-Thsang. This
Chinese pilgrim had visited India from 629 to
645 A.D., for the purpose of learning Sanskrit,
and translating from Sanskrit into Chinese some
important works on the religion and philosophy
of the Buddhists; and his account of the geography,
the social, religious, and political state of India at
the beginning of the seventh century is invaluable
for studying the practical working of that religion
at a time when its influence began to decline, and
when it was soon to be supplanted by modern
Brahmanism and Mohammedanism.

It was no easy task for M. Barthélemy Saint-
Hilaire to make himself acquainted with all these
works. The study of Buddhism would almost seem
to be beyond the power of any single individual,
if it required a practical acquaintance with all the
languages in which the doctrines of Buddha have

been written down. Burnouf was probably the only man who, in addition to his knowledge of Sanskrit, did not shrink from acquiring a practical knowledge of Tibetan, Pâli, Singhalese, and Burmese, in order to prepare himself for such a task. The same scholar had shown, however, that though it was impossible for a Tibetan, Mongolian, or Chinese scholar to arrive, without a knowledge of Sanskrit, at a correct understanding of the doctrines of Buddha, a knowledge of Sanskrit was sufficient for entering into their spirit, for comprehending their origin and growth in India, and their modification in the different countries where they took root in later times. Assisted by his familiarity with Sanskrit, and bringing into the field, as a new and valuable auxiliary, his intimate acquaintance with nearly all the systems of philosophy and religion of both the ancient and modern worlds, M. Barthélemy Saint-Hilaire has succeeded in drawing a picture, both lively and correct, of the origin, the character, the strong as well as weak points, of the religion of Buddha. He has become the first historian of Buddhism. He has not been carried away by a temptation which must have been great for one who is able to read in the past the lessons for the present or the future. He has not used Buddhism either as a bugbear or as a *beau idéal.* He is satisfied with stating in his preface that many lessons might be learned by modern philosophers from a study of Buddhism, but in the body of the work he never perverts the chair of the historian into the pulpit of the preacher.

'This book may offer one other advantage,' he writes, 'and I regret to say that at present it may

seem to come opportunely. It is the misfortune
of our times that the same doctrines which form
the foundation of Buddhism meet at the hands of
some of our philosophers with a favour which they
ill deserve. For some years we have seen systems
arising in which metempsychosis and transmigration
are highly spoken of, and attempts are made to
explain the world and man without either a God
or a Providence, exactly as Buddha did. A future
life is refused to the yearnings of mankind, and the
immortality of the soul is replaced by the immortality of works. God is dethroned, and in His
place they substitute man, the only being, we are
told, in which the Infinite becomes conscious of
itself. These theories are recommended to us sometimes in the name of science, or of history, or philology, or even of metaphysics; and though they are
neither new nor very original, yet they can do much
injury to feeble hearts. This is not the place to
examine these theories, and their authors are both
too learned and too sincere to deserve to be con-
demned summarily and without discussion. But
it is well that they should know by the example,
too little known, of Buddhism, what becomes of
man if he depends on himself alone, and if his
meditations, misled by a pride of which he is hardly
conscious, bring him to the precipice where Buddha
was lost. I am well aware of all the differences, and
I am not going to insult our contemporary philosophers by confounding them indiscriminately with
Buddha, although addressing to both the same re-
proof. I acknowledge willingly all their additional
merits, which are considerable. But systems of philosophy must always be judged by the conclusions to

which they lead, whatever road they may follow in reaching them; and their conclusions, though obtained by different means, are not therefore less objectionable. Buddha arrived at his conclusions 2,400 years ago. He proclaimed and practised them with an energy which is not likely to be surpassed, even if it be equalled. He displayed a childlike intrepidity which no one can exceed, nor can it be supposed that any system in our days could again acquire so powerful an ascendency over the souls of men. It would be useful, however, if the authors of these modern systems would just cast a glance at the theories and destinies of Buddhism. It is not philosophy in the sense in which we understand this great name, nor is it religion in the sense of ancient paganism, of Christianity, or of Mohammedanism; but it contains elements of all worked up into a perfectly independent doctrine which acknowledges nothing in the universe but man, and obstinately refuses to recognise anything else, though confounding man with nature in the midst of which he lives. Hence all those aberrations of Buddhism which ought to be a warning to others. Unfortunately, if people rarely profit by their own faults, they profit yet more rarely by the faults of others.' (Introduction, p. vii.)

But though M. Barthélemy Saint-Hilaire does not write history merely for the sake of those masked batteries which French writers have used with so much skill at all times, but more particularly during the late years of Imperial sway, it is clear, from the remarks just quoted, that our author is not satisfied with simply chronicling the dry facts of Buddhism, or turning into French the tedious discourses of its founder. His work is an animated

sketch, giving too little rather than too much. It
is just the book which was wanted to dispel the
erroneous notions about Buddhism, which are still
current among educated men, and to excite an
interest which may lead those who are naturally
frightened by the appalling proportions of Buddhist
literature, and the uncouth sounds of Buddhist
terminology, to a study of the quartos of Burnouf,
Turnour, and others. To those who may wish for
more detailed information on Buddhism, than could
be given by M. Barthélemy Saint Hilaire, consist-
ently with the plan of his work, we can strongly
recommend the work of a German writer, 'Die
Religion des Buddha,' von Köppen, Berlin, 1857.
It is founded on the same materials as the French
work, but being written by a scholar and for scholars,
it enters on a more minute examination of all that
has been said or written on Buddha and Buddhism.
In a second volume the same learned and industrious
student has lately published a history of Buddhism
in Tibet.

M. Barthélemy Saint-Hilaire's work is divided into
three portions. The first contains an account of the
origin of Buddhism, a life of Buddha, and an examination of Buddhist ethics and metaphysics. In the
second he describes the state of Buddhism in India
in the seventh century of our era, from the materials
supplied by the travels of Hiouen-Thsang. The
third gives a description of Buddhism as actually
existing in Ceylon, and as lately described by an
eye-witness, the Rev. Spence Hardy. We shall
confine ourselves chiefly to the first part, which
treats of the life and teaching of Buddha.

M. Barthélemy Saint-Hilaire, following the ex-

ample of Burnouf, Lassen, and Wilson, accepts the
date of the Ceylonese era 543 B. C. as the date of
Buddha's death. Though we cannot enter here
into long chronological discussions, we must remark,
that this date was clearly obtained by the Buddhists of Ceylon by calculation, not by historical
tradition, and that it is easy to point out in that
calculation a mistake of about seventy years. The
more plausible date of Buddha's death is 477 B. C.
For the purposes, however, which M. Barthélemy
Saint-Hilaire had in view, this difference is of
small importance. We know so little of the history of India during the sixth and fifth centuries
B. C., that the stage on which he represents Buddha as preaching and teaching would have had
very much the same background, the same cos-
tume and accessories, for the sixth as for the fifth
century, B. C.

In the life of Buddha, which extends from p. 1
to 79, M. Barthélemy Saint-Hilaire follows almost
exclusively the Lalita-Vistara. This is one of the
most popular works of the Buddhists. It forms
part of the Buddhist canon; and as we know of a
translation into Chinese, which M. Stanislas Julien
ascribes to the year 76 A. D., we may safely refer its
original composition to an ante-Christian date. It
has been published in Sanskrit by Babu Rajendralal
Mittra, and we owe to M. Foucaux an edition of
the same work in its Tibetan translation, the first
Tibetan text printed in Europe. From specimens
that we have seen, we should think it would be
highly desirable to have an accurate translation of
the Chinese text, such as M. Stanislas Julien alone

is able to give us.[7] Few people, however, except
scholars, would have the patience to read this work
either in its English or French translation, as may
be seen from the following specimen, containing the
beginning of Babu Rajendralal Mittra's version:

'Om! Salutation to all Buddhas, Bodhisattvas,
Âryas, *S*râvakas, and Pratyeka Buddhas of all
times, past, present, and future; who are adored
throughout the farthest limits of the ten quarters
of the globe. Thus hath it been heard by me, that
once on a time Bhagavat sojourned in the garden.
of Anâthapi*n*dada, at *G*etavana, in *S*râvastî, accom-

---

[7] The advantages to be derived from these Chinese translations
have been pointed out by M. Stanislas Julien. The analytical
structure of that language imparts to Chinese translations the
character almost of a gloss; and though we need not follow impli-
citly the interpretations of the Sanskrit originals, adopted by the
Chinese translators, still their antiquity would naturally impart to
them a considerable value and interest. The following specimens
were kindly communicated to me by M. Stanislas Julien:

'Je ne sais si je vous ai communiqué autrefois les curieux
passages qui suivent: On lit dans le Lotus français, p. 271, l. 14,
C'est que c'est une chose difficile à rencontrer que la naissance d'un
bouddha, aussi difficile à rencontrer que la fleur de l'Udumbara,
que l'introduction du col d'une tortue dans l'ouverture d'un joug
formé par le grand océan.

'Il y a en chinois: un bouddha est difficile à rencontrer, comme
les fleurs Udumbara et Palâça; et en outre comme si une tortue
borgne voulait rencontrer un trou dans un bois flottant (litt. le trou
d'un bois flottant).

'Lotus français, p. 39, l. 110 (les créatures), enchaînées par la
concupiscence comme par la queue du Yak, perpétuellement
aveuglées en ce monde par les désirs, elles ne cherchent pas le
Buddha.

'Il y a en chinois: Profondément attachées aux cinq désirs—
Elles les aiment comme le Yak aime sa queue. Par la concupiscence et l'amour, elles s'aveuglent elles-mêmes, etc.'

panied by a venerable body of 12,000 Bhikshukas.
There likewise accompanied him 32,000 Bodhisattvas, all linked together by unity of caste, and
perfect in the virtues of pâramitâ; who had made
their command over Bodhisattva knowledge a pas-
time, were illumined with the light of Bodhisattva
dhâranis, and were masters of the dhâranis themselves; who were profound in their meditations, all
submissive to the lord of Bodhisattvas, and possessed
absolute control over samâdhi; great in self-com-
mand, refulgent in Bodhisattva forbearance, and re-
plete with the Bodhisattva element of perfection.
Now then, Bhagavat arriving in the great city of
Srâvasti, sojourned therein, respected, venerated,
revered, and adored, by the fourfold congregation;
by kings, princes, their counsellors, prime ministers,
and followers; by retinues of kshatriyas, brâhmanas,
householders, and ministers; by citizens, foreigners,
srâmanas, brâhmanas, recluses, and ascetics; and
although regaled with all sorts of edibles and sauces,
the best that could be prepared by purveyors, and
supplied with cleanly mendicant apparel, begging
pots, couches, and pain-assuaging medicaments, the
benevolent lord, on whom had been showered the
prime of gifts and applauses, remained unattached
to them all, like water on a lotus leaf; and the
report of his greatness as the venerable, the absolute
Buddha, the learned and well-behaved, the god of
happy exit, the great knower of worlds, the valiant,
the all-controlling charioteer, the teacher of gods
and men, the quinocular lord Buddha fully manifest
spread far and wide in the world. And Bhagavat,
having by his own power acquired all knowledge
regarding this world and the next, comprising devas,

mâras, brâhmyas (followers of Brahmâ), srâmaṇas, and brâhmaṇas, as subjects, that is both gods and men, sojourned here, imparting instructions in the true religion, and expounding the principles of a brahmakarya, full and complete in its nature, holy in its import, pure and immaculate in its character, auspicious is its beginning, auspicious its middle, auspicious its end.'

The whole work is written in a similar style, and where fact and legend, prose and poetry, sense and nonsense, are so mixed together, the plan adopted by M. Barthélemy Saint-Hilaire, of making two lives out of one, the one containing all that seems possible, the other what seems impossible, would naturally recommend itself. It is not a safe process, however, to distil history out of legend by simply straining the legendary through the sieve of physical possibility. Many things are possible, and may yet be the mere inventions of later writers, and many things which sound impossible have been reclaimed as historical, after removing from them the thin film of mythological phraseology. We believe that the only use which the historian can safely make of the Lalita-Vistara, is to employ it, not as evidence of facts which actually happened, but in illustration of the popular belief prevalent at the time when it was committed to writing. Without therefore adopting the division of fact and fiction in the life of Buddha, as attempted by M. Barthélemy Saint-Hilaire, we yet believe that in order to avoid a repetition of childish absurdities, we shall best consult the interest of our readers if we follow his example, and give a short and rational abstract of the life of Buddha as handed down by tradition, and committed to writing not later than the first century B. C.

Buddha, or more correctly, the Buddha,—for Buddha is an appellative meaning Enlightened,—was born at Kapilavastu, the capital of a kingdom of the same name, situated at the foot of the mountains of Nepal, north of the present Oude. His father, the king of Kapilavastu, was of the family of the Sâkyas, and belonged to the clan of the Gautamas. His mother was Mâyâdêvî, daughter of king Suprabuddha, and need we say that she was as beautiful as he was powerful and just? Buddha was therefore by birth of the Kshatriya, or warrior caste, and he took the name of Sâkya from his family, and that of Gautama from his clan, claiming a kind of spiritual relationship with the honoured race of Gautama. The name of Buddha, or the Buddha, dates from a later period of his life, and so probably does the name Siddhârtha (he whose objects have been accomplished), though we are told that it was given him in his childhood. His mother died seven days after his birth, and the father confided the child to the care of his deceased wife's sister, who, however, had been his wife even before the mother's death. The child grew up a most beautiful and most accomplished boy, who soon knew more than his masters could teach him. He refused to take part in the games of his playmates, and never felt so happy as when he could sit alone, lost in meditation in the deep shadows of the forest. It was there that his father found him when he had thought him lost, and in order to prevent the young prince from becoming a dreamer, the king determined to marry him at once. When the subject was mentioned by the aged ministers to the future heir to the throne, he demanded seven days for reflection, and convinced at last that not even marriage could

disturb the calm of his mind, he allowed the ministers
to look out for a princess. The princess selected
was the beautiful Gopâ, the daughter of Dandapâni.
Though her father objected at first to her marrying
a young prince who was represented to him as deficient in manliness and intellect, he gladly gave his
consent when he saw the royal suitor distancing all
his rivals both in feats of arms and power of mind.
Their marriage proved one of the happiest, but the
prince remained, as he had been before, absorbed in
meditation on the problems of life and death. ' Nothing is stable on earth,' he used to say, ' nothing is
real. Life is like the spark produced by the friction
of wood. It is lighted and is extinguished—we
know not whence it came or whither it goes. It is
like the sound of a lyre, and the wise man asks in
vain from whence it came and whither it goes.
There must be some supreme intelligence where we
could find rest. If I attained it, I could bring light
to man; if I were free myself, I could deliver the
world.' The king, who perceived the melancholy
mood of the young prince, tried every thing to divert
him from his speculations : but all was in vain.
Three of the most ordinary events that could happen
to any man, proved of the utmost importance in the
career of Buddha. We quote the description of these
occurrences from M. Barthélemy Saint-Hilaire:

' One day when the prince with a large retinue was
driving through the eastern gate of the city on the
way to one of his parks, he met on the road an old
man, broken and decrepit. One could see the veins
and muscles over the whole of his body, his teeth
chattered, he was covered with wrinkles, bald, and
hardly able to utter hollow and unmelodious sounds.

He was bent on his stick, and all his limbs and joints
trembled. "Who is that man?" said the prince to
his coachman. "He is small and weak, his flesh
and his blood are dried up, his muscles stick to his
skin, his head is white, his teeth chatter, his body is
wasted away; leaning on his stick he is hardly able
to walk, stumbling at every step. Is there something peculiar in his family, or is this the common
lot of all created beings?"

'"Sir," replied the coachman, "that man is sinking
under old age, his senses have become obtuse, suffering has destroyed his strength, and he is despised
by his relations. He is without support and useless, and people have abandoned him, like a dead
tree in a forest. But this is not peculiar to his
family. In every creature youth is defeated by old
age. Your father, your mother, all your relations,
all your friends, will come to the same state; this is
the appointed end of all creatures."

'"Alas!" replied the prince, "are creatures so
ignorant, so weak and foolish, as to be proud of the
youth by which they are intoxicated, not seeing the
old age which awaits them! As for me, I go away.
Coachman, turn my chariot quickly. What have I,
the future prey of old age,—what have I to do with
pleasure?" And the young prince returned to the
city without going to his park.

'Another time the prince was driving through the
southern gate to his pleasure garden, when he perceived on the road a man suffering from illness,
parched with fever, his body wasted, covered with
mud, without a friend, without a home, hardly able
to breathe, and frightened at the sight of himself
and the approach of death. Having questioned his

coachman, and received from him the answer which
he expected, the young prince said, " Alas ! health
is but the sport of a dream, and the fear of suffering
must take this frightful form. Where is the wise
man who, after having seen what he is, could any
longer think of joy and pleasure ? " The prince
turned his chariot and returned to the city.

' A third time he was driving to his pleasure garden
through the western gate, when he saw a dead body
on the road, lying on a bier, and covered with a cloth.
The friends stood about crying, sobbing, tearing their
hair, covering their heads with dust, striking their
breasts, and uttering wild cries. The prince, again,
calling his coachman to witness this painful scene,
exclaimed, " Oh ! woe to youth, which must be
destroyed by old age! Woe to health, which must
be destroyed by so many diseases ! Woe to this life,
where a man remains so short a time ! If there were
no old age, no disease, no death; if these could be
made captive for ever !" Then betraying for the
first time his intentions, the young prince said,
" Let us turn back, I must think how to accomplish
deliverance."

' A last meeting put an end to his hesitation. He
was driving through the northern gate on the way to
his pleasure gardens, when he saw a mendicant who
appeared outwardly calm, subdued, looking downwards, wearing with an air of dignity his religious
vestment, and carrying an alms-bowl.

' " Who is this man? " asked the prince.

' " Sir," replied the coachman, " this man is one of
those who are called bhikshus, or mendicants. He
has renounced all pleasures, all desires, and leads a
life of austerity. He tries to conquer himself. He

has become a devotee. Without passion, without envy,
he walks about asking for alms."

'"This is good and well said," replied the prince.
"The life of a devotee has always been praised by
the wise. It will be my refuge, and the refuge of
other creatures; it will lead us to a real life, to happiness and immortality."

'With these words the young prince turned his
chariot and returned to the city.'

After having declared to his father and his wife
his intention of retiring from the world, Buddha left
his palace one night when all the guards that were
to have watched him were asleep. After travelling
the whole night, he gave his horse and his ornaments to his groom, and sent him back to Kapilavastu. 'A monument,' remarks the author of the
Lalita-Vistara (p. 270), 'is still to be seen on the
spot where the coachman turned back.' Hiouen-
Thsang (II. 330) saw the same monument at the edge
of a large forest, on his road to Kusinâgara, a city
now in ruins, and situated about fifty miles E.S.E.
from Gorakpur[8].

Buddha first went to Vaisâlî, and became the pupil
of a famous Brahman, who had gathered round him
300 disciples. Having learnt all that the Brahman
could teach him, Buddha went away disappointed.
He had not found the road to salvation. He then
tried another Brahman at Râgagriha, the capital of

---

[8] The geography of India at the time of Buddha, and later at
the time of Fahian and Hiouen-Thsang, has been admirably treated
by M. L. Vivien de Saint-Martin, in his 'Mémoire Analytique sur
la Carte de l'Asie Centrale et de l'Inde,' in the third volume of
M. Stanislas Julien's 'Pèlerins Bouddhistes.'

Magadha or Behar, who had 700 disciples, and there
too he looked in vain for the means of deliverance.
He left him, followed by five of his fellow-students,
and for six years retired into solitude, near a village named Uruvilva, subjecting himself to the most
severe penances, previous to his appearing in the
world as a teacher. At the end of this period, however, he arrived at the conviction that asceticism,
far from giving peace of mind and preparing the
way to salvation, was a snare and a stumbling-block
in the way of truth. He gave up his exercises, and
was at once deserted as an apostate by his five disciples. Left to himself he now began to elaborate
his own system. He had learnt that neither the
doctrines nor the austerities of the Brahmans were
of any avail for accomplishing the deliverance of man,
and freeing him from the fear of old age, disease, and
death. After long meditations, and ecstatic visions,
he at last imagined that he had arrived at that true
knowledge which discloses the cause, and thereby
destroys the fear, of all the changes inherent in life.
It was from the moment when he arrived at this
knowledge, that he claimed the name of Buddha, the
Enlightened. At that moment we may truly say
that the fate of millions of millions of human beings
trembled in the balance. Buddha hesitated for a
time whether he should keep his knowledge to himself, or communicate it to the world. Compassion
for the sufferings of man prevailed, and the young
prince became the founder of a religion which, after
more than 2000 years, is still professed by 455,000,000
of human beings[9].

---

[9] Though truth is not settled by majorities, it would be interesting
to know which religion counts at the present moment the largest

The further history of the new teacher is very
simple. He proceeded to Benares, which at all times
was the principal seat of learning in India, and the
first converts he made were the five fellow-students
who had left him when he threw off the yoke of the
Brahmanical observances. Many others followed;
but as the Lalita-Vistara breaks off at Buddha's
arrival at Benares, we have no further consecutive
account of the rapid progress of his doctrine. From
what we can gather from scattered notices in the
Buddhist canon, he was invited by the king of
Magadha, Bimbisâra, to his capital, Râgagriha. Many
of his lectures are represented as having been delivered at the monastery of Kalantaka, with which
the king or some rich merchant had presented him;
others on the Vulture Peak, one of the five hills that
surrounded the ancient capital.

Three of his most famous disciples, Sâriputra,
Kâtyâyana, and Maudgalyâyana, joined him during

---

numbers of believers. Berghaus, in his ' Physical Atlas,' gives the
following division of the human race according to religion :

Buddhists	31.2 per cent.
Christians	30.7 „
Mohammedans	15.7 „
Brahmanists	13.4 „
Heathens	8.7 „
Jews	0.3 „

As Berghaus does not distinguish the Buddhists in China from the
followers of Confucius and Laotse, the first place on the scale belongs really to Christianity. It is difficult in China to say to what
religion a man belongs, as the same person may profess two or
three. The emperor himself, after sacrificing according to the
ritual of Confucius, visits a Tao-ssé temple, and afterwards bows
before an image of Fo in a Buddhist chapel. (' Mélanges Asiatiques
de St. Pétersbourg,' vol. ii. p. 374.)

his stay in Magadha, where he enjoyed for many years the friendship of the king. That king was afterwards assassinated by his son, Agâtasatru, and then we hear of Buddha as settled for a time at Srâvastî, north of the Ganges, where Anâthapindada, a rich merchant, had offered him and his disciples a magnificent building for their residence. Most of Buddha's lectures or sermons were delivered at Srâvasti, the capital of Kosala; and the king of Kosala himself, Prasênagit, became a convert to his doctrine. After an absence of twelve years we are told that Buddha visited his father at Kapilavastu, on which occasion he performed several miracles, and converted all the Sâkyas to his faith. His own wife became one of his followers, and, with his aunt, offers the first instance of female Buddhist devotees in India. We have fuller particulars again of the last days of Buddha's life. He had attained the good age of three score and ten, and had been on a visit to Râgagriha, where the king, Agâtasatru, the former enemy of Buddha, and the assassin of his own father, had joined the congregation, after making a public confession of his crimes. On his return he was followed by a large number of disciples, and when on the point of crossing the Ganges, he stood on a square stone, and turning his eyes back towards Râgagriha, he said, full of emotion, ' This is the last time that I see that city.' He likewise visited Vaisâlî, and after taking leave of it, he had nearly reached the city of Kusinâgara, when his vital strength began to fail. He halted in a forest, and while sitting under a sâl tree, he gave up the ghost, or, as a Buddhist would say, entered into Nirvâna.

This is the simple story of Buddha's life. It reads

much better in the eloquent pages of M. Barthélemy
Saint-Hilaire, than in the turgid language of the
Buddhists. If a critical historian, with the materials
we possess, entered at all on the process of separating
truth from falsehood, he would probably cut off much
of what our biographer has left. Professor Wilson,
in his Essay on Buddha and Buddhism, considers it
doubtful whether any such person as Buddha ever
actually existed. He dwells on the fact that there
are at least twenty different dates assigned to his
birth, varying from 2420 to 453 b. c. He points out
that the clan of the Sâkyas is never mentioned by
early Hindu writers, and he lays much stress on the
fact that most of the proper names of the persons
connected with Buddha suggest an allegorical signification. The name of his father means, he whose
food is pure; that of his mother signifies illusion;
his own secular appellation, Siddhârtha, he by whom
the end is accomplished. Buddha itself means, the
Enlightened, or, as Professor Wilson translates it less
accurately, he by whom all is known. The same
distinguished scholar goes even further, and maintaining that Kapilavastu, the birthplace of Buddha,
has no place in the geography of the Hindus, suggests
that it may be rendered, the substance of Kapila;
intimating, in fact, the Sânkhya philosophy, the doctrine of Kapila Muni, upon which the fundamental
elements of Buddhism, the eternity of matter, the
principles of things, and the final extinction, are supposed to be planned. 'It seems not impossible,' he
continues, ' that Sâkya Muni is an unreal being, and
that all that is related of him is as much a fiction, as
is that of his preceding migrations, and the miracles
that attended his birth, his life, and his departure.'

This is going far beyond Niebuhr, far even beyond
Strauss. If an allegorical name had been invented
for the father of Buddha, one more appropriate than
'Clean-food' might surely have been found. His
mother is not the only queen known by the name of
Mâyâ, Mâyâdêvî, or Mâyâvatî. Why, if these names
were invented, should his wife have been allowed to
keep the prosaic name of Gopâ (cowherdess), and his
father-in-law, that of Dandapâni, 'Stick-hand?' As
to his own name, Siddhârtha, the Tibetans maintain
that it was given him by his parent, whose wish
(artha) had been fulfilled (siddha), as we hear of
Désirés and Dieu-donnés in French. One of the
ministers of Dasaratha had the same name. It is
possible also that Buddha himself assumed it in after
life, as was the case with many of the Roman sur-
names. As to the name of Buddha, no one ever
maintained that it was more than a title, the Enlightened, changed from an appellative into a proper
name, just like the name of Christos, the Anointed,
or Mohammed, the Expected [10]. Kapilavastu would
be a most extraordinary compound to express 'the
substance of the Sânkhya philosophy.' But all
doubt on the subject is removed by the fact that
both Fahian in the fifth, and Hiouen-Thsang in the
seventh centuries, visited the real ruins of that
city.

Making every possible allowance for the accumulation of fiction which is sure to gather round the life
of the founder of every great religion, we may be
satisfied that Buddhism, which changed the aspect
not only of India, but of nearly the whole of Asia,

[10] See Sprenger, 'Das Leben des Mohammed,' 1861, vol. i. p. 155.

had a real founder; that he was not a Brahman
by birth, but belonged to the second or royal caste;
that being of a meditative turn of mind, and deeply
impressed with the frailty of all created things, he
became a recluse, and sought for light and comfort
in the different systems of Brâhman philosophy and
theology. Dissatisfied with the artificial systems of
their priests and philosophers, convinced of the uselessness, nay of the pernicious influence, of their
ceremonial practices and bodily penances, shocked,
too, by their worldliness and pharisaical conceit,
which made the priesthood the exclusive property of
one caste and rendered every sincere approach of
man to his Creator impossible without their intervention, Buddha must have produced at once a powerful
impression on the people at large, when breaking
through all the established rules of caste, he assumed
the privileges of a Brahman, and throwing away the
splendour of his royal position, travelled about as a
beggar, not shrinking from the defiling contact of
sinners and publicans. Though when we now speak
of Buddhism, we think chiefly of its doctrines, the
reform of Buddha had originally much more of a
social than of a religious character. Buddha swept
away the web with which the Brahmans had encir-
cled the whole of India. Beginning as the destroyer
of an old, he became the founder of a new religion. We can hardly understand how any nation
could have lived under a system like that of the
Brahmanic hierarchy, which coiled itself round every
public and private act, and would have rendered life
intolerable to any who had forfeited the favour of
the priests. That system was attacked by Buddha.
Buddha might have taught whatever philosophy he

pleased, and we should hardly have heard his name. The people would not have minded him, and his system would only have been a drop in the ocean of philosophical speculation, by which India was deluged at all times. But when a young prince assembled round him people of all castes, of all ranks, when he defeated the Brahmans in public disputations, when he declared the sacrifices by which they made their living not only useless but sinful, when instead of severe penance or excommunications inflicted by the Brahmans sometimes for the most trifling offences, he only required public confession of sin and a promise to sin no more: when the charitable gifts hitherto monopolised by the Brahmans, began to flow into new channels, supporting hundreds and thousands of Buddhist mendicants, more had been achieved than probably Buddha himself had ever dreamt of; and he whose meditations had been how to deliver the soul of man from misery and the fear of death, had delivered the people of India from a degrading thraldom and from priestly tyranny.

The most important element of the Buddhist reform has always been its social and moral code, not its metaphysical theories. That moral code, taken by itself, is one of the most perfect which the world has ever known. On this point all testimonies from hostile and from friendly quarters agree. Spence Hardy, a Wesleyan Missionary, speaking of the Dhamma Padam, or the 'Footsteps of the Law,' admits that a collection might be made from the precepts of this work, which in the purity of its ethics could hardly be equalled from any other heathen author. M. Laboulaye, one of the most distinguished members of the French Academy, remarks in the

'Débats' of the 4th of April, 1853: 'It is difficult
to comprehend how men not assisted by revelation
could have soared so high, and approached so near to
the truth.' Besides the five great commandments
not to kill, not to steal, not to commit adultery, not
to lie, not to get drunk, every shade of vice, hypocrisy, anger, pride, suspicion, greediness, gossiping,
cruelty to animals, is guarded against by special
precepts. Among the virtues recommended, we find
not only reverence of parents, care for children, submission to authority, gratitude, moderation in time
of prosperity, submission in time of trial, equanimity
at all times, but virtues unknown in any heathen
system of morality, such as the duty of forgiving
insults and not rewarding evil with evil. All virtues,
we are told, spring from Maitrî, and this Maitrî can
only be translated by charity and love. 'I do not
hesitate,' says Burnouf[11], 'to translate by charity the
word Maitrî; it does not express friendship or the
feeling of particular affection which a man has for
one or more of his fellow-creatures, but that universal
feeling which inspires us with good-will towards all
men and constant willingness to help them.' We add
one more testimony from the work of M. Barthélemy
Saint-Hilaire:

'Je n'hésite pas à ajouter,' he writes, 'que, sauf le
Christ tout seul, il n'est point, parmi les fondateurs
de religion, de figure plus pure ni plus touchante que
celle du Bouddha. Sa vie n'a point de tâche. Son
constant héroisme égale sa conviction; et si la
théorie qu'il préconise est fausse, les exemples per-
sonnels qu'il donne sont irréprochables. Il est le

---

[11] Burnouf, 'Lotus de la bonne Loi,' p. 300.

modèle achevé de toutes les vertus qu'il prêche; son
abnégation, sa charité, son inaltérable douceur, ne
se démentent point un seul instant; il abandonne à
vingt-neuf ans la cour du roi son père pour se faire
religieux et mendiant; il prépare silencieusement sa
doctrine par six années de retraite et de méditation;
il la propage par la seule puissance de la parole et
de la persuasion, pendant plus d'un demi-siècle; et
quand il meurt entre les bras de ses disciples, c'est
avec la sérénité d'un sage qui a pratiqué le bien
toute sa vie, et qui est assuré d'avoir trouvé le
vrai.' (Page v.)

There still remain, no doubt, some blurred and doubtful pages in the history of the prince of Kapilavastu;
but we have only to look at the works on ancient
philosophy and religion published some thirty years
ago, in order to perceive the immense progress that
has been made in establishing the true historical
character of the founder of Buddhism. There was a
time when Buddha was identified with Christ. The
Manichæans were actually forced to adjure their
belief that Buddha, Christ, and Mani were one and
the same person[12]. But we are thinking rather of
the eighteenth and nineteenth centuries, when elaborate books were written, in order to prove that Buddha had been in reality the Thoth of the Egyptians,
that he was Mercury, or Wodan, or Zoroaster, or
Pythagoras. Even Sir W. Jones, as we saw, identified Buddha, first with Odin, and afterwards with
Shishak, 'who either in person or by a colony
from Egypt imported into India the mild heresy of

the ancient Bauddhas.' Now we know that neither
Egypt nor the Walhalla of Germany, neither Greece
nor Persia, could have produced either the man
himself or his doctrine. He is the offspring of
India in mind and soul. His doctrine, by the very
antagonism in which it stands to the old system of
Brahmanism, shows that it could not have sprung up
in any country except India. The ancient history of
Brahmanism leads on to Buddhism, with the same
necessity with which mediæval Romanism led to
Protestantism. Though the date of Buddha is still
liable to small chronological oscillations, his place in
the intellectual annals of India is henceforth definitely marked: Buddhism became the state religion
of India at the time of Asoka; and Asoka, the Buddhist Constantine, was the grandson of Kandragupta,
the contemporary of Seleucus Nicator. The system of
the Brahmans had run its course. Their ascendency,
at first purely intellectual and religious, had gradually assumed a political character. By means
of the system of caste this influence pervaded the
whole social fabric, not as a vivifying leaven, but as
a deadly poison. Their increasing power and self-
confidence are clearly exhibited in the successive
periods of their ancient literature. It begins with
the simple hymns of the Veda. These are followed
by the tracts, known by the name of Brâhmanas,
in which a complete system of theology is elaborated
and claims advanced in favour of the Brahmans, such
as were seldom conceded to any hierarchy. The
third period in the history of their ancient literature
is marked by their Sûtras or Aphorisms, curt and
dry formularies, showing the Brahmans in secure
possession of all their claims. Such privileges as

they then enjoyed are never enjoyed for any length of time. It was impossible for anybody to move or to assert his freedom of thought and action without finding himself impeded on all sides by the web of the Brahmanic law; nor was there anything in their religion to satisfy the natural yearnings of the human heart after spiritual comfort. What was felt by Buddha, had been felt more or less intensely by thousands; and this was the secret of his success. That success was accelerated, however, by political events. *K*andragupta had conquered the throne of Magadha, and acquired his supremacy in India in defiance of the Brahmanic law. He was of low origin, a mere adventurer, and by his accession to the throne an important mesh had been broken in the intricate system of caste. Neither he nor his successors could count on the support of the Brahmans, and it is but natural that his grandson, Asoka, should have been driven to seek support from the sect founded by Buddha. Buddha, by giving up his royal station, had broken the law of caste as much as *K*andragupta by usurping it. His school, though it had probably escaped open persecution until it rose to political importance, could never have been on friendly terms with the Brahmans of the old school. The *parvenu* on the throne saw his natural allies in the followers of Buddha, and the mendicants, who by their unostentatious behaviour had won golden opinions among the lower and middle classes, were suddenly raised to an importance little dreamt of by their founder. Those who see in Buddhism, not a social but chiefly a religious and philosophical reform, have been deceived by the later Buddhist literature, and particularly by the controversies between Buddhists and Brahmans, which in later times led to the total expulsion of the former from India, and to the political re-establishment of Brahmanism. These, no doubt, turn chiefly on philosophical problems, and are of the most abstruse and intricate character. But such was not the teaching of Buddha. If we may judge from 'the four verities,' which Buddha inculcated from the first day that he entered on his career as a teacher, his philosophy of life was very simple. He proclaims that there was nothing but sorrow in life ; that sorrow is produced by our affections, that our affections must be destroyed in order to destroy the root of sorrow, and that he could teach mankind how to eradicate all the affections, all passions, all desires. Such doctrines were intelligible; and considering that Buddha received people of all castes, who after renouncing the world and assuming their yellow robes, were sure of finding a livelihood from the charitable gifts of the people, it is not surprising that the number of his followers should have grown so rapidly. If Buddha really taught the metaphysical doctrines which are ascribed to him by subsequent writers—and this is a point which it is impossible to settle—not one in a thousand among his followers would have been capable of appreciating those speculations. They must have been reserved for a few of his disciples, and they would never have formed the nucleus for a popular religion.

Nearly all who have written on Buddhism, and M. Barthélemy Saint-Hilaire among the rest, have endeavoured to show that these metaphysical doctrines of Buddha were borrowed from the earlier systems of Brahmanic philosophy, and more particu-

larly from the Sânkhya system. The reputed founder
of that system is Kapila, and we saw before how
Professor Wilson actually changed the name of Kapilavastu, the birthplace of Buddha, into a mere alle-
gory:—Kapilavastu meaning, according to him, the
substance of Kapila or of the Sânkhya philosophy.
This is not all. Mr. Spence Hardy (p. 132) quotes
a legend in which it is said that Buddha was in a
former existence the ascetic Kapila, that the Sâkya
princes came to his hermitage, and that he pointed
out to them the proper place for founding a new
city, which city was named after him Kapilavastu.
But we have looked in vain for any definite similarities between the system of Kapila, as known to us
in the Sânkhya-sûtras, and the Abhidharma, or the
metaphysics of the Buddhists. Such similarities
would be invaluable. They would probably enable
us to decide whether Buddha borrowed from Kapila
or Kapila from Buddha, and thus determine the real
chronology of the philosophical literature of India, as
either prior or subsequent to the Buddhist era. There
are certain notions which Buddha shares in common
not only with Kapila, but with every Hindu philosopher. The idea of transmigration, the belief in the
continuing effects of our good and bad actions, extending from our former to our present and from our
present to our future lives, the sense that life is a
dream or a burden, the admission of the uselessness
of religious observances after the attainment of the
highest knowledge, all these belong, so to say, to
the national philosophy of India. We meet with these
ideas everywhere, in the poetry, the philosophy, the
religion of the Hindus. They cannot be claimed as
the exclusive property of any system in particular.

But if we look for more special coincidences between
Buddha's doctrines and those of Kapila or other
Indian philosophers, we look in vain. At first it
might seem as if the very first aphorism of Kapila,
namely, ' the complete cessation of pain, which is of
three kinds, is the highest aim of man,' was merely a
philosophical paraphrase of the events which, as we
saw, determined Buddha to renounce the world in
search of the true road to salvation. But though
the starting-point of Kapila and Buddha is the same,
a keen sense of human misery and a yearning after a
better state, their roads diverge so completely and
their goals are so far apart, that it is difficult to
understand how, almost by common consent, Buddha
is supposed either to have followed in the footsteps
of Kapila, or to have changed Kapila's philosophy
into a religion. Some scholars imagine that there
was a more simple and primitive philosophy which
was taught by Kapila, and that the Sûtras which are
now ascribed to him are of later date. It is impossible either to prove or to disprove such a view. At
present we know Kapila's philosophy from his Sûtras
only[13], and these Sûtras seem to us posterior, not
anterior, to Buddha. Though the name of Buddha
is not mentioned in the Sûtras, his doctrines are
clearly alluded to and controverted in several parts
of them.

It has been said that Buddha and Kapila were

---

[13] Of Kapila's Sûtras, together with the commentary of Vigñâna
Bhikshu, a new edition was published in 1856, by Dr. Fitz-Edward
Hall, in the ' Bibliotheca Indica.' An excellent translation of the
Aphorisms, with illustrative extracts from the commentaries, was
printed for the use of the Benares College, by Dr. Ballantyne.

both atheists, and that Buddha borrowed his atheism
from Kapila. But atheism is an indefinite term, and
may mean very different things. In one sense every
Indian philosopher was an atheist, for they all perceived that the gods of the populace could not claim
the attributes that belong to a Supreme Being. But
all the important philosophical systems of the Brahmans admit, in some form or other, the existence of
an Absolute and Supreme Being, the source of all
that exists, or seems to exist. Kapila, when accused
of atheism, is not accused of denying the existence of
an Absolute Being. He is accused of denying the
existence of Îsvara, which in general means the Lord,
but which, in the passage where it occurs, refers to
the Îsvara of the Yogins, or mystic philosophers.
They maintained that in an ecstatic state man possesses the power of seeing God face to face, and they
wished to have this ecstatic intuition included under
the head of sensuous perceptions. To this Kapila
demurred. You have not proved the existence of
your Lord, he says, and therefore I see no reason
why I should alter my definition of sensuous perception in order to accommodate your ecstatic visions.
The commentator narrates that this strong language
was used by Kapila in order to silence the wild
talk of the Mystics, and that, though he taunted his
adversaries with having failed to prove the existence
of their Lord, he himself did not deny the existence
of a Supreme Being. Kapila, however, went further.
He endeavoured to show that all the attributes
which the Mystics ascribed to their Lord are inap-
propriate. He used arguments very similar to those
which have lately been used with such ability by a
distinguished Bampton Lecturer. The supreme lord

of the Mystics, Kapila argued, is either absolute
and unconditioned (mukta), or he is bound and
conditioned (baddha). If he is absolute and unconditioned, he cannot enter into the condition of
a Creator; he would have no desires which could
instigate him to create. If, on the contrary, he is
represented as active, and entering on the work of
creation, he would no longer be the absolute and
unchangeable Being which we are asked to believe
in. Kapila, like the preacher of our own days, was
accused of paving the road to atheism, but his
philosophy was nevertheless admitted as orthodox,
because, in addition to sensuous perception and inductive reasoning, Kapila professed emphatically his
belief in revelation, i. e. in the Veda, and allowed to
it a place among the recognised instruments of knowledge. Buddha refused to allow to the Vedas any
independent authority whatever, and this consti-
tuted the fundamental difference between the two
philosophers.

Whether Kapila's philosophy was really in accordance with the spirit of the Veda, is quite a different
question. No philosophy, at least nothing like a
definite system, is to be found in the sacred hymns
of the Brahmans; and though the Vedânta philosophy does less violence to the passages which it
quotes from the Veda, the authors of the Veda would
have been as much surprised at the consequences
deduced from their words by the Vedântin, as by
the strange meaning attributed to them by Kapila.
The Vedânta philosopher, like Kapila, would deny
the existence of a Creator in the usual sense of the
word. He explained the universe as an emanation
from Brahman, which is all in all. Kapila admitted

two principles, an absolute Spirit and Nature, and
he looked upon the universe as produced by a reflection of Nature thrown on the mirror of the absolute
Spirit. Both systems seem to regard creation, or
the created world, as a misfortune, as an unfortunate
accident. But they maintain that its effects can be
neutralised, and that emancipation from the bonds
of earthly existence is possible by means of philosophy. The Vedânta philosopher imagines he is
free when he has arrived at the knowledge that
nothing exists but Brahman; that all phenomena
are merely the result of ignorance; that after the
destruction of that ignorance, and of its effects, all is
merged again in Brahman, the true source of being,
thought, and happiness. Kapila taught that the spirit
became free from all mundane fetters as soon as it
perceived that all phenomena were only passing reflections produced by nature upon the spirit, and as soon
as it was able to shut its eyes to those illusory visions.
Both systems therefore, and the same applies to all
the other philosophical systems of the Brahmans, admitted an absolute or self-existing Being as the cause
of all that exists or seems to exist. And here lies
the specific difference between Kapila and Buddha.
Buddha, like Kapila, maintained that this world had
no absolute reality, that it was a snare and an illusion. The words, ' All is perishable, all is miserable,
all is void,' must frequently have passed his lips.
But we cannot call things unreal unless we have a
conception of something that is real. Where, then,
did Buddha find a reality in comparison with which
this world might be called unreal? What remedy did
he propose as an emancipation from the sufferings of
this life? Difficult as it seems to us to conceive it,

Buddha admits of no real cause of this unreal world.
He denies the existence not only of a Creator, but of
any Absolute Being. According to the metaphysical
tenets, if not of Buddha himself, at least of his sect,
there is no reality anywhere, neither in the past nor
in the future. True wisdom consists in perceiving the
nothingness of all things, and in a desire to become
nothing, to be blown out, to enter into Nirvâna.
Emancipation is obtained by total extinction, not by
absorption in Brahman, or by a recovery of the soul's
true estate. If to be is misery, not to be must be
felicity, and this felicity is the highest reward which
Buddha promised to his disciples. In reading the
Aphorisms of Kapila, it is difficult not to see in his
remarks on those who maintain that all is void,
covert attacks on Buddha and his followers. In one
place (I. 43) Kapila argues that if people believed in
the reality of thought only, and denied the reality of
external objects, they would soon be driven to admit
that nothing at all exists, because we perceive our
thoughts in the same manner as we perceive external
objects. This naturally leads him to an examination
of that extreme doctrine, according to which all that
we perceive is void, and all is supposed to perish,
because it is the nature of things that they should
perish. Kapila remarks in reference to this view
(I. 45), that it is a mere assertion of persons who are
'not enlightened,' in Sanskrit a-buddha, a sarcastic
expression in which it is very difficult not to see an
allusion to Buddha, or to those who claimed for him
the title of the Enlightened. Kapila then proceeds
to give the best answer that could be given to those
who taught that complete annihilation must be the
highest aim of man, as the only means of a complete

cessation of suffering. 'It is not so,' he says, 'for if
people wish to be free from suffering, it is they themselves who wish to be free, just as in this life it is
they themselves who wish to enjoy happiness. There
must be a permanent soul in order to satisfy the
yearnings of the human heart, and if you deny that
soul, you have no right to speak of the highest
aim of man.'

Whether the belief in this kind of Nirvâna, i.e. in
a total extinction of being, personality, and consciousness, was at any time shared by the large masses
of the people, is difficult either to assert or deny.
We know nothing in ancient times of the religious
convictions of the millions. We only know what a
few leading spirits believed, or professed to believe.
That certain individuals should have spoken and
written of total extinction as the highest aim of man,
is intelligible. Job cursed the day on which he was
born, and Solomon praised the 'dead which are
already dead, more than the living which are yet
alive.' 'Yea, better is he than both they,' he said,
'which hath not yet been, who hath not seen the
evil work that is done under the sun.' Voltaire said
in his own flippant way, 'On aime la vie, mais le
néant ne laisse pas d'avoir du bon;' and a modern
German philosopher, who has found much favour
with those who profess to despise Kant, Schelling,
and Hegel, writes, 'Considered in its objective value,
it is more than doubtful that life is preferable to the
Nothing. I should say even, that if experience and
reflection could lift up their voices they would recommend to us the Nothing. We are what ought
not to be, and we shall therefore cease to be.' Under
peculiar circumstances, in the agonies of despair, or

under the gathering clouds of madness, such language is intelligible; but to believe, as we are asked to believe, that one half of mankind had yearned for total annihilation, would be tantamount to a belief that there is a difference in kind between man and man. Buddhist philosophers, no doubt, held this doctrine, and it cannot be denied that it found a place in the Buddhist canon. But even among the different schools of Buddhist philosophers, very different views are adopted as to the true meaning of Nirvâna, and with the modern Buddhists of Burmah, Nigban, as they call it, is defined simply as freedom from old age, disease, and death. We do not find fault with M. Barthélemy Saint-Hilaire for having so emphatically pressed the charge of nihilism against Buddha himself. In one portion of the Buddhist canon the most extreme views of nihilism are put into his mouth. All we can say is that that canon is later than Buddha, and that in the same canon[14] the founder of Buddhism, after having entered into Nirvâna, is still spoken of as living, nay, as showing himself to those who believe in him. Buddha, who denied the existence, or at least the divine nature, of the gods worshipped by the Brahmans, was raised himself to the rank of a deity by some of his followers[15] (the Aisvarikas), and we need not wonder therefore if his Nirvâna too was gradually changed

---

[14] 'L'enfant égaré,' par Ph. Ed. Foucaux, p. 19.

[15] How early this took place, we see from Clemens of Alexandria, 'Strom.' I. p. 305, A.B. (ed. Colon. 1688); 'Megasthenis Indica,' ed. Schwanbeck, p. 139, εἰσὶ δὲ τῶν Ἰνδῶν οἱ τοῖς Βοῦττα (sive Βοῦττα) πειθόμενοι παραγγέλμασιν, ὃν δι' ὑπερβολὴν σεμνότητος ὡς θεὸν τετιμήκασι.

into an Elysian field. And finally, if we may argue from human nature, such as we find it at all times and in all countries, we confess that we cannot bring ourselves to believe that the reformer of India, the teacher of so perfect a code of morality, the young prince who gave up all he had in order to help those whom he saw afflicted in mind, body, or estate, should have cared much about speculations which he knew would either be misunderstood, or not understood at all, by those whom he wished to benefit; that he should have thrown away one of the most powerful weapons in the hands of every religious teacher, the belief in a future life, and should not have seen, that if this life was sooner or later to end in nothing, it was hardly worth the trouble which he took himself, or the sacrifices which he imposed on his disciples.

April, 1862.

X.

BUDDHIST PILGRIMS[1].

M. STANISLAS JULIEN has commenced the publication of a work entitled, 'Voyages des Pèlerins Bouddhistes.' The first volume, published in the year 1853, contains the biography of Hiouen-thsang, who, in the middle of the seventh century A.D., travelled from China through Central Asia to India. The second, which has just reached us, gives us the first portion of Hiouen-thsang's own diary.

There are not many books of travel which can be compared to these volumes. Hiouen-thsang passed through countries which few had visited before him. He describes parts of the world which no one has explored since, and where even our modern maps contain hardly more than the ingenious conjectures of Alexander von Humboldt. His observations are minute; his geographical, statistical, and historical remarks most accurate and trustworthy. The chief object of

---

[1] 'Voyages des Pèlerins Bouddhistes.' Vol. I. Histoire de la Vie de Hiouen-thsang, et de ses Voyages dans l'Inde, depuis l'an 629 jusqu'en 645, par Hoeili et Yen-thsong; traduite du Chinois par Stanislas Julien.

Vol. II. Mémoires sur les Contrées Occidentales, traduits du Sanscrit en Chinois, en l'an 648, par Hiouen-thsang, et du Chinois en Français, par Stanislas Julien. Paris, 1853–1857 : B. Duprat. London and Edinburgh : Williams and Norgate.

his travels was to study the religion of Buddha, the great reformer of India. Some Chinese pilgrims visited India before, several after, his time. Hiouen-thsang, however, is considered by the Chinese themselves as the most distinguished of these pilgrims, and M. Stanislas Julien has rightly assigned to him the first place in his collection.

In order to understand what Hiouen-thsang was, and to appreciate his life and his labours, we must first cast a glance at the history of a religion which, however unattractive and even mischievous it may appear to ourselves, inspired her votary with the true spirit of devotion and self-sacrifice. That religion has now existed for 2,400 years. To millions and millions of human beings it has been the only preparation for a higher life placed within their reach. And even at the present day it counts in Asia a more numerous array of believers than any other faith, not excluding Mohammedanism or Christianity. The religion of Buddha took its origin in India about the middle of the sixth century B.C., but it did not assume its political importance till about the time of Alexander's invasion. We know little, therefore, of its first origin and spreading, because the canonical works on which we must chiefly rely for information belong to a much later period, and are strongly tinged with a legendary character. The very existence of such a being as Buddha, the son of Suddhodana, king of Kapilavastu, has been doubted. But what can never be doubted is this, that Buddhism, such as we find it in Russia[2] and Sweden[3] on the very threshold

---

[2] See W. Spottiswoode's 'Tarantasse Journey,' p. 220, Visit to the Buddhist Temple.

[3] The only trace of the influence of Buddhism among the *Kudic*

of European civilisation, in the north of Asia, in
Mongolia, Tatary, China, Tibet, Nepal, Siam, Burmah,
and Ceylon, had its origin in India. Doctrines
similar to those of Buddha existed in that country
long before his time. We can trace them like
meandering roots below the surface long before we
reach the point where the roots strike up into a stem,
and the stem branches off again into fruit-bearing
branches. What was original and new in Buddha
was his changing a philosophical system into a practical
doctrine; his taking the wisdom of the few, and
coining as much of it as he thought genuine for the
benefit of the many; his breaking with the traditional
formalities of the past, and proclaiming for the first
time, in spite of castes and creeds, the equality of the
rich and the poor, the foolish and the wise, the
'twice-born' and the outcast. Buddhism, as a religion and as a political fact, was a reaction against
Brahmanism, though it retained much of that more
primitive form of faith and worship. Buddhism, in
its historical growth, presupposes Brahmanism, and,
however hostile the mutual relation of these two

---

races, the Fins, Laps, &c., is found in the name of their priests and
sorcerers, the Shamans. Shaman is supposed to be a corruption
of *Sramana*, a name applied to Buddha, and to Buddhist priests
in general. The ancient mythological religion of the *K*udic races
has nothing in common with Buddhism. See Castren's ' Lectures on
Finnish Mythology,' 1853. Finland was ceded by Sweden to Russia
in 1809. See the Author's ' Survey of Languages,' second edition,
p. 116. Shamanism found its way from India to Siberia viâ Tibet,
China, and Mongolia. Rules on the formation of magic figures, on
the treatment of diseases by charms, on the worship of evil spirits, on
the acquisition of supernatural powers, on charms, incantations, and
other branches of Shaman witchcraft, are found in the Stan-gyour, or
the second part of the Tibetan canon, and in some of the late Tantras
of the Nepalese collection.

religions may have been at different periods of Indian
history, it can be shown, without much difficulty,
that the latter was but a natural consequence of the
former.

The ancient religion of the Aryan inhabitants of
India had started, like the religion of the Greeks, the
Romans, the Germans, Slaves, and Celts, with a simple
and intelligible mythological phraseology. In the
Veda—for there is but one real Veda—the names of
all the so-called gods or Devas betray their original
physical character and meaning without disguise.
The fire was praised and invoked by the name of
Agni (ignis); the earth by the name of Prithvi (the
broad); the sky by the name of Dyu (Jupiter), and
afterwards of Indra; the firmament and the waters
by the name of Varuna or Οὐρανός. The sun was
invoked by many names such as Sûrya, Savitri, Vishnu
or Mitra; and the dawn rejoiced in such titles as
Ushas, Urvasî, Ahanâ, and Sûryâ. Nor was the
moon forgotten. For though it is mentioned but
rarely under its usual name of Kandra, it is alluded
to under the more sacred appellation of Soma; and
each of its four phases had received its own denomi-
nation. There is hardly any part of nature, if it
could impress the human mind in any way with the
ideas of a higher power, of order, eternity, or bene-
ficence—whether the winds, or the rivers, or the
trees, or the mountains—without a name and representative in the early Hindu Pantheon. No doubt
there existed in the human mind, from the very
beginning, something, whether we call it a suspicion,
an innate idea, an intuition, or a sense of the Divine.
What distinguishes man from the rest of the animal
creation is chiefly that ineradicable feeling of depen-

dence and reliance upon some higher power, a consciousness of bondage from which the very name of
' religion ' was derived. ' It is He that hath made us,
and not we ourselves.' The presence of that power
was felt everywhere, and nowhere more clearly and
strongly than in the rising and setting of the sun, in
the change of day and night, of spring and winter, of
birth and death. But, although the Divine presence
was felt everywhere, it was impossible in that early
period of thought, and with a language incapable
as yet of expressing anything but material objects,
to conceive the idea of God in its purity and fulness,
or to assign to it an adequate and worthy expression.
Children cannot think the thoughts of men, and the
poets of the Veda could not speak the language
of Aristotle. It was by a slow process that the
human mind elaborated the idea of one absolute
and supreme Godhead; and by a still slower process
that the human language matured a word to express
that idea. A period of growth was inevitable, and
those who, from a mere guess of their own, do
not hesitate to speak authoritatively of a primeval
revelation which imparted to the Pagan world the
idea of the Godhead in all its purity, forget that,
however pure and sublime and spiritual that revelation might have been, there was no language
capable as yet of expressing the high and immaterial
conceptions of that Heaven-sent message. The real
history of religion, during the earliest mythological
period, represents to us a slow process of fermenta-
tion in thought and language, with its various interruptions, its overflowings, its coolings, its deposits,
and its gradual clearing from all extraneous and
foreign admixture. This is not only the case among

the Indo-European or Aryan races in India, in Greece, and in Germany. In Peru, and wherever the primitive formations of the intellectual world crop out, the process is exactly the same. 'The religion of the sun,' as it has been boldly said by the author of the 'Spanish Conquest in America,' 'was inevitable.' It was like a deep furrow which that heavenly luminary drew, in its silent procession from east to west, over the virgin mind of the gazing multitude; and in the impression left there by the first rising and setting of the sun there lay the dark seed of a faith in a more than human being, the first intimation of a life without beginning, of a world without end. Manifold seed fell afterwards into the soil once broken. Something divine was discovered in everything that moved and lived. Names were stammered forth in anxious haste, and no single name could fully express what lay hidden in the human mind and wanted expression, —the idea of an absolute, and perfect, and supreme, and immortal Essence. Thus a countless host of nominal gods was called into being, and for a time seemed to satisfy the wants of a thoughtless multitude. But there were thoughtful men at all times, and their reason protested against the contradictions of a mythological phraseology, though it had been hallowed by sacred customs and traditions. That rebellious reason had been at work from the very first, always ready to break the yoke of names and formulas which no longer expressed what they were intended to express. The idea which had yearned for utterance was the idea of a supreme and absolute Power, and that yearning was not satisfied by such names as Kronos, Zeus, and Apollon. The very sound

of such a word as 'God,' used in the plural, jarred on
the ear, as if we were to speak of two universes, or
of a single twin. There are many words, as Greek
and Latin grammarians tell us, which, if used in the
plural, have a different meaning from what they have
in the singular. The Latin æde s means a temple;
if used in the plural it means a house. De u s and
Θεός ought to be added to the same class of words.
The idea of supreme perfection excluded limitation,
and the idea of God excluded the possibility of
many gods. This may seem language too abstract
and metaphysical for the early times of which we
are speaking. But the ancient poets of the Vedic
hymns have expressed the same thought with perfect
clearness and simplicity. In the Rig-veda I. 164, 46,
we read:

'That which is one the sages speak of in many
ways—they call it Agni, Yama, Mâtarisvan.'

Besides the plurality of gods, which was sure to
lead to their destruction, there was a taint of mortality
which they could not throw off. They all derived
their being from the life of nature. The god who
represented the sun was liable, in the mythological
language of antiquity, to all the accidents which
threatened the solar luminary. Though he might rise
in immortal youth in the morning, he was conquered
by the shadows of the night, and the powers of winter
seemed to overthrow his heavenly throne. There is
nothing in nature free from change, and the gods of
nature fell under the thraldom of nature's laws. The
sun must set, and the solar gods and heroes must die.
There must be one God, there must be one unchang-
ing Deity; this was the silent conviction of the
human mind. There are many gods, liable to all the

vicissitudes of life; this was everywhere the answer of mythological religion.

It is curious to observe in how various ways these two opposite principles were kept for a time from open conflict, and how long the heathen temples resisted the enemy which was slowly and imperceptibly undermining their very foundations. In Greece this mortal element, inherent in all gods, was eliminated to a great extent by the conception of heroes. Whatever was too human in the ancient legends told of Zeus and Apollon was transferred to so-called half-gods or heroes, who were represented as the sons or favourites of the gods, and who bore their fate under a slightly altered name. The twofold character of Herakles as a god and as a hero is acknowledged even by Herodotus, and some of his epithets would have been sufficient to indicate his solar and originally divine character. But, in order to make some of the legends told of the solar deity possible or conceivable, it was necessary to represent Herakles as a more human being, and to make him rise to the seat of the Immortals only after he had endured toils and sufferings incompatible with the dignity of an Olympian god. We find the same idea in Peru, only that there it led to different results. A thinking, or, as he was called, a freethinking, Inca[4] remarked that this perpetual travelling of the sun was a sign of servitude[5], and he threw doubts upon the divine nature of such an unquiet thing as that great luminary appeared to him

[4] Helps, 'The Spanish Conquest,' vol. iii. p. 503 : 'Que cosa tam inquieta non le parescia ser Dios.'

[5] On the servitude of the gods, see the Essay on Comparative Mythology, 'Oxford Essays,' 1856, p. 69.

to be. And this misgiving led to a tradition which, even should it be unfounded in history, had some truth in itself, that there was in Peru an earlier worship, that of an invisible Deity, the Creator of the world, Pachacamac. In Greece, also, there are signs of a similar craving after the 'Unknown God.' A supreme God was wanted, and Zeus, the stripling of Creta, was raised to that rank. He became God above all gods—ἀπάντων κύριος, as Pindar calls him. Yet more was wanted than a mere Zeus; and thus a supreme Fate or Spell was imagined before which all the gods, and even Zeus, had to bow. And even this Fate was not allowed to remain supreme, and there was something in the destinies of man which was called ὑπέρμορον or 'beyond Fate.' The most awful solution, however, of the problem belongs to Teutonic mythology. Here, also, some heroes were introduced; but their death was only the beginning of the final catastrophe. 'All gods must die.' Such is the last word of that religion which had grown up in the forests of Germany, and found a last refuge among the glaciers and volcanoes of Iceland. The death of Sigurd, the descendant of Odin, could not avert the death of Balder, the son of Odin; and the death of Balder was soon to be followed by the death of Odin himself, and of all the immortal gods.

All this was inevitable, and Prometheus, the man of forethought, could safely predict the fall of Zeus. The struggles by which reason and faith overthrow tradition and superstition vary in different countries and at different times; but the final victory is always on their side. In India the same antagonism manifested itself, but what there seemed a victory of reason threatened to become the destruction of all religious faith. At first there was hardly a struggle. On the primitive mythological stratum of thought two new formations arose—the Brahmanical philosophy and the Brahmanical ceremonial; the one opening the widest avenues of philosophical thought, the other fencing all religious feeling within the narrowest barriers. Both derived their authority from the same source. Both professed to carry out the meaning and purpose of the Veda. Thus we see on the one side, the growth of a numerous and powerful priesthood, and the establishment of a ceremonial which embraced every moment of a man's life from his birth to his death. There was no event which might have moved the heart to a spontaneous outpouring of praise or thanksgiving, which was not regulated by priestly formulas. Every prayer was prescribed, every sacrifice determined. Every god had his share, and the claims of each deity on the adoration of the faithful were set down with such punctiliousness, the danger of offending their pride was represented in such vivid colours, that no one would venture to approach their presence without the assistance of a well-paid staff of masters of divine ceremonies. It was impossible to avoid sin without the help of the Brahmans. They alone knew the food that might properly be eaten, the air which might properly be breathed, the dress which might properly be worn. They alone could tell what god should be invoked, what sacrifice be offered, and the slightest mistake of pronunciation, the slightest neglect about clarified butter, or the length of the ladle in which it was to be offered, might bring destruction upon the head of the unassisted worshipper. No nation was ever so completely priestridden as the Hindus under the sway of the ·

Brahmanic law. Yet, on the other side, the same people were allowed to indulge in the most unrestrained freedom of thought, and in the schools of their philosophy the very names of their gods were never mentioned. Their existence was neither denied nor asserted; they were of no greater importance in the system of the world of thought than trees or mountains, men or animals; and to offer sacrifices to them with a hope of rewards, so far from being meritorious, was considered as dangerous to that emancipation to which a clear perception of philosophical truth was to lead the patient student. There was one system which taught that there existed but one Being, without a second; that everything else which seemed to exist was but a dream and illusion, and that this illusion might be removed by a true knowledge of the one Being. There was another system which admitted two principles—one a subjective and self-existent mind, the other matter, endowed with qualities. Here the world, with its joys and sorrows, was explained as the result of the subjective Self, reflecting itself in the mirror of matter; and final emancipation was obtained by turning away the eyes from the play of nature, and being absorbed in the knowledge of the true and absolute Self. A third system started with the admission of atoms, and explained every effect, including the elements and the mind, animals, men, and gods, from the concurrence of these atoms. In fact, as M. Cousin remarked many years ago, the history of the philosophy of India is 'un abrégé de l'histoire de la philosophie.' The germs of all these systems are traced back to the Vedas, Brâhmanas, and the Upanishads, and the man who believed in any of them was considered as orthodox as the devout worshipper of the gods—the one was saved by knowledge and faith, the other by works and faith.

Such was the state of the Hindu mind when Buddhism arose; or, rather, such was the state of the Hindu mind which gave rise to Buddhism. Buddha himself went through the school of the Brahmans. He performed their penances, he studied their philosophy, and he at last claimed the name of the Buddha, or the Enlightened, when he threw away the whole ceremonial, with its sacrifices, superstitions, penances, and castes, as worthless, and changed the complicated systems of philosophy into a short doctrine of salvation. This doctrine of salvation has been called pure Atheism and Nihilism, and it no doubt was liable to both charges in its metaphysical character, and in that form in which we chiefly know it. It was Atheistic, not because it denied the existence of such gods as Indra and Brahma. Buddha did not even condescend to deny their existence. But it was called Atheistic, like the Sânkhya philosophy, which admitted but one subjective Self, and considered creation as an illusion of that Self, imaging itself for a while in the mirror of nature. As there was no reality in creation, there could be no real Creator. All that seemed to exist was the result of ignorance. To remove that ignorance was to remove the cause of all that seemed to exist. How a religion which taught the annihilation of all existence, of all thought, of all individuality and personality, as the highest object of all endeavours, could have laid hold of the minds of millions of human beings, and how at the same time, by enforcing the duties of morality, justice, kindness, and self-sacrifice, it could have exercised a decided beneficial influence, not only on the natives of India, but on the lowest barbarians of Central Asia, is a riddle which no one has been able to solve. We must distinguish, it seems, between Buddhism as a religion, and Buddhism as a philosophy. The former addressed itself to millions, the latter to a few isolated thinkers. It is from these isolated thinkers, however, and from their literary compositions, that we are apt to form our notions of what Buddhism was, while, as a matter of fact, not one in a thousand would have been capable of following these metaphysical speculations. To the people at large Buddhism was a moral and religious, not a philosophical reform. Yet even its morality has a metaphysical tinge. The morality which it teaches is not a morality of expediency and rewards. Virtue is not enjoined because it necessarily leads to happiness. No; virtue is to be practised, but happiness is to be shunned, and the only reward for virtue is that it subdues the passions, and thus prepares the human mind for that knowledge which is to end in complete annihilation. There are ten commandments which Buddha imposes on his disciples[6]. They are—

1. Not to kill.
2. Not to steal.
3. Not to commit adultery.
4. Not to lie.
5. Not to get intoxicated.
6. To abstain from unseasonable meals.
7. To abstain from public spectacles.

---

[6] See Burnouf, 'Lotus de la bonne Loi,' p. 444. Barthélemy Saint-Hilaire, 'Du Bouddhisme,' p. 132. Ch. F. Neumann, ' Catechism of the Shamans.'

8. To abstain from expensive dresses.

9. Not to have a large bed.

10. Not to receive silver or gold.

The duties of those who embraced a religious life were more severe. They were not allowed to wear any dress except rags collected in cemeteries, and these rags they had to sew together with their own hands. A yellow cloak was to be thrown over these rags. Their food was to be extremely simple, and they were not to possess anything, except what they could get by collecting alms from door to door in their wooden bowls. They had but one meal in the morning, and were not allowed to touch any food after midday. They were to live in forests, not in cities, and their only shelter was to be the shadow of a tree. There they were to sit, to spread their carpet, but not to lie down, even during sleep. They were allowed to enter the nearest city or village in order to beg, but they had to return to their forest before night, and the only change which was allowed, or rather prescribed, was when they had to spend some nights in the cemeteries, there to meditate on the vanity of all things. And what was the object of all this asceticism? Simply to guide each individual towards that path which would finally bring him to Nirvâna, to utter extinction or annihilation. The very definition of virtue was that it helped man to cross over to the other shore, and that other shore was not death, but cessation of all being. Thus charity was considered a virtue; modesty, patience, courage, contemplation, and science, all were virtues, but they were practised only as a means of arriving at deliverance. Buddha himself exhibited the perfection of all these virtues. His charity knew no bounds. When he saw a tigress

starved, and unable to feed her cubs, he is said to
have made a charitable oblation of his body to be
devoured by them.   Hiouen-thsang visited the place
on the banks of the Indus where this miracle was
supposed to have happened, and he remarks that the
soil is still red there from the blood of Buddha, and
that the trees and flowers have the same colour[7].   As
to the modesty of Buddha, nothing could exceed it.
One day, king Prasenagit, the protector of Buddha,
called on him to perform miracles, in order to silence
his adversaries, the Brahmans.   Buddha consented.
He performed the required miracles; but he exclaimed, 'Great king, I do not teach the law to my
pupils, telling them, Go, ye saints, and before the
eyes of the Brahmans and householders perform, by
means of your supernatural powers, miracles greater
than any man can perform.   I tell them, when I
teach them the law, Live, ye saints, hiding your good
works and showing your sins.'   And yet, all this
self-sacrificing charity, all this self-sacrificing humi-
lity, by which the life of Buddha was distinguished
throughout, and which he preached to the multitudes
that came to listen to him, had, we are told, but one
object, and that object was final annihilation.   It is
impossible almost to believe it, and yet when we turn
away our eyes from the pleasing picture of that high
morality which Buddha preached for the first time to
all classes of men, and look into the dark pages of
his code of religious metaphysics, we can hardly find
another explanation.   Fortunately, the millions who
embraced the doctrines of Buddha, and were saved
by it from the depths of barbarism, brutality, and

---

[7] Vol. i. p. 89, vol. ii. p. 167.

selfishness, were unable to fathom the meaning of his
metaphysical doctrines. With them the Nirvâna to
which they aspired, became only a relative deliverance from the miseries of human life; nay, it took
the bright colours of a paradise, to be regained by
the pious worshipper of Buddha. But was this the
meaning of Buddha himself? In his 'Four Verities'
he does not, indeed, define Nirvâna, except by cessation of all pain; but when he traces the cause of
pain, and teaches the means of destroying not only
pain itself, but the cause of pain, we shall see that
his Nirvâna assumes a very different meaning. His
'Four Verities' are very simple. The first asserts the
existence of pain; the second asserts that the cause
of pain lies in sin; the third asserts that pain may
cease by Nirvâna; the fourth shows the way that
leads to Nirvâna. This way to Nirvâna consists in
eight things—right faith (orthodoxy), right judgment
(logic), right language (veracity), right purpose
(honesty), right practice (religious life), right obedience (lawful life), right memory, and right meditation. All these precepts might be understood as part
of a simply moral code, closing with a kind of mystic
meditation on the highest object of thought, and with
a yearning after deliverance from all worldly ties.
Similar systems have prevailed in many parts of the
world, without denying the existence of an absolute
Being, or of a something towards which the human
mind tends, in which it is absorbed or even annihilated. Awful as such a mysticism may appear, yet it
leaves still something that exists, it acknowledges a
feeling of dependence in man. It knows of a first
cause, though it may have nothing to predicate of it
except that it is τὸ κινοῦν ἀκίνητόν. A return is possible

from that desert. The first cause may be called to
life again. It may take the names of Creator, Pre-
server, Ruler; and when the simplicity and helplessness of the child have re-entered the heart of man,
the name of father will come back to the lips which
had uttered in vain all the names of a philosophical
despair. But from the Nirvâ*n*a of the Buddhist
metaphysician there is no return. He starts from
the idea that the highest object is to escape pain.
Life in his eyes is nothing but misery; birth the cause
of all evil, from which even death cannot deliver him,
because he believes in an eternal cycle of existence,
or in transmigration. There is no deliverance from
evil, except by breaking through the prison walls, not
only of life, but of existence, and by extirpating the
last cause of existence. What, then, is the cause of
existence? The cause of existence, says the Buddhist metaphysician, is attachment — an inclination
towards something; and this attachment arises from
thirst or desire. Desire presupposes perception of
the object desired; perception presupposes contact;
contact, at least a sentient contact, presupposes the
senses; and, as the senses can only perceive what
has form and name, or what is distinct, distinction is
the real cause of all the effects which end in existence,
birth, and pain. Now, this distinction is itself the
result of conceptions or ideas; but these ideas, so far
from being, as in Greek philosophy, the true and ever-
lasting forms of the Absolute, are here represented
as mere illusions, the effects of ignorance (avidyâ).
Ignorance, therefore, is really the primary cause of all
that seems to exist. To know that ignorance, as the
root of all evil, is the same as to destroy it, and with
it all effects that flowed from it. In order to see how

this doctrine affects the individual, let us watch the
last moments of Buddha as described by his disciples.
He enters into the first stage of meditation when he
feels freedom from sin, acquires a knowledge of the
nature of all things, and has no desire except that of
Nirvâna. But he still feels pleasure; he even uses
his reasoning and discriminating powers. The use of
these powers ceases in the second stage of meditation,
when nothing remains but a desire after Nirvâna,
and a general feeling of satisfaction, arising from
his intellectual perfection. That satisfaction, also,
is extinguished in the third stage. Indifference suc-
ceeds; yet there is still self-consciousness, and a certain amount of physical pleasure. These last remnants
are destroyed in the fourth stage; memory fades
away, all pleasure and pain are gone, and the doors of
Nirvâna now open before him. After having passed
these four stages once, Buddha went through them a
second time, but he died before he attained again to
the fourth stage. We must soar still higher, and
though we may feel giddy and disgusted, we must sit
out this tragedy till the curtain falls. After the four
stages of meditation [8] are passed, the Buddha (and
every being is to become a Buddha) enters into the
infinity of space; then into the infinity of intelligence;
and thence he passes into the region of nothing. But
even here there is no rest. There is still something
left—the idea of the nothing in which he rejoices.
That also must be destroyed, and it is destroyed in

[8] These 'four stages' are described in the same manner in the
canonical books of Ceylon and Nepal, and may therefore safely be
ascribed to that original form of Buddhism, from which the Southern
and the Northern schools branched off at a later period. See
Burnouf, 'Lotus de la bonne Loi,' p. 800.

the fourth and last region, where there is not even
the idea of a nothing left, and where there is complete
rest, undisturbed by nothing, or what is not nothing[9].
There are few persons who will take the trouble of
reasoning out such hallucinations; least of all, persons who are accustomed to the sober language of
Greek philosophy; and it is the more interesting to
hear the opinion which one of the best Aristotelian
scholars of the present day, after a patient examination
of the authentic documents of Buddhism, has formed
of its system of metaphysics.   M. Barthélemy Saint-
Hilaire, in a review on Buddhism, published in the
' Journal des Savants,' says:

' Buddhism has no God; it has not even the con-
fused and vague notion of a Universal Spirit in which
the human soul, according to the orthodox doctrine of
Brahmanism, and the Sânkhya philosophy, may be
absorbed.   Nor does it admit nature, in the proper
sense of the word, and it ignores that profound
division between spirit and matter which forms the
system and the glory of Kapila.   It confounds man
with all that surrounds him, all the while preaching
to him the laws of virtue.   Buddhism, therefore, cannot unite the human soul, which it does not even
mention, with a God, whom it ignores; nor with
nature, which it does not know better.   Nothing
remained but to annihilate the soul; and in order to
be quite sure that the soul may not re-appear under
some new form in this world, which has been cursed
as the abode of illusion and misery, Buddhism
destroys its very elements, and never gets tired of
glorying in this achievement.   What more is wanted?

---

[9] See Burnouf, ' Lotus de la bonne Loi,' p. 814.

If this is not the absolute nothing, what is Nirvâna ?'

Such religion, we should say, was made for a mad-
house. But Buddhism was an advance, if compared
with Brahmanism; it has stood its ground for centuries, and if truth could be decided by majorities,
the show of hands, even at the present day, would be
in favour of Buddha. The metaphysics of Buddhism,
like the metaphysics of most religions, not excluding
our own Gnosticism and Mysticism, were beyond the
reach of all except a few hardened philosophers or
ecstatic dreamers. Human nature could not be
changed. Out of the very nothing it made a new
paradise; and he who had left no place in the whole
universe for a Divine Being, was deified himself by
the multitudes who wanted a person whom they
could worship, a king whose help they might invoke,
a friend before whom they could pour out their most
secret griefs. And there remained the code of a pure
morality, proclaimed by Buddha. There remained
the spirit of charity, kindness, and universal pity with
which he had inspired his disciples[10]. There remained
the simplicity of the ceremonial he had taught,
the equality of all men which he had declared, the

[10] See the 'Dhammapadam,' a Pâli work on Buddhist ethics, lately
edited by V. Fausböll, a distinguished pupil of Professor Westergaard,
at Copenhagen. The Rev. Spence Hardy ('Eastern Monachism,'
p. 169) writes: 'A collection might be made from the precepts of
this work, that in the purity of its ethics could scarcely be equalled
from any other heathen author.' Mr. Knighton, when speaking of
the same work in his 'History of Ceylon' (p. 77), remarks: 'In it
we have exemplified a code of morality, and a list of precepts,
which, for pureness, excellence, and wisdom, is only second to that
of the Divine Lawgiver himself.'

religious toleration which he had preached from the
beginning. There remained much, therefore, to account for the rapid strides which his doctrine made
from the mountain peaks of Ceylon to the Tundras
of the Samoyedes, and we shall see in the simple
story of the life of Hiouen-thsang that Buddhism,
with all its defects, has had its heroes, its martyrs,
and its saints.

Hiouen-thsang, born in China more than a thousand years after the death of Buddha, was a believer
in Buddhism. He dedicated his whole life to the
study of that religion ; travelling from his native
country to India, visiting every place mentioned in
Buddhist history or tradition, acquiring the ancient
language in which the canonical books of the Buddhists were written, studying commentaries, discussing
points of difficulty, and defending the orthodox faith
at public councils against disbelievers and schismatics.
Buddhism had grown and changed since the death
of its founder, but it had lost nothing of its vitality.
At a very early period a proselytizing spirit awoke
among the disciples of the Indian reformer, an element
entirely new in the history of ancient religions.   No
Jew, no Greek, no Roman, no Brahman ever thought
of converting people to his own national form of
worship. Religion was looked upon as private or
national property. It was to be guarded against
strangers. The most sacred names of the gods, the
prayers by which their favour could be gained, were
kept secret. No religion, however, was more exclusive than that of the Brahmans. A Brahman was
born, nay, twice-born. He could not be made. Not
even the lowest caste, that of the Súdras, would
open its ranks to a stranger. Here lay the secret of

Buddha's success. He addressed himself to castes
and outcasts. He promised salvation to all; and he
commanded his disciples to preach his doctrine in all
places and to all men. A sense of duty, extending
from the narrow limits of the house, the village, and
the country to the widest circle of mankind, a feeling
of sympathy and brotherhood towards all men, the
idea, in fact, of humanity, was in India first pronounced by Buddha. In the third Buddhist Council,
the acts of which have been preserved to us in the
' Mahavansa[11],' we hear of missionaries being sent to
the chief countries beyond India. This Council, we are
told, took place 30? B.C., 235 years after the death of
Buddha, in the 17th year of the reign of the famous
king 'Asoka, whose edicts have been preserved to us
on rock inscriptions in various parts of India. There
are sentences in these inscriptions of Asoka which
might be read with advantage by our own missionaries, though they are now more than 2000 years old.
Thus it is written on the rocks of Girnar, Dhauli, and
Kapurdigiri—

' Piyadasi, the king beloved of the gods, desires
that the ascetics of all creeds might reside in all
places. All these ascetics profess alike the command
which people should exercise over themselves, and
the purity of the soul. But people have different
opinions, and different inclinations.'

And again:

' A man ought to honour his own faith only; but
he should never abuse the faith of others. It is
thus that he will do no harm to anybody. There are
even circumstances where the religion of others ought

---

[11] 'Mahavanso,' ed. G. Turnour, Ceylon, 1837, p. 71.

to be honoured. And in acting thus, a man fortifies
his own faith, and assists the faith of others. He
who acts otherwise, diminishes his own faith, and
hurts the faith of others.'

Those who have no time to read the voluminous
works of the late E. Burnouf on Buddhism, his 'Introduction à l'Histoire du Buddhisme,' and his translation of ' Le Lotus de la bonne Loi,' will find a very
interesting and lucid account of these councils, and
edicts, and missions, and the History of Buddhism in
general, in a work lately published by Mrs. Speir,
' Life in Ancient India.' Buddhism spread in the
south to Ceylon, in the north to Kashmir, the Himalayan countries, Tibet, and China. One Buddhist missionary is mentioned in the Chinese annals as early as
217 b.c.[12]; and about the year 120 b.c. a Chinese
General, after defeating the barbarous tribes north of
the Desert of Gobi, brought back as a trophy a golden
statue, the statue of Buddha.[13] It was not, however,
till the year 65 a.d. that Buddhism was officially
recognised by the Emperor Ming-ti[14] as a third state
religion in China. Ever since, it has shared equal
honours with the doctrines of Confucius and Lao-tse,
in the Celestial Empire, and it is but lately that these
three established religions have had to fear the encroachments of a new rival in the creed of the Chief
of the rebels.

After Buddhism had been introduced into China,
the first care of its teachers was to translate the
sacred works from Sanskrit, in which they were

---

[12] See 'Foe Koue Ki,' p. 41, and xxxviii. preface.
[13] See 'Foe Koue Ki,' p. 41.
[14] 'Lalita-Vistara,' ed. Foucaux, p. xvii. n.

originally written, into Chinese. We read of the
Emperor Ming-ti[15], of the dynasty of Han, sending
Tsaï-in and other high officials to India, in order to
study there the doctrine of Buddha. They engaged
the services of two learned Buddhists, Matânga and
Tchou-fa-lan, and some of the most important Buddhist works were translated by them into Chinese.
' The Life of Buddha,' the ' Lalita-Vistara[16],' a Sanskrit
work which, on account of its style and language,
had been referred by Oriental scholars to a much
more modern period of Indian literature, can now
safely be ascribed to an ante-Christian era, if, as we
are told by Chinese scholars, it was translated from
Sanskrit into Chinese, as one of the canonical books
of Buddhism, as early as the year 76 A. D. The
same work was translated also into Tibetan ; and an
edition of it—the first Tibetan work printed in
Europe—published in Paris by M. E. Foucaux, re-
flects high credit on that distinguished scholar, and on
the Government which supports these studies in the
most liberal and enlightened spirit. The intellectual
intercourse between the Indian peninsula and the
northern continent of Asia remained uninterrupted
for many centuries. Missions were sent from China
to India, to report on the political and geographical
state of the country, but the chief object of interest
which attracted public embassies and private pilgrims
across the Himalayan mountains was the religion of
Buddha. About three hundred years after the public
recognition of Buddhism by the Emperor Ming-ti,

[15] ' Lalita-Vistara,' p. 17.
[16] Two parts of the Sanskrit text have been published in the
' Bibliotheca Indica.'

s 2

the great stream of Buddhist pilgrims began to flow
from China to India. The first account which we
possess of these pilgrimages refers to the travels of
Fahian, who visited India towards the end of the
fourth century. His travels have been translated by
Rémusat, but M. Julien promises a new and more
correct translation. After Fahian, we have the travels
of Hoei-seng and Song-yun, who were sent to India,
in 518, by command of the Empress, with a view of
collecting sacred books and relics. Of Hiouen-thsang,
who follows next in time, we possess, at present,
eight out of twelve books; and there is reason to
hope that the last four books of his Journal will soon
follow in M. Julien's translation.[17] After Hiouen-
thsang, the chief works of Chinese pilgrims are the
' Itineraries' of the fifty-six monks, published in 730,
and the travels of Khi-nie, who visited India in 964,
at the head of three hundred pilgrims. India was
for a time the Holy Land of China. There lay the
scene of the life and death of the great teacher;
there were the monuments commemorating the chief
events of his life; there the shrines where his relics
might be worshipped; there the monasteries where
tradition had preserved his sayings and his doings;
there the books where his doctrine might be studied in
its original purity; there the schools where the tenets
of different sects which had sprung up in the course
of time might best be acquired.

Some of the pilgrims and envoys have left us
accounts of their travels, and, in the absence of anything like an historical literature in India itself, these
Chinese works are of the utmost importance for gaining

---

[17] They have since been published.

an insight into the social, political, and religious history of that country from the beginning of our era to the time of the Mohammedan conquest. The importance of Mohammedan writers, so far as they treat on the history of India during the Middle Ages, was soon recognised, and in a memoir lately published by the most eminent Arabic scholar of France, M. Reinaud, new and valuable historical materials have been collected—materials doubly valuable in India, where no native historian has ever noted down the passing events of the day. But, although the existence of similar documents in Chinese was known, and although men of the highest literary eminence—such as Humboldt, Biot, and others—had repeatedly urged the necessity of having a translation of the early travels of the Chinese Pilgrims, it seemed almost as if our curiosity was never to be satisfied. France has been the only country where Chinese scholarship has ever flourished, and it was a French scholar, Abel Rémusat, who undertook at last the translation of one of the Chinese Pilgrims. Rémusat died before his work was published, and his translation of the travels of Fahian, edited by M. Landresse, remained for a long time without being followed up by any other. Nor did the work of that eminent scholar answer all expectations. Most of the proper names, the names of countries, towns, mountains, and rivers, the titles of books, and the whole Buddhistic phraseology, were so disguised in their Chinese dress that it was frequently impossible to discover their original form.

The Chinese alphabet was never intended to represent the sound of words. It was in its origin a hieroglyphic system, each word having its own graphic representative. Nor would it have been possible to write Chinese in any other way. Chinese is a monosyllabic language. No word is ·allowed more than one consonant and one vowel,—the vowels including diphthongs and nasal vowels. Hence the possible number of words is extremely small, and the number of significative sounds in the Chinese language is said to be no more than 450. No language, however, could be satisfied with so small a vocabulary, and in Chinese, as in other monosyllabic dialects, each word, as it was pronounced with various accents and intonations, was made to convey a large number of meanings; so that the total number of words, or rather of ideas, expressed in Chinese, is said to amount to 43,496. Hence a graphic representation of the mere sound of words would have been perfectly useless, and it was absolutely necessary to resort to hieroglyphical writing, enlarged by the introduction of determinative signs. Nearly the whole immense dictionary of Chinese—at least twenty-nine thirtieths —consists of combined signs, one part indicating the general sound, the other determining its special meaning. With such a system of writing it was possible to represent Chinese, but impossible to convey either the sound or the meaning of any other language. Besides, some of the most common sounds—such as r, b, d, and the short a—are unknown in Chinese.

How, then, were the translators to render Sanskrit names in Chinese? The most rational plan would have been to select as many Chinese signs as there were Sanskrit letters, and to express one and the same letter in Sanskrit always by one and the same sign in Chinese; or, if the conception of a consonant without a vowel, and of a vowel without a consonant, was too much for a Chinese understanding, to express at least

the same syllabic sound in Sanskrit, by one and the
same syllabic sign in Chinese. A similar system is
adopted at the present day, when the Chinese find
themselves under the necessity of writing the names
of Lord Palmerston or Sir John Bowring; but, instead
of adopting any definite system of transcribing, each
translator seems to have chosen his own signs for
rendering the sounds of Sanskrit words, and to have
chosen them at random. The result is that every
Sanskrit word as transcribed by the Chinese Buddhists is a riddle which no ingenuity is able to solve.
Who could have guessed that 'Fo-to,' or more frequently 'Fo,' was meant for Buddha? 'Ko-lo-keou-lo'
for Râhula, the son of Buddha? 'Po-lo-naï' for
Benares? 'Heng-ho' for Ganges? 'Niepan' for Nirvâna? 'Chamen' for Sramana? 'Feïto' for Veda?
'Tcha-li' for Kshattriya? 'Siu-to-lo' for Sûdra?
'Fan' or 'Fan-lon-mo' for Brahma? Sometimes, it is
true, the Chinese endeavoured to give, besides the
sounds, a translation of the meaning of the Sanskrit
words. But the translation of proper names is always
very precarious, and it required an intimate knowledge of Sanskrit and Buddhist literature to recognise
from these awkward translations the exact form of
the proper names for which they were intended. If,
in a Chinese translation of 'Thukydides,' we read of
a person called 'Leader of the people,' we might
guess his name to have been Demagogos, or Lao-
egos, as well as Agesilaos. And when the name
of the town of Sravasti was written Che-wei, which
means in Chinese 'where one hears,' it required no
ordinary power of combination to find that the name
of Sravasti was derived from a Sanskrit noun, sravas
(Greek κλέος, Lat. cluo), which means 'hearing' or

'fame,' and that the etymological meaning of the
name of *Sravasti* was intended by the Chinese ' Che-
wei.' Besides these names of places and rivers, of
kings and saints, there was the whole strange phraseology of Buddhism, of which no dictionary gives any
satisfactory explanation. How was even the best
Chinese scholar to know that the words which usually
mean 'dark shadow' must be taken in the technical
sense of Nirvâna, or becoming absorbed in the Absolute, that 'return-purity' had the same sense, and
that a third synonymous expression was to be recognised in a phrase which, in ordinary Chinese, would
have the sense of ' transport-figure-crossing-age?' A
monastery is called 'origin-door,' instead of 'black-
door.' The voice of Buddha is called ' the voice of
the dragon;' and his doctrine goes by the name of
' the door of expedients.'

Tedious as these details may seem, it was almost a
duty to state them, in order to give an idea of the
difficulties which M. Stanislas Julien had to grapple
with. Oriental scholars labour under great dis-
advantages. Few people take an interest in their
works, or, if they do, they simply accept the results, ·
but they are unable to appreciate the difficulty with
which these results were obtained. Many persons
who have read the translation of the cuneiform
inscriptions are glad, no doubt, to have the authentic
and contemporaneous records of Darius and Xerxes.
But if they followed the process by which scholars
such as Grotefend, Burnouf, Lassen, and Rawlinson
arrived at their results, they would see that the discovery of the alphabet, the language, the grammar,
and the meaning of the inscriptions of the Achæmenian dynasty deserves to be classed with the

discoveries of a Kepler, a Newton, or a Faraday.　In
a similar manner, the mere translation of a Chinese
work into French seems a very ordinary performance;
but M. Stanislas Julien, who has long been acknowledged as the first Chinese scholar in Europe, had to
spend twenty years of incessant labour in order to
prepare himself for the task of translating the
'Travels of Hiouen-thsang.'　He had to learn Sanskrit, no very easy language; he had to study the
Buddhist literature written in Sanskrit, Pâli, Tibetan,
Mongolian, and Chinese.　He had to make vast
indices of every proper name connected with Buddhism.　Thus only could he shape his own tools, and
accomplish what at last he did accomplish.　Most
persons will remember the interest with which the
travels of M.M. Huc and Gabet were read a few years
ago, though these two adventurous missionaries were
obliged to renounce their original intention of entering India by way of China and Tibet, and were not
allowed to proceed beyond the famous capital of
Lhassa.　If, then, it be considered that there was a
traveller who had made a similar journey twelve
hundred years earlier—who had succeeded in crossing
the deserts and mountain passes which separate China
from India—who had visited the principal cities of
the Indian Peninsula, at a time of which we have no
information, from native or foreign sources, as to the
state of that country—who had learned Sanskrit, and
made a large collection of Buddhist works—who had
carried on public disputations with the most eminent
philosophers and theologians of the day—who had
translated the most important works on Buddhism
from Sanskrit into Chinese, and left an account of his
travels, which still existed in the libraries of China—

nay, which had been actually printed and published
—we may well imagine the impatience with which
all scholars interested in the ancient history of India,
and in the subject of Buddhism, looked forward to
the publication of so important a work.   Hiouen-
thsang's name had first been mentioned in Europe by
Abel Rémusat and Klaproth.   They had discovered
some fragments of his travels in a Chinese work on
foreign countries and foreign nations.   Rémusat wrote
to China to procure, if possible, a complete copy of
Hiouen-thsang's works.   He was informed by Mor-
rison that they were out of print.   Still, the few
specimens which he had given at the end of his translation of the ' Foe Koue Ki' had whetted the appetite
of Oriental scholars.   M. Stanislas Julien succeeded
in procuring a copy of Hiouen-thsang in 1838; and
after nearly twenty years spent in preparing a translation of the Chinese traveller, his version is now
before us.   If there are but few who know the difficulty of a work like that of M. Stanislas Julien, it
becomes their duty to speak out, though, after all,
perhaps the most intelligible eulogium would be, that
in a branch of study where there are no monopolies
and no patents, M. Stanislas Julien is acknowledged
to be the only man in Europe who could produce
the article which he has produced in the work
before us.

  We shall devote the rest of our space to a short
account of the life and travels of Hiouen-thsang.
Hiouen-thsang was born in a provincial town of China,
at a time when the empire was in a chronic state of
revolution.   His father had left the public service,
and had given most of his time to the education of
his four children.   Two of them distinguished them-

selves at a very early age—one of them was Hiouen-
thsang, the future traveller and theologian. The boy
was sent to school at a Buddhist monastery, and,
after receiving there the necessary instruction, partly
from his elder brother, he was himself admitted as a
monk at the early age of thirteen. During the next
seven years, the young monk travelled about with
his brother from place to place, in order to follow the
lectures of some of the most distinguished professors.
The horrors of war frequently broke in upon his
quiet studies, and forced him to seek refuge in the
more distant provinces of the empire. At the age of
twenty he took priest's orders, and had then already
become famous by his vast knowledge. He had
studied the chief canonical books of the Buddhist
faith, the records of Buddha's life and teaching, the
system of ethics and metaphysics; and he was versed
in the works of Confucius and Lao-tse. But still his
own mind was agitated by doubts. Six years he
continued his studies in the chief places of learning
in China, and where he came to learn he was frequently asked to teach. At last, when he saw that
none, even the most eminent theologians, were able
to give him the information he wanted, he formed his
resolve of travelling to India. The works of earlier
pilgrims, such as Fahian and others, were known to
him. He knew that in India he should find the
originals of the works which in their Chinese translation left so many things doubtful in his mind; and
though he knew from the same sources the dangers of
his journey, yet 'the glory,' as he says, 'of recovering the Law, which was to be a guide to all men and
the means of their salvation, seemed to him worthy of
imitation.' In common with several other priests, he

addressed a memorial to the Emperor to ask leave for
their journey. Leave was refused, and the courage of
his companions failed. Not that of Hiouen-thsang.
His own mother had told him that, soon before she
gave birth to him, she had seen her child travelling
to the Far West in search of the Law. He was himself haunted by similar visions, and having long
surrendered worldly desires, he resolved to brave all
dangers, and to risk his life for the only object for
which he thought it worth while to live. He proceeded
to the Yellow River, the Hoang-ho, and to the place
where the caravans bound for India used to meet,
and, though the Governor had sent strict orders not to
allow any one to cross the frontier, the young priest,
with the assistance of his co-religionists, succeeded
in escaping the vigilance of the Chinese 'douaniers.'
Spies were sent after him. But so frank was his
avowal, and so firm his resolution, which he expressed
in the presence of the authorities, that the Governor
himself tore his hue and cry to pieces, and allowed
him to proceed. Hitherto he had been accompanied
by two friends. They now left him, and Hiouen-
thsang found himself alone, without a friend and
without a guide. He sought for strength in fervent
prayer. The next morning a person presented himself, offering his services as a guide. This guide conducted him safely for some distance, but left him
when they approached the desert. There were still
five watch-towers to be passed, and there was nothing
to indicate the road through the desert, except the
hoof-marks of horses, and skeletons. The traveller
followed this melancholy track, and, though misled by
the 'mirage' of the desert, he reached the first tower.
Here the arrows of the watchmen would have put an

end to his existence and his cherished expedition.
But the officer in command, himself a zealous Buddhist, allowed the courageous pilgrim to proceed, and
gave him letters of recommendation to the officers
of the next towers. The last tower, however, was
guarded by men inaccessible to bribes, and deaf to
reasoning. In order to escape their notice, Hiouen-
thsang had to make a long détour. He passed
through another desert, and lost his way. The bag
in which he carried his water burst, and then even
the courage of Hiouen-thsang failed. He began to
retrace his steps. But suddenly he stopped. 'I
took an oath,' he said, 'never to make a step backward till I had reached India. Why, then, have I
come here? It is better I should die proceeding to
the West than return to the East and live.' Four
nights and five days he travelled through the desert
without a drop of water. He had nothing to refresh
himself except his prayers—and what were they?
Texts from a work which taught that there was no
god, no Creator, no creation,—nothing but mind,
minding itself. It is incredible in how exhausted an
atmosphere the divine spark within us will glimmer
on, and even warm the dark chambers of the human
heart. Comforted by his prayers, Hiouen-thsang
proceeded, and arrived after some time at a large
lake. He was in the country of the Oïgour Tatars.
They received him well, nay, too well. One of the
Tatar Khans, himself a Buddhist, sent for the Buddhist pilgrim, and insisted on his staying with him
to instruct his people. Remonstrances proved of no
avail. But Hiouen-thsang was not to be conquered.
'I know,' he said, 'that the king, in spite of his
power, has no power over my mind and my will;'

and he refused all nourishment in order to put an
end to his life. Θανοῦμαι καὶ ἐλευθερήσομαι Three
days he persevered, and at last the Khan, afraid of
the consequences, was obliged to yield to the poor
monk. He made him promise to visit him on his
return to China, and then to stay three years with
him. At last, after a delay of one month, during
which the Khan and his Court came daily to hear
the lessons of their pious guest, the traveller continued his journey with a numerous escort, and with
letters of introduction from the Khan to twenty-four
Princes whose territories the little caravan had to
pass. Their way lay through what is now called
Dsungary, across the Musur-dabaghan mountains, the
northern portion of the Belur-tag, the Yaxartes valley,
Bactria, and Kabulistân. We cannot follow them
through all the places they passed, though the accounts which he gives of their adventures are most
interesting, and the description of the people most
important. Here is a description of the Musur-dabaghan mountains:

'The top of the mountain rises to the sky. Since
the beginning of the world the snow has been accu-
mulating, and is now transformed into vast masses of
ice, which never melt, either in spring or summer.
Hard and brilliant sheets of snow are spread out till
they are lost in the infinite, and mingle with the
clouds. If one looks at them, the eyes are dazzled
by the splendour. Frozen peaks hang down over
both sides of the road, some hundred feet high, and
twenty feet or thirty feet thick. It is not without
difficulty and danger that the traveller can clear
them or climb over them. Besides, there are squalls
of wind, and tornadoes of snow which attack the

pilgrims. Even with double shoes, and in thick furs, one cannot help trembling and shivering.'

During the seven days that Hiouen-thsang crossed these Alpine passes he lost fourteen of his companions.

What is most important, however, in this early portion of the Chinese traveller is the account which he gives of the high degree of civilisation among the tribes of Central Asia. We had gradually accustomed ourselves to believe in an early civilisation of Egypt, of Babylon, of China, of India; but now that we find the hordes of Tatary possessing in the seventh century the chief arts and institutions of an advanced society, we shall soon have to drop the name of barbarians altogether. The theory of M. Oppert, who ascribes the original invention of the cuneiform letters and a civilisation anterior to that of Babylon and Nineveh to a Turanian or Scythian race, will lose much of its apparent improbability; for no new wave of civilisation had reached these countries between the cuneiform period of their literature and history and the time of Hiouen-thsang's visit. In the kingdom of Okini, on the western frontier of China, Hiouen-thsang found an active commerce, gold, silver, and copper coinage; monasteries, where the chief works of Buddhism were studied, and an alphabet, derived from Sanskrit. As he travelled on he met with mines, with agriculture, including pears, plums, peaches, almonds, grapes, pomegranates, rice, and wheat. The inhabitants were dressed in silk and woollen materials. There were musicians in the chief cities who played on the flute and the guitar. Buddhism was the prevailing religion, but there were traces of an earlier worship, the Bactrian fire-worship.

The country was everywhere studded with halls, monasteries, monuments, and statues. Samarkand formed at that early time a kind of Athens, and its manners were copied by all the tribes in the neighbourhood. Balkh, the old capital of Bactria, was still an important place on the Oxus, well fortified, and full of sacred buildings. And the details which our traveller gives of the exact circumference of the cities, the number of their inhabitants, the products of the soil, the articles of trade, can leave no doubt in our minds that he relates what he had seen and heard himself. A new page in the history of the world is here opened, and new ruins pointed out, which would reward the pickaxe of a Layard.

But we must not linger. Our traveller, as we said, had entered India by way of Kabul. Shortly before he arrived at Pou-lou-cha-pou-lo, i. e. the Sanskrit Purushapura, the modern Peshawer, Hiouen-thsang heard of an extraordinary cave where Buddha had formerly converted a dragon, and had promised his new pupil to leave him his shadow, in order that, whenever the evil passions of his dragon-nature should revive, the aspect of his master's shadowy features might remind him of his former vows. This promise was fulfilled, and the dragon-cave became a famous place of pilgrimage. Our traveller was told that the roads leading to the cave were extremely dangerous, and infested by robbers—that for three years none of the pilgrims had ever returned from the cave. But he replied, 'It would be difficult during a hundred thousand Kalpas to meet one single time with the true shadow of Buddha; how could I, having come so near, pass on without going to adore it?' He left his companions behind, and after

asking in vain for a guide, he met at last with a boy
who showed him to a farm belonging to a convent.
Here he found an old man who undertook to act as his
guide. They had hardly proceeded a few miles when
they were attacked by five robbers. The monk took
off his cap and displayed his ecclesiastical robes.
'Master,' said one of the robbers, 'where are you
going?' Hiouen-thsang replied, 'I desire to adore
the shadow of Buddha.' 'Master,' said the robber,
'have you not heard that these roads are full of
bandits?' 'Robbers are men,' Hiouen-thsang exclaimed, 'and at present, when I am going to adore
the shadow of Buddha, even though the roads were
full of wild beasts, I should walk on without fear.
Surely, then, I ought not to fear you, as you are men
whose heart is possessed of pity.' The robbers were
moved by these words, and opened their hearts to the
true faith. After this little incident, Hiouen-thsang
proceeded with his guide. He passed a stream rush-
ing down between two precipitous walls of rock. In
the rock itself there was a door which opened. All
was dark. But Hiouen-thsang entered, advanced
towards the east, then moved fifty steps backwards,
and began his devotions. He made one hundred
salutations, but he saw nothing. He reproached himself bitterly with his former sins, he cried, and abandoned himself to utter despair, because the shadow of
Buddha would not appear before him. At last, after
many prayers and invocations, he saw on the eastern
wall a dim light, of the size of a saucepan, such as
the Buddhist monks carry in their hands. But it
disappeared. He continued praying full of joy and
pain, and again he saw a light, which vanished like
lightning. Then he vowed, full of devotion and love,

that he would never leave the place till he had seen
the shadow of the 'Venerable of the age.' After two
hundred prayers, the cave was suddenly bathed in
light, and the shadow of Buddha, of a brilliant white
colour, rose majestically on the wall, as when the
clouds suddenly open and, all at once, display the
marvellous image of the 'Mountain of Light.' A
dazzling splendour lighted up the features of the
divine countenance. Hiouen-thsang was lost in contemplation and wonder, and would not turn his eyes
away from the sublime and incomparable object. . . .
After he awoke from his trance, he called in six men,
and commanded them to light a fire in the cave, in
order to burn incense; but, as the approach of the
light made the shadow of Buddha disappear, the fire
was extinguished. Then five of the men saw the
shadow, but the sixth saw nothing. The old man
who had acted as guide was astounded when-Hiouen-
thsang told him the vision. 'Master,' he said, 'without the sincerity of your faith, and the energy of your
vows, you could not have seen such a miracle.'

This is the account given by Hiouen-thsang's
biographers. But we must say, to the credit of
Hiouen-thsang himself, that in the 'Si-yu-ki,' which
contains his own diary, the story is told in a different
way. The cave is described with almost the same
words. But afterwards the writer continues: 'Formerly, the shadow of Buddha was seen in the cave,
bright, like his natural appearance, and with all the
marks of his divine beauty. One might have said,
it was Buddha himself. For some centuries, however,
it can no longer be seen completely. Though one
does see something, it is only a .feeble and doubtful
resemblance. If a man prays with sincere faith, and

if he has received from above a hidden impression, he sees the shadow clearly, but he cannot enjoy the sight for any length of time.'

From Peshawer, the scene of this extraordinary miracle, Hiouen-thsang proceeded to Kashmir, visited the chief towns of Central India, and arrived at last in Magadha, the Holy Land of the Buddhists. Here he remained five years, devoting all his time to the study of Sanskrit and Buddhist literature, and inspecting every place hallowed by the recollections of the past. He then passed through Bengal, and proceeded to the south, with a view of visiting Ceylon, the chief seat of Buddhism. Baffled in that wish, he crossed the peninsula from east to west, ascended the Malabar coast, reached the Indus, and, after numerous excursions to the chief places of North-Western India, returned to Magadha, to spend there, with his old friends, some of the happiest years of his life. The route of his journeyings is laid down in a map drawn with exquisite skill by M. Vivien de Saint-Martin. At last he was obliged to return to China, and, passing through the Penjab, Kabulistan, and Bactria, he reached the Oxus, followed its course nearly to its sources on the plateau of Pamir, and, after staying some time in the three chief towns of Turkistan, Khasgar, Yarkand, and Khoten, he found himself again, after sixteen years of travels, dangers, and studies, in his own native country. His fame had spread far and wide, and the poor pilgrim, who had once been hunted by imperial spies and armed policemen, was now received with public honours by the Emperor himself. His entry into the capital was like a triumph. The streets were covered with carpets, flowers were scattered, and banners flying. Soldiers were drawn up, the magistrates went out to meet him, and all the monks of the neighbourhood marched along in solemn procession. The trophies that adorned this triumph, carried by a large number of horses, were of a peculiar kind. First, 150 grains of the dust of Buddha; secondly, a golden statue of the great Teacher; thirdly, a similar statue of sandal-wood; fourthly, a statue of sandal-wood, representing Buddha as descending from heaven; fifthly, a statue of silver; sixthly, a golden statue of Buddha conquering the dragons; seventhly, a statue of sandal-wood, representing Buddha as a preacher; lastly, a collection of 657 works in 520 volumes. The Emperor received the traveller in the Phœnix Palace, and, full of admiration for his talents and wisdom, invited him to accept a high office in the Government. This Hiouen-thsang declined. ' The soul of the administration,' he said, ' is still the doctrine of Confucius;' and he would dedicate the rest of his life to the Law of Buddha. The Emperor thereupon asked him to write an account of his travels, and assigned him a monastery where he might employ his leisure in translating the works he had brought back from India. His travels were soon written and published, but the translation of the Sanskrit MSS. occupied the whole rest of his life. It is said that the number of works translated by him, with the assistance of a large staff of monks, amounted to 740, in 1,335 volumes. Frequently he might be seen meditating on a difficult passage, when suddenly it seemed as if a higher spirit had enlightened his mind. His soul was cheered, as when a man walking in darkness sees all at once the sun piercing the clouds and shining in its full brightness; and, unwilling to trust to his own understanding, he used to attribute his knowledge to a secret inspiration of Buddha and the Bodhisattvas. When he found that the hour of death approached, he had all his property divided among the poor. He invited his friends to come and see him, and to take a cheerful leave of that impure body of Hiouen-thsang. 'I desire,' he said, 'that whatever rewards I may have merited by good works may fall upon other people. May I be born again with them in the heaven of the blessed, be admitted to the family of Mi-le, and serve the Buddha of the future, who is full of kindness and affection. When I descend again upon earth to pass through other forms of existence, I desire at every new birth to fulfil my duties towards Buddha, and arrive at the last at the highest and most perfect intelligence. He died in the year 664—about the same time that Mohammedanism was pursuing its bloody conquests in the East, and Christianity began to shed its pure light over the dark forests of Germany.

It is impossible to do justice to the character of so extraordinary a man as Hiouen-thsang in so short a sketch as we have been able to give. If we knew only his own account of his life and travels—the volume which has just been published at Paris—we should be ignorant of the motives which guided him and of the sufferings which he underwent. Happily, two of his friends and pupils had left an account of their teacher, and M. Stanislas Julien has acted wisely in beginning his collection of the Buddhist Pilgrims with the translation of that biography. There we learn something of the man himself and of that silent enthusiasm which supported him in his arduous work. There we see him braving the dangers of the desert, scrambling along glaciers, crossing over torrents, and quietly submitting to the brutal violence of Indian Thugs. There we see him rejecting the tempting invitations of Khans, Kings, and Emperors, and quietly pursuing among strangers, within the bleak walls of the cell of a Buddhist college, the study of a foreign language, the key to the sacred literature of his faith. There we see him rising to eminence, acknowledged as an equal by his former teachers, as a superior by the most distinguished scholars of India; the champion of the orthodox faith, an arbiter at councils, the favourite of Indian kings. In his own work there is hardly a word about all this. We do not wish to disguise his weaknesses, such as they appear in the same biography. He was a credulous man, easily imposed upon by crafty priests, still more easily carried away by his own superstitions; but he deserved to have lived in better times, and we almost grudge so high and noble a character to a country not our own, and to a religion unworthy of such a man. Of selfishness we find no trace in him. His whole life belonged to the faith in which he was born, and the object of his labour was not so much to perfect himself as to benefit others. He was an honest man. And strange, and stiff, and absurd, and outlandish as his outward appearance may seem, there is something in the face of that poor Chinese monk, with his yellow skin and his small oblique eyes, that appeals to our sympathy—something in his life, and the work of his life, that places him by right among the heroes of Greece, the martyrs of Rome, the knights of the crusades, the explorers of the Arctic regions—something that makes us feel it a duty to inscribe his name on the roll of the 'forgotten worthies' of the human race. There is a higher consanguinity than

that of the blood which runs through our veins—
that of the blood which makes our hearts beat
with the same indignation and the same joy. And
there is a higher nationality than that of being
governed by the same imperial dynasty—that of our
common allegiance to the Father and Ruler of all
mankind.

It is but right to state that we owe the publication,
at least of the second volume of M. Julien's work, to
the liberality of the Court of Directors of the East-
India Company. We have had several opportunities
of pointing out the creditable manner in which that
body has patronized literary and scientific works connected with the East, and we congratulate the Chair-
man, Colonel Sykes, and the President of the Board
of Control, Mr. Vernon Smith, on the excellent choice
they have made in this instance. Nothing can be
more satisfactory than that nearly the whole edition
of a work which would have remained unpublished
without their liberal assistance, has been sold in little
more than a month.

April, 1857.

XI.

THE MEANING OF NIRVÂNA.

To the Editor of THE TIMES.

SIR,—Mr. Francis Barham, of Bath, has protested in a letter, printed in 'The Times' of the 24th of April, against my interpretations of Nirvâna, or the summum bonum of the Buddhists. He maintains that the Nirvâna in which the Buddhists believe, and which they represent as the highest goal of their religion and philosophy, means union and communion with God, or absorption of the individual soul by the divine essence, and not, as I tried to show in my articles on the 'Buddhist Pilgrims,' utter annihilation.

I must not take up much more of your space with so abstruse a subject as Buddhist metaphysics; but at the same time I cannot allow Mr. Barham's protest to pass unnoticed. The authorities which he brings forward against my account of Buddhism, and particularly against my interpretation of Nirvâna, seem formidable enough. There is Neander, the great church historian, Creuzer, the famous scholar, and Huc, the well-known traveller and missionary,—all interpreting, as Mr. Barham says, the Nirvâna of the Buddhists in the sense of an apotheosis of the human soul, as it was taught in the Vedânta philosophy of

the Brahmans, the Sufiism of the Persians, and the
Christian mysticism of Eckhart and Tauler, and not
in the sense of absolute annihilation.

Now, with regard to Neander and Creuzer, I must
observe that their works were written before the
canonical books of the Buddhists, composed in Sanskrit had been discovered, or at least before they
had been sent to Europe, and been analysed by
European scholars. Besides, neither Neander nor
Creuzer was an Oriental scholar, and their knowledge
of the subject could only be second-hand. It was in
1824 that Mr. Brian Houghton Hodgson, then resident at the Court of Nepal, gave the first intimation
of the existence of a large religious literature written
in Sanskrit, and preserved by the Buddhists of Nepal
as the canonical books of their faith. It was in 1830
and 1835 that the same eminent scholar and natu-
ralist presented the first set of these books to the
Royal Asiatic Society in London. In 1837 he made
a similar gift to the Société Asiatique of Paris, and
some of the most important works were transmitted
by him to the Bodleian Library at Oxford. It was
in 1844 that the late Eugène Burnouf published,
after a careful study of these documents, his classical
work, 'Introduction à l'Histoire du Buddhisme Indien,'
and it is from this book that our knowledge of Buddhism may be said to date. Several works have since
been published, which have added considerably to
the stock of authentic information on the doctrine
of the great Indian reformer. There is Burnouf's
translation of 'Le Lotus de la bonne Loi,' published
after the death of that lamented scholar, together
with numerous essays, in 1852. There are two interesting works by the Rev. Spence Hardy—'Eastern

Monachism,' London, 1850, and 'A Manual of Buddhism,' London, 1853; and there are the publications
of M. Stanislas Julien, E. Foucaux, the Honourable
George Turnour, Professor H. H. Wilson, and others,
alluded to in my article on the ' Buddhist Pilgrims.'
It is from these works alone that we can derive
correct and authentic information on Buddhism, and
not from Neander's ' History of the Christian Church'
or from Creuzer's ' Symbolik.'

If any one will consult these works, he will find
that the discussions on the true meaning of Nirvâna
are not of modern date, and that, at a very early
period, different philosophical schools among the
Buddhists of India, and different teachers who spread
the doctrine of Buddhism abroad, propounded every
conceivable opinion as to the orthodox explanation
of this term. Even in one and the same school we
find different parties maintaining different views on
the meaning of Nirvâna. There is the school of the
Svâbhâvikas, which still exists in Nepal. The Svâbhâvikas maintain that nothing exists but nature, or
rather substance, and that this substance exists by .
itself (svabhâvât), without a Creator or a Ruler. It
exists, however, under two forms: in the state of
Pravritti, as active, or in the state of Nirvritti, as
passive. Human beings, who, like everything else,
exist svabhâvât, 'by themselves,' are supposed to be
capable of arriving at Nirvritti, or passiveness, which
is nearly synonymous with Nirvâna. But here the
Svâbhâvikas branch off into two sects. Some believe
that Nirvritti is repose, others that it is annihilation; and the former add, 'were it even annihilation
(sûnyatâ), it would still be good, man being otherwise doomed to an eternal migration through all the

forms of nature ; the more desirable of which are
little to be wished for; and the less so, at any price
to be shunned[1].'

What was the original meaning of Nirvâna may
perhaps best be seen from the etymology of this
technical term. Every Sanskrit scholar knows that
Nirvâna means originally the blowing out, the extinction of light, and not absorption. The human
soul, when it arrives at its perfection, is blown out[2],
if we use the phraseology of the Buddhists, like a
lamp; it is not absorbed, as the Brahmans say, like
a drop in the ocean. Neither in the system of
Buddhist philosophy, nor in the philosophy from
which Buddha is supposed to have borrowed, was
there any place left for a Divine Being by which the
human soul could be absorbed. Sânkhya philosophy,
in its original form, claims the name of an-îsvara,
'lordless' or 'atheistic' as its distinctive title. Its
final object is not absorption in God, whether personal
or impersonal, but Moksha, deliverance of the soul
from all pain and illusion, and recovery by the soul
of its true nature. It is doubtful whether the term
Nirvâna was coined by Buddha. It occurs in the
literature of the Brahmans as a synonyme of Moksha,
deliverance; Nirvritti, cessation ; Apavarga, release;
Nihsreyas, summum bonum. It is used in this
sense in the Mahâbhârata, and it is explained in the
Amara-Kosha as having the meaning of ' blowing out,

[1] See Burnouf, 'Introduction,' p. 441; Hodgson, 'Asiatic
Researches,' vol. xvi.

[2] 'Calm,' 'without wind,' as Nirvâna is sometimes explained,
is expressed in Sanskrit by Nirvâta. See Amara-Kosha, sub
voce.

applied to a fire and to a sage[3].' Unless, however,
we succeed in tracing this term in works anterior to
Buddha, we may suppose that it was invented by him
in order to express that meaning of the summum
bonum which he was the first to preach, and which
some of his disciples explained in the sense of absolute annihilation.

The earliest authority to which we can go back, if
we want to know the original character of Buddhism,
is the Buddhist Canon, as settled after the death of
Buddha at the first Council. It is called Tripi*t*aka,
or the Three Baskets, the first containing the Sûtras, or
the discourses of Buddha; the second, the Vinaya, or
his code of morality; the third, the Abhidharma,
or the system of metaphysics. The first was compiled by Ananda, the second by Upâli, the third by
Kâsyapa—all of them the pupils and friends of
Buddha. It may be that these collections, as we
now possess them, were finally arranged, not at the
first, but at the third Council. Yet, even then, we
have no earlier, no more authentic, documents from
which we could form an opinion as to the original
teaching of Buddha; and the Nirvâ*n*a, as taught
in the metaphysics of Kâsyapa, and particularly in
the Pra*gn*â-pâramitâ, is annihilation, not absorption.
Buddhism, therefore, if tested by its own canonical
books, cannot be freed from the charge of Nihilism,
whatever may have been its character in the mind
of its founder, and whatever changes it may have
undergone in later times, and among races less inured
to metaphysical discussions than the Hindus.

---

[3] Different views of the Nirvâ*n*a, as conceived by the Tîrthakas,
or the Brahmans, may be seen in an extract from the Lankâvatâra,
translated by Burnouf, p. 514.

THE MEANING OF NIRVÂNA.

The ineradicable feeling of dependence on something else, which is the life-spring of all religion, was
completely numbed in the early Buddhist metaphysicians, and it was only after several generations had
passed away, and after Buddhism had become the
creed of millions, that this feeling returned with increased warmth, changing, as I said in my article,
the very Nothing into a paradise, and deifying the
very Buddha who had denied the existence of a
Deity. That this has been the case in China we
know from the interesting works of the Abbé Huc,
and from other sources, such as the 'Catechism of
the Shamans, or the Laws and Regulations of the
Priesthood of Buddha in China,' translated by Ch. F.
Neumann, London, 1831. In India, also, Buddhism,
as soon as it became a popular religion, had to speak
a more human language than that of metaphysical
Pyrrhonism. But, if it did so, it was because it was
shamed into it. This we may see from the very
nicknames which the Brahmans apply to their
opponents, the Bauddhas. They call them Nâstikas
—those who maintain that there is nothing; Sûnya-
vadins—those who maintain that there is a universal
void.

The only ground, therefore, on which we may
stand, if we wish to defend the founder of Buddhism
against the charges of Nihilism and Atheism, is this,
that, as some of the Buddhists admit, the 'Basket
of Metaphysics' was rather the work of his pupils,
not of Buddha himself[4]. This distinction between

[4] See Burnouf, 'Introduction,' p. 41. 'Abuddhoktam abhidhar-
ma-sâstram.' Ibid. p. 454. According to the Tibetan Buddhists,
however, Buddha propounded the Abhidharma when he was fifty-one
years old. 'Asiatic Researches,' vol. xx. p. 339.

the authentic words of Buddha and the canonical
books in general, is mentioned more than once. The
priesthood of Ceylon, when the manifest errors with
which their canonical commentaries abound, were
brought to their notice, retreated from their former
position, and now assert that it is only the express
words of Buddha that they receive as undoubted
truth[5]. There is a passage in a Buddhist work
which reminds us somewhat of the last page of
Dean Milman's 'History of Christianity,' and where
we read:

'The words of the priesthood are good; those of
the Rahats (saints) are better; but those of the
All-knowing are the best of all.'

This is an argument which Mr. Francis Barham
might have used with more success, and by which
he might have justified, if not the first disciples, at
least the original founder of Buddhism. Nay, there
is a saying of Buddha's which tends to show that all
metaphysical discussion was regarded by him as vain
and useless. It is a saying mentioned in one of the
MSS. belonging to the Bodleian Library. As it has
never been published before, I may be allowed to
quote it in the original: Sadasad vikâram na
sahate,—'The ideas of being and not being do not
admit of discussion,'—a tenet which, if we consider
that it was enunciated before the time of the Eleatic
philosophers of Greece, and long before Hegel's Logic,
might certainly have saved us many an intricate and
indigestible argument.

A few passages from the Buddhist writings of
Nepal and Ceylon will best show that the horror

---

[5] 'Eastern Monachism,' p. 171.

nihili was not felt by the metaphysicians of former
ages in the same degree as it is felt by ourselves.
The famous hymn which resounds in heaven when
the luminous rays of the smile of Buddha penetrate
through the clouds, is ' All is transitory, all is misery,
all is void, all is without substance.'   Again, it is
said in the Pragnâ-pâramitâ[6], that Buddha began
to think that he ought to conduct all creatures to
perfect Nirvâna.   But he reflected that there are
really no creatures which ought to be conducted, nor
creatures that conduct; and, nevertheless, he did
conduct all creatures to perfect Nirvâna.   Then,
continues the text, why is it said that there are
neither creatures which arrive at complete Nirvâna,
nor creatures which conduct there?   Because it is
illusion which makes creatures what they are.   It is
as if a clever juggler, or his pupil, made an immense
number of people to appear on the high road, and
after having made them to appear, made them to
disappear again.   Would there be anybody who had
killed, or murdered, or annihilated, or caused them
to vanish?   No.   And it is the same with Buddha.
He conducts an immense, innumerable, infinite number
of creatures to complete Nirvâna, and yet there are
neither creatures which are conducted, nor creatures
that conduct.   If a Bodhisattva, on hearing this explanation of the Law, is not frightened, then it may
be said that he has put on the great armour[7].

Soon after, we read: ' The name of Buddha is
nothing but a word.   The name of Bodhisattva is
nothing but a word.   The name of Perfect Wisdom
(Pragnâ-pâramitâ) is nothing but a word.   The name

---

[6] Burnouf, 'Introduction,' p. 462.   [7] Ibid. p. 478.

is indefinite, as if one says " I," for " I " is something
indefinite because it has no limits.'

Burnouf gives the gist of the whole Pragnâ-pâramitâ in the following words: ' The highest Wisdom,
or what is to be known, has no more real existence
than he who has to know, or the Bodhisattva; no
more than he who does know, or the Buddha.' But
Burnouf remarks that nothing of this kind is to be
found in the Sûtras, and that Gautama Sâkya-muni,
the son of Suddhodana, would never have become
the founder of a popular religion if he had started
with similar absurdities. In the Sûtras the reality
of the objective world is denied; the reality of form
is denied; the reality of the individual, or the ' I,'
is equally denied. But the existence of a subject,
of something like the Purusha, the thinking substance of the Sânkhya philosophy, is spared. Something at least exists with respect to which everything
else may be said not to exist. The germs of the
ideas, developed in the Pragnâ-pâramitâ, may indeed
be discovered here and there in the Sûtras[8]. But
they had not yet ripened into that poisonous plant
which soon became an indispensable narcotic in the
schools of the later Buddhists. Buddha himself, however, though, perhaps, not a Nihilist, was certainly
an Atheist. He does not deny distinctly either the
existence of gods, or that of God; but he ignores the
former, and he is ignorant of the latter. Therefore,
if Nirvâna in his mind was not yet complete annihilation, still less could it have been absorption into a
Divine essence. It was nothing but selfishness, in
the metaphysical sense of the word—a relapse into

---

[8] Burnouf, ' Introduction,' p. 520.

that being which is nothing but itself. This is the most charitable view which we can take of the Nirvâna, even as conceived by Buddha himself, and it is the view which Burnouf derived from the canonical books of the Northern Buddhists. On the other hand, Mr. Spence Hardy, who in his works follows exclusively the authority of the Southern Buddhists, the Pâli and Singhalese works of Ceylon, arrives at the same result. We read in his work: 'The Rahat (Arhat), who has reached Nirvâna, but is not yet a Pratyeka-buddha, or a Supreme Buddha, says: "I await the appointed time for the cessation of existence. I have no wish to live ; I have no wish to die. Desire is extinct." '

In a very interesting dialogue between Milinda and Nâgasena, communicated by Mr. Spence Hardy, Nirvâna is represented as something which has no antecedent cause, no qualities, no locality. It is something of which the utmost we may assert is, that it is.

Nâgasena. Can a man, by his natural strength, go from the city of Sàgal to the forest of Himâla?

Milinda. Yes.

Nâgasena. But could any man, by his natural strength, bring the forest of Himâla to this city of Sâgal?

Milinda. No.

Nâgasena. In like manner, though the fruition of the paths may cause the accomplishment of Nirvâna, no cause by which Nirvâna is produced can be declared. The path that leads to Nirvâna may be pointed out, but not any cause for its production. Why? because that which constitutes Nirvâna is beyond all computation,—a mystery, not to be understood. . . . It cannot be said that it is produced, nor that it is not produced; that it is past or future or present. Nor can it be said that it is the seeing of the eye, or the hearing of the ear, or the smelling of the nose, or the tasting of the tongue, or the feeling of the body.

Milinda. Then you speak of a thing that is not; you merely say that Nirvâna is Nirvâna;—therefore there is no Nirvâna.

Nâgasena. Great king, Nirvâna is.

Another question also, whether Nirvâna is something different from the beings that enter into it, has been asked by the Buddhists themselves:

Milinda. Does the being who acquires it, attain something that has previously existed?—or is it his own product, a formation peculiar to himself?

Nâgasena. Nirvâna does not exist previously to its reception; nor is it that which was brought into existence. Still to the being who attains it, there is Nirvâna.

In opposition, therefore, to the more advanced views of the Nihilistic philosophers of the North, Nâgasena maintains the existence of Nirvâna, and of the being that has entered Nirvâna. He does not say that Buddha is a mere word. When asked by king Milinda, whether the all-wise Buddha exists, he replies:

Nâgasena. He who is the most meritorious (Bhagavat) does exist.

Milinda. Then can you point out to me the place in which he exists?

Nâgasena. Our Bhagavat has attained Nirvâna, where there is no repetition of birth. We cannot say that he is here, or that he is there. When a fire is extinguished, can it be said that it is here, or that it is there? Even so, our Buddha has attained extinction (Nirvâna). He is like the sun that has set behind the Astagiri mountain. It cannot be said that he is here, or that he is there: but we can point him out by the discourses he delivered. In them he lives.

At the present moment, the great majority of Buddhists would probably be quite incapable of understanding the abstract speculation of their ancient masters. The view taken of Nirvâna in China, Mongolia, and Tatary may probably be as gross as that which most of the Mohammedans form of their paradise. But, in the history of religion, the historian must go back to the earliest and most original documents that are to be obtained. Thus only may he hope to understand the later developments which, whether for good or evil, every form of faith has had to undergo.

April, 1857.

XII.

CHINESE TRANSLATIONS

OF

SANSKRIT TEXTS[1].

WELL might M. Stanislas Julien put εὕρηκα on the title-page of his last work, in which he explains his method of deciphering the Sanskrit words which occur in the Chinese translations of the Buddhist literature of India. We endeavoured to explain the laborious character and the important results of his researches on this subject on a former occasion, when reviewing his translation of the ' Life and Travels of the Buddhist Pilgrim Hiouen-thsang.' At that time, however, M. Julien kept the key of his discoveries to himself. He gave us the results of his labours without giving us more than a general idea of the process by which those results had been obtained. He has now published his ' Méthode pour déchiffrer et transcrire les noms sanscrits qui se rencontrent dans les livres chinois,' and he has given to

---

[1] ' Méthode pour déchiffrer et transcrire les noms sanscrits qui se rencontrent dans les livres chinois.' Par M. Stanislas Julien, Membre de l'Institut. Paris, 1861.

the public his Chinese-Sanskrit dictionary, the work of sixteen years of arduous labour, containing all the Chinese characters which are used for representing phonetically the technical terms and proper names of the Buddhist literature of India.

In order fully to appreciate the labours and discoveries of M. Julien in this remote field of Oriental literature, we must bear in mind that the doctrine of Buddha arose in India about two centuries before Alexander's invasion. It became the state religion of India soon after Alexander's conquest, and it produced a vast literature, which was collected into a canon at a council held about 246 B.C. Very soon after that council, Buddhism assumed a proselytizing character. It spread in the south to Ceylon, in the north to Kashmir, the Himalayan countries, Tibet, and China. In the historical annals of China, on which, in the absence of anything like historical literature in Sanskrit, we must mainly depend for information on the spreading of Buddhism, one Buddhist missionary is mentioned as early as 217 B.C.; and about the year 120 B.C. a Chinese general, after defeating the barbarous tribes north of the desert of Gobi, brought back as a trophy a golden statue—the statue of Buddha. It was not, however, till the year 65 A.D. that Buddhism was officially recognised by the Chinese Emperor as a third state religion. Ever since, it has shared equal honours with the doctrines of Confucius and Lao-tse in the Celestial Empire; and it is but lately that these three established religions have had to fear the encroachments of a new rival in the creed of the Chief of the rebels.

Once established in China, and well provided with monasteries and benefices, the Buddhist priesthood

seems to have been most active in its literary
labours.   Immense as was the Buddhist literature
of India, the Chinese swelled it to still more appalling proportions.   The first thing to be done was to
translate the canonical books.   This seems to have
been the joint work of Chinese who had acquired a
knowledge of Sanskrit during their travels in India,
and of Hindus who settled in Chinese monasteries in
order to assist the native translators.   The translation of books which profess to contain a new religious
doctrine is under all circumstances a task of great
difficulty.   It was so particularly when the subtle
abstractions of the Buddhist religion had to be
clothed in the solid, matter-of-fact idiom of the
Chinese.   But there was another difficulty which it
seemed almost impossible to overcome.   Many words,
not only proper names, but the technical terms also
of the Buddhist creed, had to be preserved in Chinese.
They were not to be translated, but to be trans-
literated.   But how was this to be effected with a
language which, like Chinese, had no phonetic alphabet ?   Every Chinese character is a word; it has
both sound and meaning; and it is unfit, therefore,
for the representation of the sound of foreign words.
In modern times, certain characters have been set
apart for the purpose of writing the proper names
and titles of foreigners; but such is the peculiar
nature of the Chinese system of writing, that even
with this alphabet it is only possible to represent
approximatively the pronunciation of foreign words.
In the absence, however, of even such an alphabet,
the translators of the Buddhist literature seem to
have used their own discretion—or rather indiscre-
tion—in appropriating, without any system, what-

ever Chinese characters seemed to them to come
nearest to the sound of Sanskrit words. Now the
whole Chinese language consists in reality of about
four hundred words, or significative sounds, all
monosyllabic. Each of these monosyllabic sounds
embraces a large number of various meanings, and
each of these various meanings is represented by its
own sign. Thus it has happened that the Chinese
Dictionary contains 43,496 signs, whereas the Chinese
language commands only four hundred distinct utter-
ances. Instead of being restricted, therefore, to one
character which always expresses the same sound,
the Buddhist translators were at liberty to express
one and the same sound in a hundred different ways.
Of this freedom they availed themselves to the
fullest extent. Each translator, each monastery,
fixed on its own characters for representing the pronunciation of Sanskrit words. There are more than
twelve hundred Chinese characters employed by
various writers in order to represent the forty-two
simple letters of the Sanskrit alphabet. The result
has been that even the Chinese were after a time
unable to read—i. e. to pronounce—these random
transliterations. What, then, was to be expected
from Chinese scholars in Europe? Fortunately, the
Chinese, to save themselves from their own per-
plexities, had some lists drawn up, exhibiting the
principles followed by the various translators in
representing the proper names, the names of places,
and the technical terms of philosophy and religion
which they had borrowed from the Sanskrit. With
the help of these lists, and after sixteen years conse-
crated to the study of the Chinese translations of
Sanskrit works and of other original compositions

of Buddhist authors, M. Julien at last caught up the
thread that was to lead him through this labyrinth;
and by means of his knowledge of Sanskrit, which
he acquired solely for that purpose, he is now able to
do what not even the most learned among the Buddhists in China could accomplish—he is able to
restore the exact form and meaning of every word
transferred from Sanskrit into the Buddhist literature
of China.

Without this laborious process, which would have
tired out the patience and deadened the enthusiasm
of most scholars, the treasures of the Buddhist literature preserved in Chinese were really useless. Abel
Rémusat, who during his lifetime was considered the
first Chinese scholar in Europe, attempted indeed
a translation of the travels of Fahian, a Buddhist
pilgrim, who visited India about the end of the
fourth century after Christ. It was in many respects
a most valuable work, but the hopelessness of re-
ducing the uncouth Chinese terms to their Sanskrit
originals made it most tantalising to look through
its pages. Who was to guess that Ho-kia-lo was
meant for the Sanskrit Vyâkarana, in the sense of
sermons; Po-to for the Sanskrit Avadâna, para-
bles; Kia-ye-i for the Sanskrit Kâsyapîyas, the
followers of Kâsyapa? In some instances, Abel
Rémusat, assisted by Chézy, guessed rightly; and
later Sanskrit scholars, such as Burnouf, Lassen, and
Wilson, succeeded in re-establishing, with more or
less certainty, the original form of a number of
Sanskrit words, in spite of their Chinese disguises.
Still there was no system, and therefore no certainty,
in these guesses, and many erroneous conclusions
were drawn from fragmentary translations of Chinese

writers on Buddhism, which even now are not yet entirely eliminated from the works of Oriental scholars. With M. Julien's method, mathematical certainty seems to have taken the place of learned conjectures; and whatever is to be learnt from the Chinese on the origin, the history, and the true character of Buddha's doctrine may now be had in an authentic and unambiguous form.

But even after the principal difficulties have been cleared away through the perseverance of M. Stanislas Julien, and after we have been allowed to reap the fruits of his labours in his masterly translation of the 'Voyages des Pèlerins Bouddhistes,' there still remains one point that requires some elucidation. How was it that the Chinese, whose ears no doubt are of the same construction as our own, should have made such sad work of the Sanskrit names which they transcribed with their own alphabet? Much may be explained by the defects of their language. Such common sounds as v, g, r, b, d, and short a, are unknown in Chinese as initials; no compound consonants are allowed, every consonant being followed by a vowel; and the final letters are limited to a very small number. This, no doubt, explains, to a great extent, the distorted appearance of many Sanskrit words when written in Chinese. Thus, Buddha could only be written Fo to. There was no sign for an initial b, nor was it possible to represent a double consonant, such as ddh. Fo to was the nearest approach to Buddha of which Chinese, when written, was capable. But was it so in speaking? Was it really impossible for Fahian and Hiouen-thsang, who had spent so many years in India, and who were acquainted with all the intricacies of Sanskrit grammar to distinguish between the sounds of Buddha and Fo to? We cannot believe this. We are convinced that Hiouen-thsang, though he wrote, and could not but write, Fo to with the Chinese characters, pronounced Buddha just as we pronounce it, and that it was only among the unlearned that Fo to became at last the recognised name of the founder of Buddhism, abbreviated even to the monosyllabic Fo, which is now the most current appellation of 'the Enlightened.' In the same manner the Chinese pilgrims wrote Niepan, but they pronounced Nirvâna; they wrote Fan-lon-mo, and pronounced Brahma.

Nor is it necessary that we should throw all the blame of these distortions on the Chinese. On the contrary, it is almost certain that some of the discrepancies between the Sanskrit of their translations and the classical Sanskrit of Pânini were due to the corruption which, at the time when Buddhism arose, and still more at the time when Buddhism spread to China, had crept into the spoken language of India. Sanskrit had ceased to be the spoken language of the people previous to the time of Asoka. The edicts which are still preserved on the rocks of Dhauli, Girnar, and Kapurdigiri are written in a dialect which stands to Sanskrit in the same relation as Italian to Latin. Now it is true, no doubt, that the canonical books of the Buddhists are written in a tolerably correct Sanskrit, very different from the Italianised dialect of Asoka. But that Sanskrit was, like the Greek of Alexandria, like the Latin of Hungary, a learned idiom, written by the learned for the learned; it was no longer the living speech of India. Now it is curious that in many of the

canonical Buddhist works which we still possess,
the text which is written in Sanskrit prose is from
time to time interrupted by poetical portions, called
Gâthâs or ballads, in which the same things are
told in verse which had before been related in prose.
The dialect of these songs or ballads is full of what
grammarians would call irregularities, that is to say,
full of those changes which every language under-
goes in the mouths of the people. In character these
corruptions are the same as those which have been
observed in the inscriptions of Asoka, and which
afterwards appear in Pâli and the modern Prâkrit
dialects of India. Various conjectures have been
started to explain the amalgamation of the correct
prose text and the free and easy poetical version of
the same events, as embodied in the sacred literature
of the Buddhists. Burnouf, the first who instituted
a critical inquiry into the history and literature of
Buddhism, supposed that there was, besides the
canon fixed by the three convocations, another digest
of Buddhist doctrines composed in the popular style,
which may have developed itself, as he says, subsequently to the preaching of Sâkya, and which would
thus be intermediate between the regular Sanskrit
and the Pâli. He afterwards, however, inclines to
another view—namely, that these Gâthâs were written out of India by men to whom Sanskrit was no
longer familiar, and who endeavoured to write in the
·learned language, which they ill understood, with
the freedom which is imparted by the habitual use of
a popular but imperfectly determined dialect. Other
Sanskrit scholars have proposed other solutions of
this strange mixture of correct prose and incorrect
poetry in the Buddhist literature; but none of them

was satisfactory. The problem seems to have been solved at last by a native scholar, Babu Rajendralal, a curious instance of the reaction of European antiquarian research on the native mind of India. Babu Rajendralal reads Sanskrit of course with the greatest ease. He is a pandit by profession, but he is at the same time a scholar and critic in our sense of the word. He has edited Sanskrit texts after a careful collation of MSS., and in his various contributions to the 'Journal of the Asiatic Society of Bengal,' he has proved himself completely above the prejudices of his class, freed from the erroneous views on the history and literature of India in which every Brahman is brought up. and thoroughly imbued with those principles of criticism which men like Colebrooke, Lassen, and Burnouf have followed in their researches into the literary treasures of his country. His English is remarkably clear and simple, and his arguments would do credit to any Sanskrit scholar in England. We quote from his remarks on Burnouf's account of the Gâthâs, as given in that scholar's 'Histoire du Buddhisme Indien :'

'Burnouf's opinion on the origin of the Gâthâs, we venture to think, is founded on a mistaken estimate of Sanskrit style. The poetry of the Gâthâ has much artistic elegance which at once indicates that it is not the composition of men who were ignorant of the first principles of grammar. The authors display a great deal of learning, and discuss the subtlest questions of logic and metaphysics with much tact and ability, and it is difficult to conceive that men who were perfectly familiar with the most intricate forms of Sanskrit logic, who have expressed the most abstruse metaphysical ideas in precise and often in beautiful language, who composed with ease and elegance in Árya, Toṭaka, and other difficult measures, were unacquainted with the rudiments of the language in which they wrote, and were unable to conjugate the verb to be in all its forms. . . . The more reasonable conjecture appears to be that the Gâthâ is the production of bards who were contemporaries or immediate successors of Ṡâkya, who recounted to the devout congregations of the prophet of Magadha, the sayings and doings of their great teacher in popular and easy flowing verses, which in course of time came to be regarded as the most authentic source of all information connected with the founder of Buddhism. The high estimation in which the ballads and improvisations of bards are held in India and particularly in the Buddhist writings, favours this supposition; and the circumstance that the poetical portions are generally introduced in corroboration of the narration of the prose, with the words, "Thereof this may be said," affords a strong presumptive evidence.'

Now this, from the pen of a native scholar, is truly remarkable. The spirit of Niebuhr seems to have reached the shores of India, and this ballad theory comes out more successfully in the history of Buddha than in the history of Romulus. The absence of anything like cant in the mouth of a Brahman speaking of Buddhism, the *bête noire* of all orthodox Brahmans, is highly satisfactory, and our Sanskrit scholars in Europe will have to pull hard if, with such men as Babu Rajendralal in the field, they are not to be distanced in the race of scholarship.

We believe, then, that Babu Rajendralal is right, and we look upon the dialect of the Gâthâs as a specimen of the Sanskrit spoken by the followers of Buddha about the time of Asoka and later. And this will help us to understand some of the peculiar changes which the Sanskrit of the Chinese Buddhists must have undergone, even before it was disguised in the strange dress of the Chinese alphabet. The Chinese pilgrims did not hear the Sanskrit pronounced as it was pronounced in the Parishads according to the strict rules of their Sîkshâ or phonetics. They heard it as it was spoken in Buddhist monasteries, as it was sung in the Gâthâs of Buddhist minstrels, as it was preached in the Vyâkaraṇas or sermons of Buddhist friars. For instance. In the Gâthâs a short a is frequently lengthened. We find nâ instead of na, 'no.' The same occurs in the Sanskrit of the Chinese Buddhists. (See Julien, 'Méthode,' p. 18; p. 21.) We find there also vistâra instead of vistara, &c. In the dialect of the Gâthâs nouns ending in consonants, and therefore irregular, are transferred to the easier declension in a. The same process takes place in modern Greek and in the transition of Latin into Italian; it is, in fact, a general tendency of all languages which are carried on by the stream of living speech. Now this transition from one declension to another had taken place before the Chinese had appropriated the Sanskrit of the Buddhist books. The Sanskrit nabhas becomes nabha in the Gâthâs; locative nabhe, instead of nabhasi. If, therefore, we find in Chinese lo-che for the Sanskrit ragas, dust, we may ascribe the change of r into l to the inability of the Chinese to pronounce or to write an r. We may admit that the Chinese alphabet offered nothing nearer to the sound of ga than tche; but the dropping of the

final s has no excuse in Chinese, and finds its real
explanation in the nature of the Gâthâ dialect. Thus
the Chinese Fan-lun-mo does not represent the
correct Sanskrit Brahman, but the vulgar form
Brahma. The Chinese so-po for sarva, all, tho-
mo for dharma, law, find no explanation in the
dialect of the Gâthâs, but the suppression of the r
before v and m, is of frequent occurrence in the
inscriptions of Asoka. The omission of the initial s
in words like sthâna, place, sthavira, an elder, is
likewise founded on the rules of Pâli and Prâkrit,
and need not be placed to the account of the Chinese
translators. In the inscription of Girnar sthavira
is even reduced to thaira. The s of the nominative
is frequently dropped in the dialect of the Gâthâs, or
changed into o. Hence we might venture to doubt
whether it is necessary to give to the character 1780
of M. Julien's list, which generally has the value of
ta, a second value sta. This s is only wanted to
supply the final s of k a s, the interrogative pronoun,
in such a sentence as k a s tadguna*h*? what is the
use of this? Now here we are inclined to believe
that the final s of kas had long disappeared in the
popular language of India, before the Chinese came
to listen to the strange sounds and doctrines of the
disciples of Buddha. They probably heard ka tadguna, or ka tagguna, and this they represented as
best they could by the Chinese kia-to-kieou-na.

With these few suggestions we leave the work of
M. Stanislas Julien. It is in reality a work done
once for all—one huge stone and stumbling-block
effectually rolled away which for years had barred
the approach to some most valuable documents of the
history of the East. Now that the way is clear, let

us hope that others will follow, and that we shall soon have complete and correct translations of the travels of Fahian and other Buddhist pilgrims whose works are like so many Murray's 'Handbooks of India,' giving us an insight into the social, political, and religious state of that country at a time when we look in vain for any other historical documents.

March, 1861.

XIII.

THE WORKS OF CONFUCIUS[1].

IN reviewing the works of missionaries, we have repeatedly dwelt on the opportunities of scientific usefulness which are open to the messengers of the Gospel in every part of the world. We are not afraid of the common objection that missionaries ought to devote their whole time and powers to the one purpose for which they are sent out and paid by our societies. Missionaries cannot always be engaged in teaching, preaching, converting, and baptising the heathen. A missionary, like every other human creature, ought to have his leisure hours; and if those leisure hours are devoted to scientific pursuits, to the study of the languages or the literature of the people among whom he lives, to a careful description of the scenery and antiquities of the country, the manners, laws, and customs of its inhabitants, their legends, their national poetry, or popular stories, or again, to the cultivation of any branch of natural science, he may rest assured that he is not neglecting the sacred trust which he accepted, but is only bracing and invigorating his mind, and keeping it

---

[1] 'The Chinese Classics;' with a Translation, Critical and Exegetical Notes. By James Legge, D.D., of the London Missionary Society. Hong Kong, 1861.

from that stagnation which is the inevitable result
of a too monotonous employment. The staff of
missionaries which is spread over the whole globe
supplies the most perfect machinery that could be
devised for the collection of all kinds of scientific
knowledge. They ought to be the pioneers of science.
They should not only take out — they should also
bring something home; and there is nothing more
likely to increase and strengthen the support on
which our missionary societies depend, nothing more
sure to raise the intellectual standard of the men
selected for missionary labour, than a formal recognition of this additional duty. There may be exceptional cases where missionaries are wanted for
constant toil among natives ready to be instructed,
and anxious to be received as members of a Christian
community. But, as a general rule, the missionary
abroad has more leisure than a clergyman at home,
and time sits heavy on the hands of many whose congregations consist of no more than ten or twenty souls.
It is hardly necessary to argue this point, when we
can appeal to so many facts. The most successful
missionaries have been exactly those whose names are
remembered with gratitude, not only by the natives
among whom they laboured, but also by the savants
of Europe; and the labours of the Jesuit missionaries
in India and China, of the Baptist missionaries at
Serampore, of Gogerly and Spence Hardy in Ceylon,
of Caldwell in Tinnevelly, of Wilson in Bombay, of
Moffat, Krapf, and last, but not least, of Livingstone,
will live not only in the journals of our academies, but
likewise in the annals of the missionary Church.

The first volume of an edition of the Chinese
Classics, which we have just received from the

Rev. Dr. J. Legge, of the London Missionary Society, is
a new proof of what can be achieved by missionaries, if
encouraged to devote part of their time and attention
to scientific and literary pursuits. We do not care
to inquire whether Dr. Legge has been successful as
a missionary. Even if he had not converted a single
Chinese, he would, after completing the work which
he has just begun, have rendered most important
aid to the introduction of Christianity into China.
He arrived in the East towards the end of 1839,
having received only a few months' instruction in
Chinese from Professor Kidd in London. Being
stationed at Malacca, it seemed to him then—and he
adds 'that the experience of twenty-one years has
given its sanction to the correctness of the judgment'
—that he could not consider himself qualified for
the duties of his position until he had thoroughly
mastered the classical books of the Chinese, and
investigated for himself the whole field of thought
through which the sages of China had ranged, and
in which were to be found the foundations of the
moral, social, and political life of the people. He
was not able to pursue his studies without interruption, and it was only after some years, when the
charge of the Anglo-Chinese College had devolved
upon him, that he could procure the books necessary
to facilitate his progress. After sixteen years of assi-
duous study, Dr. Legge had explored the principal
works of Chinese literature; and he then felt that
he could render the course of reading through which
he had passed more easy to those who were to follow
after him, by publishing, on the model of our editions
of the Greek and Roman Classics, a critical text of
the Classics of China, together with a translation and

x 2

explanatory notes. His materials were ready, but there was the difficulty of finding the funds necessary for so costly an undertaking. Scarcely, however, had Dr. Legge's wants become known among the British and other foreign merchants in China, than one of them, Mr. Joseph Jardine, sent for the Doctor, and said to him, 'I know the liberality of the merchants in China, and that many of them would readily give their help to such an undertaking; but you need not have the trouble of canvassing the community. If you are prepared to undertake the toil of the publication, I will bear the expense of it. We make our money in China, and we should be glad to assist in whatever promises to be a benefit to it.' The result of this combination of disinterested devotion on the part of the author, and enlightened liberality on the part of his patron, lies now before us in a splendid volume of text, translation, and commentary, which, if the life of the editor is spared (and the sudden death of Mr. Jardine from the effects of the climate is a warning how busily death is at work among the European settlers in those regions), will be followed by at least six other volumes.

The edition is to comprise the books now recognised as of highest authority by the Chinese themselves. These are the five King's and the four Shoo's. King means the warp threads of a web, and its application to literary compositions rests on the same metaphor as the Latin word textus, and the Sanskrit Sûtra, meaning a yarn, and a book. Shoo simply means writings. The five King's are, 1. the Yih, or the Book of Changes; 2. the Shoo, or the Book of History; 3. the She, or the Book of Poetry; 4. the Le Ke, or Record of Rites; and 5. the Chun

Tsew, or Spring and Autumn; a chronicle extending from 721 to 480 B.C. The four Shoo's consist
of, 1. the Lun Yu, or Digested Conversations between
Confucius and his disciples; 2. Ta Hëo, or Great
Learning, commonly attributed to one of his disciples;
3. the Chung Yung, or Doctrine of the Mean, ascribed
to the grandson of Confucius; 4. of the works of
Mencius, who died 288 B.C.

The authorship of the five King's is loosely attributed to Confucius; but it is only the fifth, or 'the
Spring and Autumn,' which can be claimed as the
work of the philosopher. The Yih, the Shoo, and
the She King were not composed, but only compiled
by him, and much of the Le Ke is clearly from later
hands. Confucius, though the founder of a religion
and a reformer, was thoroughly conservative in his
tendencies, and devotedly attached to the past. He
calls himself a transmitter, not a maker, believing in
and loving the ancients (p. 59). 'I am not one who
was born in the possession of knowledge,' he says,
'I am one who is fond of antiquity, and earnest in
seeking it there' (p. 65). The most frequent themes
of his discourses were the ancient songs, the history,
and the rules of propriety established by ancient
sages (p. 64). When one of his contemporaries
wished to do away with the offering of a lamb as a
meaningless formality, Confucius reproved him with
the pithy sentence, 'You love the sheep, I love the
ceremony.' There were four things, we are told,
which Confucius taught—letters, ethics, devotion of
soul, and truthfulness (p. 66). When speaking of
himself, he said, 'At fifteen, I had my mind bent on
learning. At thirty, I stood firm. At forty, I had
no doubt. At fifty, I knew the decrees of heaven.

At sixty, my ear was an obedient organ for the reception of truth. At seventy, I could follow what
my heart desired, without transgressing what was
right' (p. 10). Though this may sound like boast-
ing, it is remarkable how seldom Confucius himself
claims any superiority above his fellow-creatures.
He offers his advice to those who are willing to
listen, but he never speaks dogmatically; he never
attempts to tyrannize over the minds or hearts of his
friends. If we read his biography, we can hardly
understand how a man whose life was devoted to
such tranquil pursuits, and whose death scarcely produced a ripple on the smooth and silent surface of
the Eastern world, could have left the impress of his
mind on millions and millions of human beings—an
impress which even now, after 2339 years, is clearly
discernible in the national character of the largest
empire of the world. Confucius died in 478 B.C.,
complaining that of all the princes of the empire
there was not one who would adopt his principles
and obey his lessons. After two generations, however, his name had risen to be a power—the rallying
point of a vast movement of national and religious
regeneration. His grandson speaks of him as the
ideal of a sage, as the sage is the ideal of humanity
at large. Though Tze-tze claims no divine honour for
his grandsire, he exalts his wisdom and virtue beyond
the limits of human nature. This is a specimen of
the language which he applies to Confucius:

'He may be compared to heaven and earth in their
supporting and containing, their overshadowing and
curtaining all things; he may be compared to the
four seasons in their alternating progress, and to
the sun and moon in their successive shining. . . .

Quick in apprehension, clear in discernment, of far-reaching intellect and all-embracing knowledge, he was fitted to exercise rule; magnanimous, generous, benign, and mild, he was fitted to exercise forbearance; impulsive, energetic, firm, and enduring, he was fitted to maintain a firm hold; self-adjusted, grave, never swerving from the Mean, and correct, he was fitted to command reverence; accomplished, distinctive, concentrative, and searching, he was fitted to exercise discrimination. . . . All-embracing and vast, he was like heaven; deep and active as a fountain, he was like the abyss. . . . Therefore his fame overspreads the Middle Kingdom and extends to all barbarous tribes. Wherever ships and carriages reach, wherever the strength of man penetrates, wherever the heavens overshadow and the earth sustains, wherever the sun and moon shine, wherever frost and dews fall, all who have blood and breath unfeignedly honour and love him. Hence it is said—He is the equal of Heaven' (p. 53).

This is certainly very magnificent phraseology, but it will hardly convey any definite impression to the minds of those who are not acquainted with the life and teaching of the great Chinese sage. These may be studied now by all who can care for the history of human thought, in the excellent work of Dr. Legge. The first volume, just published, contains the Confucian Analects, the Great Learning, and the Doctrine of the Mean, or the First, Second, and Third Shoo's, and will, we hope, soon be followed by the other Chinese Classics[2]. We must here

---

[2] Dr. Legge has since published: vol. ii. containing the works of Mencius; vol. iii. part 1. containing the first part of the Shoo King; vol. iii. part 2. containing the fifth part of the Shoo King.

confine ourselves to giving a few of the sage's sayings, selected from thousands that are to be found
in the Confucian Analects.   Their interest is chiefly
historical, as throwing light on the character of one
of the most remarkable men in the history of the
human race.   But there is besides this a charm in the
simple enunciation of simple truths; and such is the
fear of truism in our modern writers that we must go
to distant times and distant countries if we wish to
listen to that simple Solomonic wisdom which is better
than the merchandize of silver and the gain thereof
than fine gold.

Confucius shows his tolerant spirit when he says,
' The superior man is catholic, and no partisan.   The
mean man is a partisan, and not catholic' (p. 14).

There is honest manliness in his saying, ' To see what
is right, and not to do it, is want of courage' (p. 18).

His definition of knowledge, though less profound
than that of Socrates, is nevertheless full of good
sense :

' The Master said, " Shall I teach you what knowledge is?   When you know a thing, to hold that you
know it; and when you do not know a thing, to
sllow that you do not know it—this is knowledge" '
(p. 15).

Nor was Confucius unacquainted with the secrets
of the heart: ' It is only the truly virtuous man,'
he says in one place, ' who can love or who can hate
others' (p. 30).   In another place he expresses his
belief in the irresistible charm of virtue: ' Virtue is
not left to stand alone,' he says; ' he who practises
it will have neighbours.'   He bears witness to the
hidden connection between intellectual and moral
excellence : ' It is not easy,' he remarks, ' to find a man

who has learned for three years without coming to be good' (p. 76). In his ethics, the golden rule of the Gospel, ' Do ye unto others as ye would that others should do to you,' is represented as almost unattainable. Thus we read, 'Tsze-Kung said, "What I do not wish men to do to me, I also wish not to do to men." The Master said, " Tsze, you have not attained to that." ' The Brahmans, too, had a distant perception of the same truth, which is expressed, for instance, in the Hitopadesa in the following words: ' Good people show mercy unto all beings, considering how like they are to themselves.' On subjects which transcend the limits of human understanding, Confucius is less explicit; but his very reticence is remarkable, when we consider the recklessness with which Oriental philosophers launch into the deep waters of religious metaphysics. Thus we read (p. 107):

' Ke Loo asked about serving the spirits of the dead. The Master said, " While you are not able to serve men, how can you serve their spirits?"

' Ke Loo added, " I venture to ask about death." He was answered, " While you do not know life, how can you know about death?" '

And again (p. 190):

' The Master said, "I would prefer not speaking."

' Tsze-Kung said, " If you, Master, do not speak, what shall we, your disciples, have to record?"

' The Master said, " Does Heaven speak? The four seasons pursue their courses, and all things are continually being produced; but does Heaven say anything?" '

November, 1861.

XIV.

POPOL VUH.

A BOOK called 'Popol Vuh[1],' and pretending to
be the original text of the sacred writings of the
Indians of Central America, will be received by most
people with a sceptical smile. The Aztec children
who were shown all over Europe as descendants of
a race to whom, before the Spanish conquest, divine
honours were paid by the natives of Mexico, and who
turned out to be unfortunate creatures that had been
tampered with by heartless speculators, are still fresh
in the memory of most people; and the 'Livre des
Sauvages[2],' lately published by the Abbé Domenech,
under the auspices of Count Walewsky, has somewhat lowered the dignity of American studies in
general. Still, those who laugh at the 'Manuscrit
Pictographique Américain' discovered by the French
Abbé in the library of the French Arsénal, and
edited by him with so much care as a precious relic
of the old Red-skins of North America, ought not to

---

[1] 'Popol Vuh:' le Livre Sacré et les Mythes de l'Antiquité
Américaine, avec les Livres Héroïques et Historiques des Quichés.
Par l'Abbé Brasseur de Bourbourg. Paris: Durand, 1861.

[2] 'Manuscrit Pictographique Américain,' précédé d'une Notice
sur l'Idéographie des Peaux-Rouges. Par l'Abbé Em. Domenech.
Ouvrage publié sous les auspices de M. le Ministre d'Etat et de la
Maison de l'Empereur. Paris, 1860.

forget that there would be nothing at all surprising
in the existence of such a MS., containing genuine
pictographic writing of the Red Indians. The German critic of Abbé Domenech, M. Petzholdt[3], assumes
much too triumphant an air in announcing his discovery that the 'Manuscrit Pictographique' was the
work of a German boy in the backwoods of America.
He ought to have acknowledged that the Abbé himself had pointed out the German scrawls on some of
the pages of his MS.; that he had read the names
of Anna and Maria; and that he never claimed any
great antiquity for the book in question. Indeed,
though M. Petzholdt tells us very confidently that
the whole book is the work of a naughty, nasty, and
profane little boy, the son of German settlers in the
backwoods of America, we doubt whether anybody
who takes the trouble to look through all the pages
will consider this view as at all satisfactory, or even
as more probable than that of the French Abbé. We
know what boys are capable of in pictographic art
from the occasional defacements of our walls and
railings; but we still feel a little sceptical when
M. Petzholdt assures us that there is nothing extraordinary in a boy filling a whole volume with these elaborate scrawls. If M. Petzholdt had taken the trouble
to look at some of the barbarous hieroglyphics that
have been collected in North America, he would have
understood more readily how the Abbé Domenech,
who had spent many years among the Red Indians,
and had himself copied several of their inscriptions,

---

[3] 'Das Buch der Wilden im Lichte Französischer Civilisation.'
Mit Proben aus dem in Paris als 'Manuscrit Pictographique Améri-
cain,' veröffentlichten Schmierbuche eines Deutsch-Amerikanischen
Hinterwälder Jungen. Von J. Petzholdt. Dresden, 1861.

should have taken the pages preserved in the library of the Arsénal at Paris as genuine specimens of American pictography. There is a certain similarity between these scrawls and the figures scratched on rocks, tombstones, and trees by the wandering tribes of North America; and though we should be very sorry to endorse the opinion of the enthusiastic Abbé, or to start any conjecture of our own as to the real authorship of the 'Livre des Sauvages,' we cannot but think that M. Petzholdt would have written less confidently, and certainly less scornfully, if he had been more familiar than he seems to be with the little that is known of the picture-writing of the Indian tribes. As a preliminary to the question of the authenticity of the 'Popol Vuh,' a few words on the pictorial literature of the Red Indians of North America will not be considered out of place. The 'Popol Vuh' is not indeed a 'Livre des Sauvages,' but a literary composition in the true sense of the word. It contains the mythology and history of the civilised races of Central America, and comes before us with credentials that will bear the test of critical inquiry. But we shall be better able to appreciate the higher achievements of the South after we have examined, however cursorily, the rude beginnings in literature among the savage races of the North.

Colden, in his 'History of the Five Nations,' informs us that when, in 1696, the Count de Frontenac marched a well-appointed army into the Iroquois country, with artillery and all other means of regular military offence, he found, on the banks of the Onondaga, now called Oswego River, a tree, on the trunk of which the Indians had depicted the French army, and deposited two bundles of cut rushes at its foot, consisting of 1434 pieces; an act of symbolical defiance on their part, which was intended to warn their Gallic invaders that they would have to encounter this number of warriors.

This warlike message is a specimen of Indian picture-writing. It belongs to the lowest stage of graphic representation, and hardly differs from the primitive way in which the Persian ambassadors communicated with the Greeks, or the Romans with the Carthaginians. Instead of the lance and the staff of peace between which the Carthaginians were asked to choose, the Red Indians would have sent an arrow and a pipe, and the message would have been equally understood. This, though not yet *peindre la parole*, is nevertheless a first attempt at *parler aux yeux*. It is a first beginning which may lead to something more perfect in the end. We find similar attempts at pictorial communication among other savage tribes, and they seem to answer every purpose. In Freycinet and Arago's 'Voyage to the Eastern Ocean' we are told of a native of the Carolina Islands, a Tamor of Sathoual, who wished to avail himself of the presence of a ship to send to a trader at Botta, M. Martinez, some shells which he had promised to collect in exchange for a few axes and some other articles. He expressed to the captain, who gave him a piece of paper to make the drawing, and satisfactorily executed the commission. The figure of a man at the top denoted the ship's captain, who by his outstretched hands represented his office as a messenger between the parties. The rays or ornaments on his head denote rank or authority. The vine beneath him is a type of friendship. In the left column are depicted the number and kinds of shells

sent; in the right column the things wished for in
exchange—namely, seven fish-hooks, three large and
four small, two axes, and two pieces of iron.

The inscriptions which are found on the Indian
graveboards mark a step in advance. Every warrior
has his crest, which is called his totem, and is
painted on his tombstone. A celebrated war-chief,
the Adjetatig of Wabojceg, died on Lake Superior,
about 1793. He was of the clan of the Addik, or
American reindeer. The fact is symbolized by the
figure of the deer. The reversed position denotes
death. His own personal name, which was White
Fisher, is not noticed. But there are seven transverse strokes on the left, and these have a meaning—
namely, that he had led seven war parties. Then
there are three perpendicular lines below his crest,
and these again are readily understood by every
Indian. They represent the wounds received in
battle. The figure of a moose's head is said to relate
to a desperate conflict with an enraged animal of this
kind; and the symbols of the arrow and the pipe
are drawn to indicate the chief's influence in war and
peace.

There is another graveboard of the ruling chief
of Sandy Lake on the Upper Mississippi. Here the
reversed bird denotes his family name or clan, the
Crane. Four transverse lines above it denote that
he had killed four of his enemies in battle. An
analogous custom is mentioned by Aristotle ('Poli-
tica,' vii. 2, p. 220, ed. Göttling). Speaking of the
Iberians, he states that they placed as many obelisks
round the grave of a warrior as he had killed enemies
in battle.

But the Indians went further; and though they

never arrived at the perfection of the Egyptian hieroglyphics, they had a number of symbolic emblems which were perfectly understood by all their tribes. Eating is represented by a man's hand lifted to his mouth. Power over man is symbolized by a line drawn in the figure from the mouth to the heart; power in general by a head with two horns. A circle drawn around the body at the abdomen denotes full means of subsistence. A boy drawn with waved lines from each ear and lines leading to the heart represents a pupil. A figure with a plant as head, and two wings, denotes a doctor skilled in medicine, and endowed with the power of ubiquity. A tree with human legs, a herbalist or professor of botany. Night is represented by a finely crossed or barred sun, or a circle with human legs. Rain is figured by a dot or semicircle filled with water and placed on the head. The heaven with three disks of the sun is understood to mean three days' journey, and a landing after a voyage is represented by a tortoise. Short sentences, too, can be pictured in this manner. A prescription ordering abstinence from food for two, and rest for four, days is written by drawing a man with two bars on the stomach and four across the legs. We are told even of war-songs and love songs composed in this primitive alphabet; but it would seem as if, in these cases, the reader required even greater poetical imagination than the writer. There is one war-song consisting of four pictures—

1. The sun rising.

2. A figure pointing with one hand to the earth and the other extended to the sky.

3. The moon with two human legs.

4. A figure personifying the Eastern woman, i. e. the evening star.

These four symbols are said to convey to the Indian the following meaning:

> I am rising to seek the war path ;
> The earth and the sky are before me;
> I walk by day and by night;
> And the evening star is my guide.

The following is a specimen of a love song:

1. Figure representing a god (monedo) endowed with magic power.

2. Figure beating the drum and singing; lines from his mouth.

3. Figure surrounded by a secret lodge.

4. Two bodies joined with one continuous arm.

5. A woman on an island.

6. A woman asleep; lines from his ear towards her.

7. A red heart in a circle.

This poem is intended to express these sentiments:

1. It is my form and person that make me great—

2. Hear the voice of my song, it is my voice.

3. I shield myself with secret coverings.

4. All your thoughts are known to me, blush!

5. I could draw you hence were you ever so far—

6. Though you were on the other hemisphere—

7. I speak to your naked heart.

All we can say is, that if the Indians can read this writing, they are greater adepts in the mysteries of love than the judges of the old *Cours d'amour.* But it is much more likely that these war-songs and love-songs are known to the people beforehand, and that their writings are only meant to revive what exists in the memory of the reader. It is a kind of

mnemonic writing, and it has been used by missionaries for similar purposes, and with considerable success.   Thus, in a translation of the Bible in the Massa-
chusetts language by Eliot, the verses from 25 to 32
in the thirtieth chapter of Proverbs, are expressed by
'an ant, a coney, a locust, a spider, a river (symbol of
motion), a lion, a greyhound, a he-goat and king, a
man foolishly lifting himself to take hold of the
heavens.'   No doubt these symbols would help the
reader to remember the proper order of the verses, but
they would be perfectly useless without a commentary
or without a previous knowledge of the text.

We are told that the famous Testéra, brother of the
chamberlain of François I., who came to America eight
or nine years after the taking of Mexico, finding it
impossible to learn the language of the natives, taught
them the Bible history and the principal doctrines of
the Christian religion, by means of pictures, and that
these diagrams produced a greater effect on the minds
of the people, who were accustomed to this style of
representation, than all other means employed by the
missionaries.   But here again, unless these pictures
were explained by interpreters, they could by themselves convey no meaning to the gazing crowds of
the natives.   The fullest information on this subject
is to be found in a work by T. Baptiste, 'Hiéro-
glyphes de la conversion, où par des estampes et des
figures on apprend aux naturels à desirer le ciel.'

There is no evidence to show that the Indians of
the North ever advanced beyond the rude attempts
which we have thus described, and of which numerous
specimens may be found in the voluminous work of
Schoolcraft, published by authority of Congress, ' Historical and Statistical Information respecting the

History, Condition, and Prospects of the Indian Tribes
of the United States,' Philadelphia, 1851–1855. There
is no trace of anything like literature among the
wandering tribes of the North, and until a real ' Livre
des Sauvages' turns up to fill this gap, they must
continue to be classed among the illiterate races[4].

It is very different if we turn our eyes to the
people of Central and South America, to the races
who formed the population of Mexico, Guatemala,
and Peru, when conquered by the Spaniards. The
Mexican hieroglyphics published by Lord Kings-
borough are not to be placed in the same category
with the totems and the pictorial scratches of the
Red-skins. They are, first of all, of a much more
artistic character, more conventional in their structure, and hence more definite in their meaning. They
are coloured, written on paper, and in many respects
quite on a level with the hieroglyphic inscriptions
and hieratic papyri of Egypt. Even the conception
of speaking to the ear through the eye, of expressing sound by means of outlines, was familiar to the
Mexicans, though they seem to have applied their
phonetic signs to the writing of the names of places
and persons only. The principal object, indeed, of
the Mexican hieroglyphic manuscripts was not to
convey new information, but rather to remind the
reader by means of mnemonic artifices of what he
had learnt beforehand. This is acknowledged by
the best authorities, by men who knew the Indians
shortly after their first intercourse with Europeans,
and whom we may safely trust in what they tell us
of the oral literature and hieroglyphic writings of

---

[4] ' Manuscrit Pictographique,' pp. 26, 29.

the natives.   Acosta, in his ' Historia natural y moral,
vi. 7, tells us that the Indians were still in the habit
of reciting from memory the addresses and speeches
of their ancient orators, and numerous songs composed by their national poets.   As it was impossible
to acquire these by means of hieroglyphics or written
characters such as were used by the Mexicans, care
was taken that those speeches and poems should be
learnt by heart.   There were colleges and schools
for that purpose, where these and other things were
taught to the young by the aged in whose memory
they seemed to be engraved.   The young men who
were brought up to be orators themselves had to
learn the ancient compositions word by word; and
when the Spaniards came and taught them to read
and write the Spanish language, the Indians soon
began to write for themselves, a fact attested by
many eye-witnesses.

Las Casas, the devoted friend of the Indians, writes
as follows:

'It ought to be known that in all the republics of
this country, in the kingdoms of New Spain and
elsewhere, there was amongst other professions, that
of the chroniclers and historians.   They possessed a
knowledge of the earliest times, and of all things
concerning religion, the gods, and their worship.   They
knew the founders of cities, and the early history of
their kings and kingdoms.   They knew the modes of
election and the right of succession; they could tell
the number and characters of their ancient kings,
their works, and memorable achievements whether
good or bad, and whether they had governed well or
ill.   They knew the men renowned for virtue and
heroism in former days, what wars they had waged,

and how they had distinguished themselves; who
had been the earliest settlers, what had been their
ancient customs, their triumphs and defeats.   They
knew, in fact, whatever belonged to history; and
were able to give an account of all the events of the
past. . . . These chroniclers had likewise to calculate
the days, months, and years; and though they had
no writing like our own, they had their symbols and
characters through which they understood everything; they had their great books, which were composed with such ingenuity and art that our alphabet
was really of no great assistance to them. . . . Our
priests have seen those books, and I myself have
seen them likewise, though many were burnt at the
instigation of the monks, who were afraid that they
might impede the work of conversion.   Sometimes
when the Indians who had been converted had forgotten certain words, or particular points of the
Christian doctrine, they began—as they were unable
to read our books—to write very ingeniously with
their own symbols and characters, drawing the figures
which corresponded either to the ideas or to the
sounds of our words.   I have myself seen a large ·
portion of the Christian doctrine written in figures
and images, which they read as we read the characters
of a letter; and this is a very extraordinary proof of
their genius. . . . There never was a lack of those
chroniclers.   It was a profession which passed from
father to son, highly respected in the whole republic;
each historian instructed two or three of his relatives.
He made them practise constantly, and they had
recourse to him whenever a doubt arose on a point
of history. . . . But not these young historians only
went to consult him; kings, princes, and priests came

to ask his advice. Whenever there was a doubt as to ceremonies, precepts of religion, religious festivals, or anything of importance in the history of the ancient kingdoms, every one went to the chroniclers to ask for information.

In spite of the religious zeal of Dominican and Franciscan friars, a few of these hieroglyphic MSS. escaped the flames, and may now be seen in some of our public libraries, as curious relics of a nearly extinct and forgotten literature. The first collection of these MSS. and other American antiquities was due to the zeal of the Milanese antiquarian, Boturini, who had been sent by the Pope in 1736 to regulate some ecclesiastical matters, and who devoted the eight years of his stay in the New World to rescuing whatever could be rescued from the scattered ruins of ancient America. Before, however, he could bring these treasures safe to Europe, he was despoiled of his valuables by the Spanish Viceroy; and when at last he made his escape with the remnants of his collection, he was taken prisoner by an English cruiser, and lost everything. The collection, which remained at Mexico, became the subject of several lawsuits, and after passing through the hands of Veytia and Gama, who both added to it considerably, it was sold at last by public auction. Humboldt, who was at that time passing through Mexico, acquired some of the MSS., which he gave to the Royal Museum at Berlin. Others found their way into private hands, and after many vicissitudes they have mostly been secured by the public libraries or private collectors of Europe. The most valuable part of that unfortunate shipwreck is now in the hands of M. Aubin, who was sent to Mexico in 1830 by the French Government, and who devoted nearly twenty years to the same work which Boturini had commenced a hundred years before. He either bought the dispersed fragments of the collections of Boturini, Gama, and Pichardo, or procured accurate copies; and he has brought to Europe, what is, if not the most complete, at least the most valuable and most judiciously arranged collection of American antiquities. We likewise owe to M. Aubin the first accurate knowledge of the real nature of the ancient Mexican writing; and we look forward with confident hope to his still achieving in his own field as great a triumph as that of Champollion, the decipherer of the hieroglyphics of Egypt.

One of the most important helps towards the deciphering of the hieroglyphic MSS. of the Americans is to be found in certain books which, soon after the conquest of Mexico, were written down by natives who had learnt the art of alphabetic writing from their conquerors, the Spaniards. Ixtlilxochitl, descended from the royal family of Tetzcuco, and employed as interpreter by the Spanish Government, wrote the history of his own country from the earliest time to the arrival of Cortez. In writing this history he followed the hieroglyphic paintings as they had been explained to him by the old chroniclers. Some of these very paintings, which formed the text-book of the Mexican historian, have been recovered by M. Aubin; and as they helped the historian in writing his history, that history now helps the scholar in deciphering their meaning. It is with the study of works like that of Ixtlilxochitl that American philology ought to begin. They are to the student of American antiquities what Manetho is to the student of Egyptian hieroglyphics, or Berosus to the decipherer of the cuneiform inscriptions. They are written in dialects not more than three hundred years old, and still spoken by large numbers of natives, with such modifications as three centuries are certain to produce. They give us whatever was known of history, mythology, and religion among the people whom the Spaniards found in Central and South America in the possession of most of the advantages of a long-established civilisation. Though we must not expect to find in them what we are accustomed to call history, they are nevertheless of great historical interest, as supplying the vague out-lines of a distant past, filled with migrations, wars, dynasties, and revolutions, such as were cherished in the memory of the Greeks at the time of Solon, and believed in by the Romans at the time of Cato. They teach us that the New World which was opened to Europe a few centuries ago, was in its own eyes an old world, not so different in character and feelings from ourselves as we are apt to imagine when we speak of the Red-skins of America, or when we read the accounts of the Spanish conquerors, who denied that the natives of America possessed human souls, in order to establish their own right of treating them like wild beasts.

The 'Popol Vuh,' or the sacred book of the people of Guatemala, of which the Abbé Brasseur de Bour-bourg has just published the original text, together with a literal French Translation, holds a very pro-minent rank among the works composed by natives in their own native dialects, and written down by them with the letters of the Roman alphabet. There are but two works that can be compared to it in

their importance to the student of American antiquities and American languages, namely, the 'Codex
Chimalpopoca' in Nahuatl, the ancient written language of Mexico, and the 'Codex Cakchiquel' in the
dialect of Guatemala.   These, together with the work
published by the Abbé Brasseur de Bourbourg under
the title of 'Popol Vuh,' must form the starting-point
of all critical inquiries into the antiquities of the
American people.

The first point which has to be determined with
regard to books of this kind is whether they are
genuine or not; whether they are what they pretend
to be—compositions about three centuries old, founded
on the oral traditions and the pictographic documents
of the ancient inhabitants of America, and written
in the dialects as spoken at the time of Columbus, ·
Cortez, and Pizarro.   What the Abbé Brasseur de
Bourbourg has to say on this point amounts to
this:—The manuscript was first discovered by Father
Francisco Ximenes towards the end of the seventeenth century.   He was curé of Santo-Tomas Chi-
chicastenango, situated about three leagues south of
Santa-Cruz del Quiché, and twenty-two leagues
north-east of Guatemala.   He was well acquainted
with the languages of the natives of Guatemala, and
has left a dictionary of their three principal dialects,
his 'Tesoro de las Lenguas Quiché, Cakchiquel y
Tzutohil.'   This work, which has never been printed,
fills two volumes, the second of which contains the
copy of the MS. discovered by Ximenes.   Ximenes
likewise wrote a history of the province of the
preachers of San-Vincente de Chiapas y Guatemala,
in four volumes.   Of this he left two copies.   But
three volumes only were still in existence when the

Abbé Brasseur de Bourbourg visited Guatemala, and they are said to contain valuable information on the history and traditions of the country. The first volume contains the Spanish translation of the manuscript which occupies us at present. The Abbé Brasseur de Bourbourg copied that translation in 1855. About the same time a German traveller, Dr. Scherzer, happened to be at Guatemala, and had copies made of the works of Ximenes. These were published at Vienna, in 1856[5]. The French Abbé, however, was not satisfied with a mere reprint of the text and its Spanish translation by Ximenes, a translation which he characterises as untrustworthy and frequently unintelligible. During his travels in America he acquired a practical knowledge of several of the native dialects, particularly of the Quiché, which is still spoken in various dialects by about six hundred thousand people. As a priest he was in daily intercourse with these people; and it was while residing among them and able to consult them like living dictionaries, that, with the help of the MSS. of Ximenes, he undertook his own translation of the ancient chronicles of the Quichés. From the time of the discovery of Ximenes, therefore, to the time of the publication of the Abbé Brasseur de Bourbourg, all seems clear and satisfactory. But there is still a century to be accounted for, from the end of the sixteenth century, when the original is supposed to have been written, to the end of the seventeenth, when it was first discovered by Ximenes at Chichi-

---

[5] Mr. A. Helps was the first to point out the importance of this work in his excellent 'History of the Spanish Conquest in America.'

castenango. These years are not bridged over. We
may appeal, however, to the authority of the MS.
itself, which carries the royal dynasties down to the
Spanish Conquest, and ends with the names of the
two princes, Don Juan de Rojas and Don Juan
Cortes, the sons of Tecum and Tepepul. These
princes, though entirely subject to the Spaniards,
were allowed to retain the insignia of royalty to the
year 1558, and it is shortly after their time that the
MS. is supposed to have been written. The author
himself says in the beginning that he wrote ' after
the word of God (chabal Dios) had been preached,
in the midst of Christianity; and that he did so
because people could no longer see the " Popol Vuh,"
wherein it was clearly shown that they came from
the other side of the sea, the account of our living
in the land of shadow, and how we saw light and
life.' There is no attempt at claiming for his work
any extravagant age or mysterious authority. It is
acknowledged to have been written when the Castilians were the rulers of the land; when bishops were
preaching the word of Dios, the new God; when the
ancient traditions of the people were gradually dying
out. Even the title of ' Popol Vuh,' which the Abbé
Brasseur de Bourbourg has given to this work, is not
claimed for it by its author. He says that he wrote
when the ' Popol Vuh' was no longer to be seen.
Now ' Popol Vuh' means the book of the people, and
referred to the traditional literature in which all that
was known about the early history of the nation,
their religion and ceremonies, was handed down from
age to age.

It is to be regretted that the Abbé Brasseur de
Bourbourg should have sanctioned the application of

this name to the Quiché MS. discovered by Father Ximenes, and that he should apparently have translated it by ' Livre sacré' instead of ' Livre national,' or ' Libro del comun,' as proposed by Ximenes. Such small inaccuracies are sure to produce great confusion. Nothing but a desire to have a fine sounding title could have led the editor to commit this mistake, for he himself confesses that the work published by him has no right to the title ' Popol Vuh,' and that ' Popol Vuh ' does not mean ' Livre sacré.' Nor is there any more reason to suppose, with the learned Abbé, that the first two books of the Quiché MS. contain an almost literal transcript of the ' Popol Vuh,' or that the ' Popol Vuh ' was the original of the ' Teo-Amoxtli,' or the sacred book of the Toltecs. All we know is, that the author wrote his anonymous work because the ' Popol Vuh '—the national book, or the national tradition—was dying out, and that he comprehended in the first two sections the ancient traditions common to the whole race, while he devoted the last two to the historical annals of the Quichés, the ruling nation at the time of the Conquest in what is now the republic of Guatemala. If we look at the MS. in this light, there is nothing at all suspicious in its character and its contents. The author wished to save from destruction the stories which he had heard as a child of his gods and his ancestors. Though the general outline of these stories may have been preserved partly in the schools, partly in the pictographic MSS., the Spanish Conquest had thrown everything into confusion, and the writer had probably to depend chiefly on his own recollections. To extract consecutive history from these recollections, is simply impossible. All is vague, contradictory, miraculous, absurd. Consecutive history is altogether a modern idea, of which few only of the ancient nations had any conception. If we had the exact words of the 'Popol Vuh,' we should probably find no more history there than we find in the Quiché MS. as it now stands. Now and then, it is true, one imagines one sees certain periods and landmarks, but in the next page all is chaos again. It may be difficult to confess that with all the traditions of the early migrations of Cecrops and Danaus into Greece, with the Homeric poems of the Trojan war, and the genealogies of the ancient dynasties of Greece, we know nothing of Greek history before the Olympiads, and very little even then. Yet the true historian does not allow himself to indulge in any illusions on this subject, and he shuts his eyes even to the most plausible reconstructions.

The same applies with a force increased a hundred-fold to the ancient history of the aboriginal races of America, and the sooner this is acknowledged, the better for the credit of American scholars. Even the traditions of the migrations of the Chichimecs, Colhuas, and Nahuas, which form the staple of all American antiquarians, are no better than the Greek traditions about Pelasgians, Æolians, and Ionians; and it would be a mere waste of time to construct out of such elements a systematic history, only to be destroyed again sooner or later by some Niebuhr, Grote, or Lewis.

But if we do not find history in the stories of the ancient races of Guatemala, we do find materials for studying their character, for analysing their religion and mythology, for comparing their principles of morality, their views of virtue, beauty, and heroism,

to those of other races of mankind. This is the
charm, the real and lasting charm, of such works
as that presented to us for the first time in a trustworthy translation by the Abbé Brasseur de Bourbourg. Unfortunately there is one circumstance
which may destroy even this charm. It is just
possible that the writers of this and other American
MSS. may have felt more or less consciously the
influence of European and Christian ideas, and if so,
we have no sufficient guarantee that the stories they
tell represent to us the American mind in its pristine
and genuine form. There are some coincidences between the Old Testament and the Quiché MS. which
are certainly startling. Yet even if a Christian influence has to be admitted, much remains in these
American traditions which is so different from anything else in the national literatures of other countries,
that we may safely treat it as the genuine growth
of the intellectual soil of America. We shall give,
in conclusion, some extracts to bear out our remarks;
but we ought not to part with Abbé Brasseur de
Bourbourg without expressing to him our gratitude
for his excellent work, and without adding a hope
that he may be able to realise his plan of publishing
a 'Collection of documents written in the indigenous
languages, to assist the student of the history and philology of ancient America,' a collection of which the
work now published is to form the first volume.

Extracts from the 'Popol Vuh.'

The Quiché MS. begins with an account of the
creation. If we read it in the literal translation
of the Abbé Brasseur de Bourbourg, with all the
uncouth names of divine and other beings that have

to act their parts in it, it does not leave any very
clear impression on our minds.   Yet after reading it
again and again, some salient features stand out
more distinctly, and make us feel that there was a
groundwork of noble conceptions which has been
covered and distorted by an aftergrowth of fantastic
nonsense.   We shall do best for the present to leave
out all proper names, which only bewilder the memory
and which convey no distinct meaning even to the
scholar.   It will require long-continued research
before it can be determined whether the names so
profusely applied to the Deity were intended as the
names of so many distinct personalities, or as the
names of the various manifestations of one and the
same Power.   At all events, they are of no importance
to us till we can connect more distinct ideas than it is
possible to gather from the materials now at hand,
with such inharmonious sounds as Tzakol, Bitol, Alom,
Qaholom, Hun-Ahpu-Vuch, Gucumatz, Quax-Cho,&c.
Their supposed meanings are in some cases very
appropriate, such as the Creator, the Fashioner, the
Begetter, the Vivifier, the Ruler, the Lord of the
green planisphere, the Lord of the azure surface, the
Heart of heaven; in other cases we cannot fathom
the original intention of names such as the feathered
serpent, the white boar, *le tireur de sarbacane au
sarigue*, and others; and they therefore sound to our
ears simply absurd.   Well, the Quichés believed that
there was a time when all that exists in heaven and
earth was made.   All was then in suspense, all was
calm and silent; all was immovable, all peaceful, and
the vast space of the heavens was empty.   There
was no man, no animal, no shore, no trees; heaven
alone existed.   The face of the earth was not to be

seen; there was only the still expanse of the sea
and the heaven above. Divine Beings were on the
waters like a growing light. Their voice was heard
as they meditated and consulted, and when the dawn
rose, man appeared. Then the waters were commanded to retire, the earth was established that she
might bear fruit and that the light of day might shine
on heaven and earth.

'For, they said, we shall receive neither glory
nor honour from all we have created until there is
a human being — a being endowed with reason.
"Earth," they said, and in a moment the earth was
formed. Like a vapour it rose into being, mountains
appeared from the waters like lobsters, and the great
mountains were made. Thus was the creation of
the earth, when it was fashioned by those who are
the Heart of heaven, the Heart of the earth; for
thus were they called who first gave fertility to
them, heaven and earth being still inert and sus-
pended in the midst of the waters.'

Then follows the creation of the brute world, and
the disappointment of the gods when they command
the animals to tell their names and to honour those
who had created them. Then the gods said to the
animals:

'You will be changed, because you cannot speak.
We have changed your speech. You shall have your
food and your dens in the woods and crags; for our
glory is not perfect, and you do not invoke us. There
will be beings still that can salute us; we shall make
them capable of obeying. Do your task; as to your
flesh, it will be broken by the tooth.'

Then follows the creation of man. His flesh was
made of earth (*terre glaise*). But man was without

cohesion or power, inert and aqueous; he could not turn his head, his sight was dim, and though he had the gift of speech, he had no intellect. He was soon consumed again in the water.

And the gods consulted a second time how to create beings that should adore them, and after some magic ceremonies, men were made of wood, and they multiplied. But they had no heart, no intellect, no recollection of their Creator; they did not lift up their heads to their Maker, and they withered away and were swallowed up by the waters.

Then follows a third creation, man being made of a tree called tzité, woman of the marrow of a reed called sibac. They too, did neither think nor speak before him who had made them, and they were likewise swept away by the waters and destroyed. The whole nature—animals, trees, and stones—turned against men to revenge the wrongs they had suffered at their hands, and the only remnant of that early race is to be found in small monkeys which still live in the forests.

Then follows a story of a very different character, and which completely interrupts the progress of events. It has nothing to do with the creation, though it ends with two of its heroes being changed into sun and moon. It is a story very much like the fables of the Brahmans or the German Mährchen. Some of the principal actors in it are clearly divine beings who have been brought down to the level of human nature, and who perform feats and tricks so strange and incredible that in reading them we imagine ourselves in the midst of the Arabian Nights. In the struggles of the two favourite heroes against the cruel princes of Xibalba, there may be

reminiscences of historical events; but it would be
perfectly hopeless to attempt to extricate these from
the mass of fable by which they are surrounded. The
chief interest of the American tale consists in the
points of similarity which it exhibits with the tales
of the Old World. We shall mention two only—the
repeated resuscitation of the chief heroes, who, even
when burnt and ground to powder and scattered on
the water, are born again as fish and changed into
men; and the introduction of animals endowed with
reason and speech. As in the German tales, certain
peculiarities in the appearance and natural habits of
animals are frequently accounted for by events that
happened 'once upon a time'—for instance, the
stumpy tail of the bear, by his misfortune when he
went out fishing on the ice—so we find in the American tales, 'that it was when the two principal
heroes (Hun-Ahpu and Xbalanqué) had caught the
rat and were going to strangle it over the fire, that
le rat commença à porter une queue sans poil. Thus,
because a certain serpent swallowed a frog who was
sent as a messenger, therefore *aujourd'hui encore les
serpents engloutissent les crapauds.*'

The story, which well deserves the attention of
those who are interested in the origin and spreading
of popular tales, is carried on to the end of the second
book, and it is only in the third that we hear once
more of the creation of man.

Three attempts, as we saw, had been made and
had failed. We now hear again that before the
beginning of dawn, and before the sun and moon
had risen, man had been made, and that nourishment
was provided for him which was to supply his blood,
namely, yellow and white maize. Four men are

mentioned as the real ancestors of the human race,
or rather of the race of the Quichés. They were
neither begotten by the gods nor born of woman, but
their creation was a wonder wrought by the Creator.
They could reason and speak, their sight was un-
limited, and they knew all things at once. When
they had rendered thanks to their Creator for their
existence, the gods were frightened and they breathed
a cloud over the eyes of men that they might see a
certain distance only, and not be like the gods themselves. Then while the four men were asleep, the
gods gave them beautiful wives, and these became
the mothers of all tribes, great and small. These
tribes, both black and white, lived and spread in
the East. They did not yet worship the gods, but
only turned their faces up to heaven, hardly knowing
what they were meant to do here below. Their
features were sweet, so was their language, and their
intellect was strong.

We now come to a most interesting passage, which
is intended to explain the confusion of tongues. No
nation, except the Jews, has dwelt much on the problem why there should be many languages instead of
one. Grimm, in his ' Essay on the Origin of Language,'
remarks: 'It may seem surprising that neither the
ancient Greeks nor the ancient Indians attempted to
propose or to solve the question as to the origin and
the multiplicity of human speech. Holy Writ strove
to solve at least one of these riddles, that of the
multiplicity of languages, by means of the tower of
Babel. I know only one other poor Esthonian legend
which might be placed by the side of this biblical
solution. "The old god," they say, "when men
found their first seats too narrow, resolved to spread

them over the whole earth, and to give to each nation its own language. For this purpose he placed a caldron of water on the fire, and commanded the different races to approach it in order, and to select for themselves the sounds which were uttered by the singing of the water in its confinement and torture." '

Grimm might have added another legend which is current among the Thlinkithians, and was clearly framed in order to account for the existence of different languages. The Thlinkithians are one of the four principal races inhabiting Russian America. They are called Kaljush, Koljush, or Kolosh by the Russians, and inhabit the coast from about 60° to 45° N.L., reaching therefore across the Russian frontier as far as the Columbia River, and they likewise hold many of the neighbouring islands. Weniaminow estimates their number, both in the Russian and English colonies, at 20 to 25,000. They are evidently a decreasing race, and their legends, which seem to be numerous and full of original ideas, would well deserve the careful attention of American ethnologists. Wrangel suspected a relationship between them and the Aztecs of Mexico. These Thlinkithians believe in a general flood or deluge, and that men saved themselves in a large floating building. When the waters fell, the building was wrecked on a rock, and by its own weight burst into two pieces. Hence arose the difference of languages. The Thlinkithians with their language remained on one side; on the other side were all the other races of the earth.[6]

---

[6] Holmberg, 'Ethnographische Skizzen über die Völker des Russischen Amerika.' Helsingfors, 1855.

Neither the Esthonian nor the Thlinkithian legend, however, offers any striking points of coincidence with the Mosaic accounts.   The analogies, therefore, as well as the discrepancies, between the ninth chapter of Genesis and the chapter here translated from the Quiché MS. require special attention:

'All had but one language, and they did not invoke as yet either wood or stones; they only remembered the word of the Creator, the Heart of heaven and earth.

'And they spoke while meditating on what was hidden by the spring of day; and full of the sacred word, full of love, obedience, and fear, they made their prayers, and lifting their eyes up to heaven, they asked for sons and daughters:

'"Hail! O Creator and Fashioner, thou who seest and hearest us! do not forsake us, O God, who art in heaven and earth, Heart of the sky, Heart of the earth!   Give us offspring and descendants as long as the sun and dawn shall advance.   Let there be seed and light.   Let us always walk on open paths, on roads where there is no ambush.   Let us always be quiet and in peace with those who are ours.   May our lives run on happily.   Give us a life secure from reproach.   Let there be seed for harvest, and let there be light."

'They then proceeded to the town of Tulan, where they received their gods.

'And when all the tribes were there gathered together, their speech was changed, and they did not understand each other after they arrived at Tulan. It was there that they separated, and some went to the East, others came here.   Even the language of the four ancestors of the human race became different.

" Alas," they said, " we have left our language. How has this happened? We are ruined! How could we have been led into error? We had but one language when we came to Tulan; our form of worship was but one. What we have done is not good," replied all the tribes in the woods, and under the lianas.'

The rest of the work, which consists altogether of four books, is taken up with an account of the migrations of the tribes from the East, and their various settlements. The four ancestors of the race seem to have had a long life, and when at last they came to die, they disappeared in a mysterious manner, and left to their sons what is called the Hidden Majesty, which was never to be opened by human hands. What it was we do not know. There are many subjects of interest in the chapters which follow, only we must not look there for history, although the author evidently accepts as truly historical what he tells us about the successive generations of kings. But when he brings us down at last, after sundry migrations, wars, and rebellions, to the arrival of the Castilians, we find that between the first four ancestors of the human or of the Quiché race and the last of their royal dynasties, there intervene only fourteen generations, and the author, whoever he was, ends with the confession:

'This is all that remains of the existence of Quiché; for it is impossible to see the book in which formerly the kings could read everything, as it has disappeared. It is over with all those of Quiché! It is now called Santa Cruz!'

March, 1862

XV

SEMITIC MONOTHEISM[1].

A WORK such as M. Renan's 'Histoire Générale et Système Comparé des Langues Sémitiques' can only be reviewed chapter by chapter. It contains a survey not only, as its title would lead us to suppose, of the Semitic languages, but of the Semitic languages and nations; and considering that the whole history of the civilized world has hitherto been acted by two races only, the Semitic and the Aryan, with occasional interruptions produced by the inroads of the Turanian race, M. Renan's work comprehends in reality half of the history of the ancient world. We have received as yet the first volume only of this important work, and before the author had time to finish the second, he was called upon to publish a second edition of the first, which appeared in 1858, with important additions and alterations.

In writing the history of the Semitic race it is necessary to lay down certain general characteristics

---

[1] 'Histoire Générale et Système Comparé des Langues Sémitiques.' Par Ernest Renan, Membre de l'Institut. Seconde édition. Paris, 1858.

'Nouvelles Considérations sur le Caractère Général des Peuples Sémitiques, et en particulier sur leur Tendance au Monothéisme.' Par Ernest Renan. Paris, 1859.

common to all the members of that race, before
we can speak of nations so widely separated
from each other as the Jews, the Babylonians,
Phenicians, Carthaginians, and Arabs, as one race
or family. The most important bond which binds
these scattered tribes together into one ideal whole
is to be found in their language. There can be as
little doubt that the dialects of all the Semitic
nations are derived from one common type as there
is about the derivation of French, Spanish, and
Italian from Latin, or of Latin, Greek, German,
Celtic, Slavonic, and Sanskrit from the primitive
idiom of the ancestors of the Aryan race. The
evidence of language would by itself be quite sufficient to establish the fact that the Semitic nations
descended from common ancestors, and constitute
what, in the science of language, may be called a
distinct race. But M. Renan was not satisfied with
this single criterion of the relationship of the Semitic
tribes, and he has endeavoured to draw, partly from
his own observations, partly from the suggestions of
other scholars, such as Ewald and Lassen, a more
complete portrait of the Semitic man. This was no
easy task. It was like drawing the portrait of a
whole family, omitting all that is peculiar to each
individual member, and yet preserving the features
which constitute the general family likeness. The
result has been what might be expected. Critics
most familiar with one or the other branch of the
Semitic family have each and all protested that they
can see no likeness in the portrait. It seems to some
to contain features which it ought not to contain,
whereas others miss the very expression which
appears to them most striking.

The following is a short abstract of what M. Renan
considers the salient points in the Semitic character:

'Their character,' he says, 'is religious rather than
political, and the mainspring of their religion is the
conception of the unity of God. Their religious
phraseology is simple, and free from mythological
elements. Their religious feelings are strong, exclusive, intolerant, and sustained by a fervour which
finds its peculiar expression in prophetic visions.
Compared to the Aryan nations, they are found
deficient in scientific and philosophical originality.
Their poetry is chiefly subjective or lyrical, and we
look in vain among their poets for excellence in epic
and dramatic compositions. Painting and the plastic
arts have never arrived at a higher than the decora-
tive stage. Their political life has remained patri-
archal and despotic, and their inability to organise
on a large scale has deprived them of the means of
military success. Perhaps the most general feature
of their character is a negative one,—their inability
to perceive the general and the abstract, whether in
thought, language, religion, poetry, or politics; and,
on the other hand, a strong attraction towards the
individual and personal, which makes them monotheistic in religion, lyrical in poetry, monarchical
in politics, abrupt in style, and useless for speculation.'

One cannot look at this bold and rapid outline of
the Semitic character without perceiving how many
points it contains which are open to doubt and discussion. We shall confine our remarks to one point,
which, in our mind, and, as far as we can see, in
M. Renan's mind likewise, is the most important of
all—namely, the supposed monotheistic tendency of

the Semitic race. M. Renan asserts that this tendency belongs to the race by instinct,—that it
forms the rule, not the exception; and he seems
to imply that without it the human race would
never have arrived at the knowledge or worship of
the One God.

If such a remark had been made fifty years ago, it
would have roused little or no opposition. 'Semitic'
was then used in a more restricted sense, and hardly
comprehended more than the Jews and Arabs. Of
this small group of people it might well have been
said, with such limitations as are tacitly implied in
every general proposition on the character of individuals or nations, that the work set apart for them
by a Divine Providence in the history of the world
was the preaching of a belief in one God. Three
religions have been founded by members of that
more circumscribed Semitic family—the Jewish, the
Christian, the Mohammedan; and all three proclaim,
with the strongest accent, the doctrine that there is
but one God.

Of late, however, not only have the limits of the
Semitic family been considerably extended, so as to
embrace several nations notorious for their idolatrous
worship, but the history of the Jewish and Arab
tribes has been explored so much more fully, that
even there traces of a wide-spread tendency to polytheism have come to light.

The Semitic family is divided by M. Renan into
two great branches, differing from each other in the
form of their monotheistic belief, yet both, according
to their historian, imbued from the beginning with
the instinctive faith in one God:

1. The nomad branch, consisting of Arabs, Hebrews,

and the neighbouring tribes of Palestine, commonly
called the descendants of Terah; and

2. The political branch, including the nations of
Phenicia, of Syria, Mesopotamia, and Yemen.

Can it be said that all these nations, comprising
the worshippers of Elohim, Jehovah, Sabaoth, Moloch,
Nisroch, Rimmon, Nebo, Dagon, Ashtaroth, Baal or
Bel, Baal-peor, Baal-zebub, Chemosh, Milcom, Adram-
melech, Annamelech, Nibhaz and Tartak, Ashima,
Nergal, Succoth-benoth, the Sun, Moon, planets, and
all the host of heaven, were endowed with a monotheistic instinct?　M. Renan admits that monotheism
has always had its principal bulwark in the nomadic
branch, but he maintains that it has by no means
been so unknown among the members of the political
branch as is commonly supposed.　But where are
the criteria by which, in the same manner as their
dialects, the religions of the Semitic races could be
distinguished from the religions of the Aryan and
Turanian races?　We can recognise any Semitic
dialect by the triliteral character of its roots.　Is it
possible to discover similar radical elements in all
the forms of faith, primary or secondary, primitive or
derivative, of the Semitic tribes?　M. Renan thinks
that it is.　He imagines that he hears the key-note
of a pure monotheism through all the wild shoutings
of the priests of Baal and other Semitic idols, and he
denies the presence of that key-note in any of the
religious ' systems of the Aryan nations, whether
Greeks or Romans, Germans or Celts, Hindus or
Persians.　Such an assertion could not but rouse
considerable opposition, and so strong seems to have
been the remonstrances addressed to M. Renan by
several of his colleagues in the French Institute

that, without awaiting the publication of the second volume of his great work, he has thought it right to publish part of it as a separate pamphlet. In his 'Nouvelles Considérations sur le Caractère Général des Peuples Sémitiques, et en particulier sur leur Tendance au Monothéisme,' he endeavours to silence the objections raised against the leading idea of his history of the Semitic race. It is an essay which exhibits not only the comprehensive knowledge of the scholar, but the warmth and alacrity of the advocate. With M. Renan the monotheistic character of the descendants of Shem is not only a scientific tenet, but a moral conviction. He wishes that his whole work should stand or fall with this thesis, and it becomes, therefore, all the more the duty of the critic, to inquire whether the arguments which he brings forward in support of his favourite idea are valid or not.

It is but fair to M. Renan that, in examining his statements, we should pay particular attention to any slight modifications which he may himself have adopted in his last memoir. In his history he asserts with great confidence, and somewhat broadly, that 'le monothéisme résume et explique tous les caractères de la race Sémitique.' In his later pamphlet he is more cautious. As an experienced pleader he is ready to make many concessions in order to gain all the more readily our assent to his general proposition. He points out himself with great candour the weaker points of his argument, though, of course, only in order to return with unabated courage to his first position,—that of all the races of mankind the Semitic race alone was endowed with the instinct of monotheism. As it is impossible to deny the fact

that the Semitic nations, in spite of this supposed
monotheistic instinct, were frequently addicted to the
most degraded forms of a polytheistic idolatry, and
that even the Jews, the most monotheistic of all,
frequently provoked the anger of the Lord by burning incense to other gods, M. Renan remarks that
when he speaks of a nation in general he only
speaks of the intellectual aristocracy of that nation.
He appeals in self-defence to the manner in which
historians lay down the character of modern nations.
' The French,' he says, ' are repeatedly called " *une
nation spirituelle*," and yet no one would wish to
assert either that every Frenchman is *spirituel*, or
that no one could be *spirituel* who is not a Frenchman.' Now, here we may grant to M. Renan that if
we speak of ' *esprit* ' we naturally think of the intellectual minority only, and not of the whole bulk of a
nation; but if we speak of religion, the case is different. If we say that the French believe in one
God only, or that they are Christians, we speak not
only of the intellectual aristocracy of France but of
every man, woman, and child born and bred in
France. Even if we say that the French are Roman
Catholics, we do so only because we know that there
is a decided majority in France in favour of the
unreformed system of Christianity. But if, because
some of the most distinguished writers of France
have paraded their contempt for all religious dogmas,
we were to say broadly that the French are a nation
without religion, we should justly be called to order
for abusing the legitimate privileges of generaliza-
tion. The fact that Abraham, Moses, Elijah, and
Jeremiah were firm believers in one God could not
be considered sufficient to support the general pro-

position that the Jewish nation was monotheistic by
instinct. And if we remember that among the other
Semitic races we should look in vain for even four
such names, the case would seem to be desperate to
any one but M. Renan.

We cannot believe that M. Renan would be satisfied with the admission that there had been among
the Jews a few leading men who believed in one God,
or that the existence of but one God was an article
of faith not quite unknown among the other Semitic
races; yet he has hardly proved more. He has
collected, with great learning and ingenuity, all
traces of monotheism in the annals of the Semitic
nations; but he has taken no pains to discover the
traces of polytheism, whether faint or distinct, which
are disclosed in the same annals. In acting the part
of an advocate he has for a time divested himself of
the nobler character of the historian.

If M. Renan had looked with equal zeal for the scattered vestiges both of a monotheistic and of a polytheistic worship, he would have drawn, perhaps, a less
striking, but we believe a more faithful, portrait of
the Semitic man. We may accept all the facts of
M. Renan, for his facts are almost always to be
trusted; but we cannot accept his conclusions, because they would be in contradiction to other facts
which M. Renan places too much in the background,
or ignores altogether. Besides, there is something
in the very conclusions to which he is driven by
his too partial evidence which jars on our ears, and
betrays a want of harmony in the premises on which
he builds. Taking his stand on the fact that the
Jewish race was the first of all the nations of
the world to arrive at the knowledge of one God,

M. Renan proceeds to argue that, if their monotheism
had been the result of a persevering mental effort
—if it had been a discovery like the philosophical
or scientific discoveries of the Greeks, it would be
necessary to admit that the Jews surpassed all other
nations of the world in intellect and vigour of speculation. This, he admits, is contrary to fact:

'Apart la supériorité de son culte, le peuple juif
n'en a aucune autre; c'est un des peuples les moins
doués pour la science et la philosophie parmi les
peuples de l'antiquité; il n'a une grande position ni
politique ni militaire. Ses institutions sont pure-
ment conservatrices; les prophètes, qui représentent
excellemment son génie, sont des hommes essentielle-
ment réactionnaires, se reportant toujours vers un
idéal antérieur. Comment expliquer, au sein d'une
société aussi étroite et aussi peu développée, une
révolution d'idées qu'Athènes et Alexandrie n'ont
pas réussi à accomplir ?'

M. Renan then defines the monotheism of the Jews,
and of the Semitic nations in general, as the result
of a low, rather than of a high state of intellectual
cultivation: ' I'l s'en faut,' he writes (p. 40), 'que le
monothéisme soit le produit d'une race qui a des
idées exaltées en fait de religion; c'est en réalité
le fruit d'une race qui a peu de besoins religieux.
C'est comme *minimum* de religion, en fait de dogmes
et en fait de pratiques extérieures, que le monothéisme
est surtout accommodé aux besoins des populations
nomades.'

But even this *minimum* of religious reflection, which
is required, according to M. Renan, for the perception
of the unity of God, he grudges to the Semitic nations,
and he is driven in the end (p. 73) to explain the

Semitic Monotheism as the result of a religious instinct, analogous to the instinct which led each race to the formation of its own language.

Here we miss the clearness and precision which distinguish most of M. Renan's works. It is always dangerous to transfer expressions from one branch of knowledge to another. The word 'instinct' has its legitimate application in natural history, where it is used of the unconscious acts of unconscious beings. We say that birds build their nests by instinct, that fishes swim by instinct, that cats catch mice by instinct; and, though no natural philosopher has yet explained what instinct is, yet we accept the term as a conventional expression for an unknown power working in the animal world.

If we transfer this word to the unconscious acts of conscious beings, we must necessarily alter its definition. We may speak of an instinctive motion of the arm, but we only mean a motion which has become so habitual as to require no longer any special effort of the will.

If, however, we transfer the word to the conscious thoughts of conscious beings, we strain the word beyond its natural capacities, we use it in order to avoid other terms which would commit us to the admission either of innate ideas or inspired truths. We use a word in order to avoid a definition. It may sound more scientific to speak of a monotheistic instinct rather than of the inborn image or the revealed truth of the One living God; but is instinct less mysterious than revelation? Can there be an instinct without an instigation or an instigator? And whose hand was it that instigated the Semitic mind to the worship of one God? Could the same hand

have instigated the Aryan mind to the worship of
many gods?   Could the monotheistic instinct of the
Semitic race, if an instinct, have been so frequently
obscured, or the polytheistic instinct of the Aryan
race, if an instinct, so completely annihilated, as to
allow the Jews to worship on all the high places
round Jerusalem, and the Greeks and Romans to become believers in Christ?   Fishes never fly, and cats
never catch frogs.   These are the difficulties into
which we are led; and they arise simply and solely
from our using words for their sound rather than for
their meaning.   We begin by playing with words, but
in the end the words will play with us.

There are, in fact, various kinds of monotheism,
and it becomes our duty to examine more carefully
what they mean and how they arise.   There is one
kind of monotheism, though it would more properly
be called theism, or henotheism, which forms the
birthright of every human being.   What distinguishes
man from all other creatures, and not only raises him
above the animal world, but removes him altogether
from the confines of a merely natural existence, is the
feeling of sonship inherent in and inseparable from
human nature.   That feeling may find expression in
a thousand ways, but there breathes through all of
them the inextinguishable conviction, 'It is He that
hath made us, and not we ourselves.'   That feeling of
sonship may with some races manifest itself in fear
and trembling, and it may drive whole generations
into religious madness and devil worship.   In other
countries it may tempt the creature into a fatal
familiarity with the Creator, and end in an apotheosis
of man, or a headlong plunging of the human into
the divine.   It may take, as with the Jews, the

form of a simple assertion that 'Adam was the son
of God,' or it may be clothed in the mythological
phraseology of the Hindus, that Manu, or man, was
the descendant of Svayambhu, the Self-existing. But,
in some form or other, the feeling of dependence on
a higher Power breaks through in all the religions of
the world, and explains to us the meaning of St.
Paul, 'that God, though in times past He suffered all
nations to walk in their own ways, nevertheless He
left not Himself without witness, in that He did good
and gave us rain from heaven, and fruitful seasons,
filling our hearts with food and gladness.'

This primitive intuition of God and the ineradicable feeling of dependence on God, could only have
been the result of a primitive revelation, in the
truest sense of that word. Man, who owed his
existence to God, and whose being centred and rested
in God, saw and felt God as the only source of his
own and of all other existence. By the very act of
the creation, God had revealed Himself. There He
was, manifested in His works, in all His majesty and
power, before the face of those to whom He had
given eyes to see and ears to hear, and into whose
nostrils He had breathed the breath of life, even the
Spirit of God.

This primitive intuition of God, however, was in
itself neither monotheistic nor polytheistic, though
it might become either, according to the expression
which it took in the languages of man. It was this
primitive intuition which supplied either the subject
or the predicate in all the religions of the world, and
without it no religion, whether true or false, whether
revealed or natural, could have had even its first
beginning. It is too often forgotten by those who

believe that a polytheistic worship was the most
natural unfolding of religious life, that polytheism
must everywhere have been preceded by a more or
less conscious theism. In no language does the plural
exist before the singular. No human mind could
have conceived the idea of gods without having previously conceived the idea of a god. It would be,
however, quite as great a mistake to imagine, because
the idea of a god must exist previously to that of
gods, that therefore a belief in One God preceded
everywhere the belief in many gods. A belief in
God as exclusively One, involves a distinct negation
of more than one God, and that negation is possible
only after the conception, whether real or imaginary,
of many gods.

The primitive intuition of the Godhead is neither
monotheistic nor polytheistic, and it finds its most
natural expression in the simplest and yet the most
important article of faith—that God is God. This
must have been the faith of the ancestors of mankind
previously to any division of race or confusion of
tongues. It might seem, indeed, as if in such a faith
the oneness of God, though not expressly asserted,
was implied, and that it existed, though latent,
in the first revelation of God. History, however,
proves that the question of oneness was yet unde-
cided in that primitive faith, and that the intuition
of God was not yet secured against the illusions of a
double vision. There are, in reality, two kinds of
oneness which, when we enter into metaphysical
discussions, must be carefully distinguished, and
which for practical purposes are well kept separate
by the definite and indefinite articles. There is one
kind of oneness which does not exclude the idea of

plurality; there is another which does. When we /
say that Cromwell was a Protector of England, we
do not assert that he was the only protector. But if
we say that he was the Protector of England, it is
understood that he was the only man who enjoyed
that title. If, therefore, an expression had been
given to that primitive intuition of the Deity, which
is the mainspring of all later religion, it would have
been—' There is a God,' but not yet ' There is but
" One God." ' The latter form of faith, the belief in
One God, is properly called monotheism, whereas the '
term of henotheism would best express the faith in
a single god.

We must bear in mind that we are here speaking
of a period in the history of mankind when, together
with the awakening of ideas, the first attempts only
were being made at expressing the simplest conceptions by means of a language most simple, most
sensuous, and most unwieldy. There was as yet no
word sufficiently reduced by the wear and tear of
thought to serve as an adequate expression for the
abstract idea of an immaterial and supernatural
Being. There were words for walking and shouting,
for cutting and burning, for dog and cow, for house
and wall, for sun and moon, for day and night.
Every object was called by some quality which had
struck the eye as most peculiar and characteristic.
But what quality should be predicated of that Being
of which man knew as yet nothing but its existence?
Language possessed as yet no auxiliary verbs. The
very idea of being without the attributes of quality
or action, had never entered into the human mind.
How then was that Being to be called which had
revealed its existence, and continued to make itself

done

felt by everything that most powerfully impressed the awakening mind, but which as yet was known only like a subterraneous spring by the waters which it poured forth with inexhaustible strength? When storm and lightning drove a father with his helpless family to seek refuge in the forests, and the fall of mighty trees crushed at his side those who were most dear to him, there were, no doubt, feelings of terror and awe, of helplessness and dependence, in the human heart which burst forth in a shriek for pity or help from the only Being that could command the storm. But there was no name by which He could be called. There might be names for the storm-wind and the thunderbolt, but these were not the names applicable to Him that rideth upon the heaven of heavens, which were of old. Again, when after a wild and tearful night the sun dawned in the morning, smiling on man—when after a dreary and death-like winter spring came again with its sunshine and flowers, there were feelings of joy and gratitude, of love and adoration in the heart of every human being, but though there were names for the sun and the spring, for the bright sky and the brilliant dawn, there was no word by which to call the source of all this gladness, the giver of light and life.

At the time when we may suppose that the first attempts at finding a name for God were made, the divergence of the languages of mankind had commenced. We cannot dwell here on the causes which led to the multiplicity of human speech; but whether we look on the confusion of tongues as a natural or supernatural event, it was an event which the

science of language has proved to have been inevitable. The ancestors of the Semitic and the
Aryan nations had long become unintelligible to each
other in their conversations on the most ordinary
topics, when they each in their own way began to
look for a proper name for God. Now one of the
most striking differences between the Aryan and the
Semitic forms of speech was this:—In the Semitic
languages the roots expressive of the predicates
which were to serve as the proper names of any
subjects, remained so distinct within the body of a
word, that those who used the word were unable to
forget its predicative meaning, and retained in most
cases a distinct consciousness of its appellative power.
In the Aryan languages, on the contrary, the significative element, or the root of a word, was apt to
become so completely absorbed by the derivative
elements, whether prefixes or suffixes, that most substantives ceased almost immediately to be appellative, and were changed into mere names or proper
names. What we mean can best be illustrated by
the fact that the dictionaries of Semitic languages
are mostly arranged according to their roots. When
we wish to find the meaning of a word in Hebrew or
Arabic we first look for its root, whether triliteral or
biliteral, and then look in the dictionary for that
root and its derivatives. In the Aryan languages,
on the contrary, such an arrangement would be extremely inconvenient. In many words it is impossible to detect the radical element. In others, after
the root is discovered, we find that it has not given
birth to any other derivatives which would throw
their converging rays of light on its radical meaning.
In other cases, again, such seems to have been the

boldness of the original name-giver that we can
hardly enter into the idiosyncrasy which assigned
such a name to such an object.

This peculiarity of the Semitic and Aryan languages must have had the greatest influence on the
formation of their religious phraseology. The Semitic
man would call on God in adjectives only, or in words
which always conveyed a predicative meaning. Every
one of his words was more or less predicative, and he
was therefore restricted in his choice to such words
as expressed some one or other of the abstract
qualities of the Deity. The Aryan man was less
fettered in his choice. Let us take an instance.
Being startled by the sound of thunder, he would at
first express his impression by the single phrase, It
thunders,—βροντᾷ. Here the idea of God is understood rather than expressed, very much in the same
manner as the Semitic proper names Zabd (present),
Abd (servant), Aus (present), are habitually used
for Abd-allah, Zabd-allah, Aus-allah, — the
servant of God, the gift of God. It would be more
in accordance with the feelings and thoughts of
those who first used these so-called impersonal verbs
to translate them by He thunders, He rains, He
snows. Afterwards, instead of the simple impersonal verb He thunders, another expression naturally suggested itself. The thunder came from
the sky, the sky was frequently called Dyaus (the
bright one), in Greek Ζεύς; and though it was not
the bright sky which thundered, but the dark,
yet Dyaus had already ceased to be an expressive predicate, it had become a traditional name,
and hence there was nothing to prevent an Aryan
man from saying Dyaus, or the sky thunders,

in Greek Ζεὺς βροντᾷ. Let us here mark the almost irresistible influence of language on the mind. The word Dyaus, which at first meant bright, had lost its radical meaning, and now meant simply sky. It then entered into a new stage. The idea which had first been expressed by the pronoun or the termination of the third person, He thunders, was taken up into the word Dyaus, or sky. He thunders, and Dyaus thunders, became synonymous expressions, and by the mere habit of speech He became Dyaus, and Dyaus became He. Henceforth Dyaus remained as an appellative of that unseen though ever present Power, which had revealed its existence to man from the beginning, but which remained without a name long after every beast of the field and every fowl of the air had been named by Adam.

Now, what happened in this instance with the name of Dyaus, happened again and again with other names. When men felt the presence of God in the great and strong wind, in the earthquake, or the fire, they said at first, He storms, He shakes, He burns. But they likewise said, the storm (Marut) blows, the fire (Agni) burns, the subterraneous fire (Vulcanus) upheaves the earth. And after a time the result was the same as before, and the words meaning originally wind or fire were used, under certain restrictions, as names of the unknown God. As long as all these names were remembered as mere names or attributes of one and the same Divine Power, there was as yet no polytheism, though, no doubt, every new name threatened to obscure more and more the primitive intuition of God. At first, the names of God, like fetishes

or statues, were honest attempts at expressing or
representing an idea which could never find an
adequate expression or representation. But the
eidolon, or likeness, became an idol; the no-
men, or name, lapsed into a numen, or demon,
as soon as they were drawn away from their
original intention. If the Greeks had remembered that Zeus was but a name or symbol of
the Deity, there would have been no more harm
in calling God by that name than by any other.
If they had remembered that Kronos, and Uranos,
and Apollon were all but so many attempts at nam-
ing the various sides, or manifestations, or aspects,
or persons of the Deity, they might have used
these names in the hours of their various needs,
just as the Jews called on Jehovah, Elohim, and
Sabaoth, or as Roman Catholics implore the help of
Nunziata, Dolores, and Notre-Dame-de-Grace.

What, then, is the difference between the Aryan
and Semitic nomenclature for the Deity? Why are
we told that the pious invocations of the Aryan
world turned into a blasphemous mocking of the
Deity, whereas the Semitic nations are supposed to
have found from the first the true name of God?
Before we look anywhere else for an answer to the
question, we must look to language itself, and here
we see that the Semitic dialects could never, by any
possibility, have produced such names as the Sanskrit Dyaus (Zeus), Varuna (Uranos), Marut (Storm,
Mars), or Ushas (Eos). They had no doubt names
for the bright sky, for the tent of heaven, and for
the dawn. But these names were so distinctly felt
as appellatives, that they could never be thought of as
proper names, whether as names of the Deity, or as

names of deities. This peculiarity has been illustrated
with great skill by M. Renan. We differ from him
when he tries to explain the difference between the
mythological phraseology of the Aryan and the theological phraseology of the Semitic races, by assigning
to each a peculiar theological instinct. We cannot,
in fact, see how the admission of such an instinct, i.e.
of an unknown and incomprehensible power, helps us
in any way whatsoever to comprehend this curious
mental process. His problem, however, is exactly the
same as ours, and it would be impossible to state that
problem in a more telling manner than he has done.

' The rain,' he says (p. 79), ' is represented, in all the
primitive mythologies of the Aryan race, as the fruit
of the embraces of Heaven and Earth.' ' The bright
sky,' says Æschylus, in a passage which one might
suppose was taken from the Vedas, ' loves to penetrate
the earth; the earth on her part aspires to the
heavenly marriage. Rain falling from the loving sky
impregnates the earth, and she produces for mortals
pastures of the flocks and the gifts of Ceres.' In the
Book of Job[2], on the contrary, it is God who tears
open the waterskins of Heaven (xxxviii. 37), who
opens the courses for the floods (ibid. 25), who en-
genders the drops of dew (ibid. 28):

' He draws towards Him the mists from the waters,
Which pour down as rain, and form their vapours.
Afterwards the clouds spread them out,
They fall as drops on the crowds of men.' (Job
    xxxvi. 27, 28.)

---

[2] We give the extracts according to M. Renan's translation of the
Book of Job (Paris, 1859, Michel Lévy).

' He charges the night with damp vapours,
He drives before Him the thunder-bearing cloud.
It is driven to one side or the other by His com-
  mand.
To execute all that He ordains
On the face of the universe,
Whether it be to punish His creatures
Or to make thereof a proof of his mercy.' (Job
  xxxvii. 11–13.)

Or, again, Proverbs xxx. 4:
' Who hath gathered the wind in His fists? Who
hath bound the waters in a garment? Who hath
established all the ends of the earth? What is His
name, and what is His Son's name, if thou canst
tell?'

It has been shown by ample evidence from the
Rig-veda how many mythes were suggested to the
Aryan world by various names of the dawn, the
day-spring of life. The language of the ancient
Aryans of India had thrown out many names for that
heavenly apparition, and every name, as it ceased to
be understood, became, like a decaying seed, the germ
of an abundant growth of mythe and legend. Why
should not the same have happened to the Semitic
names for the dawn? Simply and solely because the
Semitic words had no tendency to phonetic corruption; simply and solely because they continued to
be felt as appellatives, and would inevitably have
defeated every attempt at mythological phraseology
such as we find in India and Greece. When the
dawn is mentioned in the book of Job (ix. 7), it is
God ' who commandeth the sun and it riseth not, and
sealeth up the stars.' It is His power which causeth

the day-spring to know its place, that it might take
hold of the ends of the earth, that the wicked might
be shaken out of it (Job xxxviii. 12, 13; Renan,
'Livre de Job,' pref. 71). Shahar, the dawn, never
becomes an independent agent; she is never spoken
of as Eos rising from the bed of her husband Ti-
thonos (the setting sun), solely and simply because
the word retained its power as an appellative,
and thus could not enter into any mythological
metamorphosis.

Even in Greece there are certain words which have
remained so pellucid as to prove unfit for mythological refraction. Selene in Greek is so clearly the
moon that her name would pierce through the darkest
clouds of mythe and fable. Call her Hecate, and
she will bear any disguise, however fanciful. It is
the same with the Latin Luna. She is too clearly
the moon to be mistaken for anything else, but call
her Lucina, and she will readily enter into various
mythological phases. If, then, the names of sun and
moon, of thunder and lightning, of light and day, of
night and dawn could not yield to the Semitic races
fit appellatives for the Deity, where were they to be
found? If the names of Heaven or Earth jarred on
their ears as names unfit for the Creator, where could
they find more appropriate terms? They would not
have objected to real names such as Jupiter Optimus Maximus, or Ζεὺς κύδιστος μέγιστος, if such
words could have been framed in their dialects, and
the names of Jupiter and Zeus could have been so
ground down as to become synonymous with the
general term for 'God.' Not even the Jews could
have given a more exalted definition of the Deity
than that of Optimus Maximus—the Best and the

Greatest; and their very name of God, Jehovah, is generally supposed to mean no more than what the Peleiades of Dodona said of Zeus, Ζεὺς ἦν, Ζεὺς ἐστίν, Ζεὺς ἔσσεται· ὦ μεγάλε Ζεῦ, ' He was, He is, He will be, Oh great Zeus !' Not being able to form such substantives as Dyaus, or Varuna, or Indra, the descendants of Shem fixed on the predicates which in the Aryan prayers follow the name of the Deity, and called Him the Best and the Greatest, the Lord and King. If we examine the numerous names of the Deity in the Semitic dialects we find that they are all adjectives, expressive of moral qualities. There is El, strong; Bel or Baal, Lord; Beel-samin, Lord of Heaven; Adonis (in Phenicia), Lord; Marnas (at Gaza), our Lord; Shet, Master, afterwards a demon; Moloch, Milcom, Malika, King; Eliun, the Highest (the God of Melchisedek); Ram and Rimmon, the Exalted; and many more names, all originally adjectives and expressive of certain general qualities of the Deity, but all raised by one or the other of the Semitic tribes to be the names of God or of that idea which the first breath of life, the first sight of this world, the first consciousness of existence, had for ever impressed and implanted in the human mind.

But do these names prove that the people who invented them had a clear and settled idea of the unity of the Deity? Do we not find among the Aryan nations that the same superlatives, the same names of Lord and King, of Master and Father, are used when the human mind is brought face to face with the Divine, and the human heart pours out in prayer and thanksgiving the feelings inspired by the presence of God? Brahman, in Sanskrit, meant originally Power,

the same as El. It resisted for a long time the
mythological contagion, but at last it yielded like
all other names of God, and became the name of one
God. By the first man who formed or fixed these
names, Brahman, like El, and like every name of
God, was meant, no doubt, as the best expression that
could be found for the image reflected from the
Creator upon the mind of the creature. But in none
of these words can we see any decided proof that
those who framed them had arrived at the clear perception of One God, and were thus secured against
the danger of polytheism. Like Dyaus, like Indra,
like Brahman, Baal and El and Moloch were names of
God, but not yet of the One God.

And we have only to follow the history of these
Semitic names in order to see that, in spite of their
superlative meaning, they proved no stronger bul-
warks against polytheism than the Latin Optimus
Maximus. The very names which we saw ex-
plained before as meaning the Highest, the Lord, the
Master, are represented in the Phenician mythology
as standing to each other in the relation of Father
and Son. (Renan, p. 60.) There is hardly one single
Semitic tribe which did not at times forget the ori-
ginal meaning of the names by which they called on
God. If the Jews had remembered the meaning of
El, the Omnipotent, they could not have worshipped
Baal, the Lord, as different from El. But as the
Aryan tribes bartered the names of their gods, and
were glad to add the worship of Zeus to that of
Uranos, the worship of Apollon to that of Zeus,
the worship of Hermes to that of Apollon, the
Semitic nations likewise were ready to try the
gods of their neighbours. If there had been in the

Semitic race a truly monotheistic instinct, the history
of those nations would become perfectly unintelligible.   Nothing is more difficult to overcome than
an instinct: naturam expellas furcâ, tamen
usque recurret.   But the history even of the
Jews is made up of an almost uninterrupted series
of relapses into polytheism.   Let us admit, on the contrary, that God had in the beginning revealed Himself
as the same to the ancestors of the whole human race.
Let us then observe the natural divergence of the
languages of man, and consider the peculiar difficulties
that had to be overcome in framing names for God,
and the peculiar manner in which they were overcome in the Semitic and Aryan languages, and
everything that follows will be intelligible.   If we
consider the abundance of synonymes into which all
ancient languages burst out at their first starting—
if we remember that there were hundreds of names
for the earth and the sky, the sun and the moon, we
shall not be surprised at meeting with more'than one
name for God both among the Semitic and the Aryan
nations.   If we consider how easily the radical or
significative elements of words were absorbed and
obscured in the Aryan, and how they stood out in
bold relief in the Semitic languages, we shall appreciate the difficulty which the Shemites experienced in
framing any name that should not seem to take too
one-sided a view of the Deity by predicating but one
quality, whether strength, dominion, or majesty; and
we shall equally perceive the snare which their very
language laid for the Aryan nations, by supplying
them with a number of words which, though they
seemed harmless as meaning nothing except what by
tradition or definition they were made to mean, yet

were full of mischief owing to the recollections which,
at any time, they might revive. Dyaus in itself was
as good a name as any for God, and in some respects
more appropriate than its derivative deva, the Latin
deus, which the Romance nations still use without
meaning any harm. But Dyaus had meant sky for
too long a time to become entirely divested of all the
old mythes or sayings which were true of Dyaus,
the sky, but could only be retained as fables, if transferred to Dyaus, God. Dyaus, the Bright, might
be called the husband of the earth; but when the
same mythe was repeated of Zeus, the god, then
Zeus became the husband of Demeter, Demeter
became a goddess, a daughter sprang from their
union, and all the sluices of mythological madness
were opened. There were a few men, no doubt, at
all times, who saw through this mythological phraseology, who called on God, though they called him
Zeus, or Dyaus, or Jupiter. Xenophanes, one of the
earliest Greek heretics, boldly maintained that there
was but 'one God, and that he was not like unto
men, either in body or mind.[3]' A poet in the Veda
asserts distinctly, 'They call him Indra, Mitra,
Varuna, Agni; then He is the well-winged heavenly Garutmat; that which is One the wise
call it many ways—they call it Agni, Yama, Mâtarisvan[4].'

But, on the whole, the charm of mythology prevailed among the Aryan nations, and a return to the

---

[3] Xenophanes, about contemporary with Cyrus, as quoted by
Clemens Alex., Strom. v. p. 601,—εἷς θεὸς ἔν τε θεοῖσι καὶ ἀνθρώποισι
μέγιστος, οὔτε δέμας θνητοῖσιν ὁμοίιος οὐδὲ νόημα.

[4] 'History of Ancient Sanskrit Literature,' by M. M., p. 567.

primitive intuition of God and a total negation of all
gods, were rendered more difficult to the Aryan than
to the Semitic man. The Semitic man had hardly
ever to resist the allurements of mythology. The
names with which he invoked the Deity did not trick
him by their equivocal character. Nevertheless, these
Semitic names, too, though predicative in the beginning, became subjective, and from being the various
names of One Being, lapsed into names of various
beings. Hence arose a danger which threatened
well-nigh to bar to the Semitic race the approach to
the conception and worship of the One God.

Nowhere can we see this danger more clearly than
in the history of the Jews. The Jews had, no doubt,
preserved from the beginning the idea of God, and
their names of God contained nothing but what
might by right be ascribed to Him. They worshipped a single God, and, whenever they fell into
idolatry, they felt that they had fallen away from
God. But that God, under whatever name they
invoked Him, was especially their God, their own
national God, and His existence did not exclude the
existence of other gods or demons. Of the ancestors of Abraham and Nachor, even of their father
Terah, we know that in old time, when they dwelt on
the other side of the flood, they served other gods
(Joshua xxiv. 2). At the time of Joshua these gods
were not yet forgotten, and instead of denying their
existence altogether, Joshua only exhorts the people
to put away the gods which their fathers served on
the other side of the flood and in Egypt, and to serve
the Lord: 'Choose ye this day,' he says, 'whom you
will serve; whether the gods which your fathers served
that were on the other side of the flood, or the gods

of the Amorites, in whose land ye dwell; but as for me and my house, we will serve the Lord.'

Such a speech, exhorting the people to make their choice between various gods, would have been unmeaning if addressed to a nation which had once conceived the unity of the Godhead. Even images of the gods were not unknown to the family of Abraham, for, though we know nothing of the exact form of the teraphim, or images which Rachel stole from her father, certain it is that Laban calls them his gods (Genesis xxxi. 19, 30). But what is much more significant than these traces of polytheism and idolatry is the hesitating tone in which some of the early patriarchs speak of their God. When Jacob flees before Esau into Padan-Aram and awakes from his vision at Bethel, he does not profess his faith in the One God, but he bargains, and says, 'If God will be with me, and will keep me in this way that I go, and will give me bread to eat, and raiment to put on, so that I come again to my father's house in peace, then' shall the Lord be my God: and this stone, which I have set for a pillar, shall be God's house: and of all that thou shalt give me, I will surely give the tenth unto thee ' (Genesis xxviii. 20-22). Language of this kind evinces not only a temporary want of faith in God, but it shows that the conception of God had not yet acquired that complete universality which alone deserves to be called monotheism, or belief in the One God. To him who has seen God face to face there is no longer any escape or doubt as to who is to be his god; God is his god, whatever befall. But this Jacob learnt not until he had struggled and wrestled with God, and committed himself to His care at the very time when no one

else could have saved him. In that struggle Jacob
asked for the true name of God, and he learnt from
God that His name was secret (Genesis xxxii. 29).
After that, his God was no longer one of many gods.
His faith was not like the faith of Jethro (Exodus
xxvii. 11), the priest of Midian, the father-in-law of
Moses, who when he heard of all that God had
done for Moses acknowledged that God (Jehovah)
was greater than all gods (Elohim).   This is not yet
faith in the One God. It is a faith hardly above the
faith of the people who were halting between Jehovah
and Baal, and who only when they saw what the
Lord did for Elijah, fell on their faces and said, 'The
Lord He is the God.'

   And yet this limited faith in Jehovah as the God
of the Jews, as a God more powerful than the gods of
the heathen, as a God above all gods, betrays itself
again and again in the history of the Jews. The idea
of many gods is there, and wherever that idea exists,
wherever the plural of god is used in earnest, there is
polytheism. It is not so much the names of Zeus,
Hermes, &c., which constitute the polytheism of the
Greeks; it is the plural θεοί, gods, which contains the
fatal spell. We do not know what M. Renan means
when he says that Jehovah with the Jews 'n'est pas
le plus grand entre plusieurs dieux; c'est le Dieu
unique.'   It was so with Abraham, it was so after
Jacob had been changed into Israel, it was so with
Moses, Elijah, and Jeremiah.   But what is the meaning of the very first commandment, 'Thou shalt have
no other gods before me?'   Could this command have
been addressed to a nation to whom the plural of God
was a nonentity?   It might be answered that the
plural of God was to the Jews as revolting as it is to

us, that it was revolting to their faith, if not to their reason. But how was it that their language tolerated the plural of a word which excludes plurality as much as the word for the centre of a sphere? No man who had clearly perceived the unity of God, could say with the Psalmist (lxxxvi. 8), 'Among the gods there is none like unto Thee, O Lord, neither are there any works like unto Thy works.' Though the same poet says, 'Thou art God alone,' he could not have compared God with other gods, if his idea of God had really reached that all-embracing character which it had with Abraham, Moses, Elijah, and Jeremiah. Nor would God have been praised as the 'great king above all gods' by a poet in whose eyes the gods of the heathen had been recognised as what they were —mighty shadows, thrown by the mighty works of God, and intercepting for a time the pure light of the Godhead.

We thus arrive at a different conviction from that which M. Renan has made the basis of the history of the Semitic race. We can see nothing that would justify the admission of a monotheistic instinct, granted to the Semitic, and withheld from the Aryan race. They both share in the primitive intuition of God, they are both exposed to dangers in framing names for God, and they both fall into polytheism. What is peculiar to the Aryan race is their mythological phraseology, superadded to their polytheism; what is peculiar to the Semitic race is their belief in a national god—in a god chosen by his people as his people had been chosen by him.

No doubt, M. Renan might say that we ignored his problem, and that we have not removed the difficulties which drove him to the admission of a mono-

theistic instinct.   How is the fact to be explained, he
might ask, that the three great religions of the world
in which the unity of the Deity forms the key-note,
are of Semitic origin, and that the Aryan nations,
wherever they have been brought to a worship of the
One God, invoke Him with names borrowed from the
Semitic languages?

But let us look more closely at the facts before we
venture on theories.   Mohammedanism, no doubt, is
a Semitic religion, and its very core is monotheism.
But did Mohammed invent monotheism?   Did he invent even a new name of God? (Renan, p. 23.)   Not
at all.   His object was to destroy the idolatry of the
Semitic tribes of Arabia, to dethrone the angels, the
Jin, the sons and daughters who had been assigned
to Allah, and to restore the faith of Abraham in one
God. (Renan, p. 37.)

And how is it with Christianity?   Did Christ come
to preach a faith in a new God?   Did He or His
disciples invent a new name of God?   No, Christ
came not to destroy, but to fulfil; and the God whom
He preached was the God of Abraham.

And who is the God of Jeremiah, of Elijah, and of
Moses?   We answer again, the God of Abraham.

Thus the faith in the One living God, which seemed
to require the admission of a monotheistic instinct,
grafted in every member of the Semitic family, is
traced back to one man, to him 'in whom all families of the earth shall be blessed' (Genesis xii. 3,
Acts iii. 25, Galatians iii. 8).   If from our earliest
childhood we have looked upon Abraham, the friend
of God, with love and veneration; if our first im-
pressions of a truly god-fearing life were taken
from him, who left the land of his fathers to

live a stranger in the land whither God had called
him, who always listened to the voice of God,
whether it conveyed to him the promise of a son
in his old age, or the command to sacrifice that son,
his only son Isaac, his venerable figure will assume
still more majestic proportions when we see in him ?
the life-spring of that faith which was to unite all the (
nations of the earth, and the author of that blessing
which was to come on the Gentiles through Jesus
Christ.

And if we are asked how this one Abraham possessed not only the primitive intuition of God as He
had revealed Himself to all mankind, but passed
through the denial of all other gods to the know-)
ledge of the one God, we are content to answer that)
it was by a special Divine Revelation. We do not
indulge in theological phraseology, but we mean
every word to its fullest extent. The Father of Truth
chooses His own prophets, and He speaks to them in
a voice stronger than the voice of thunder. It is the
same inner voice through which God speaks to all of
us. That voice may dwindle away, and become
hardly audible; it may lose its Divine accent, and
sink into the language of worldly prudence; but it
may also, from time to time, assume its real nature,
with the chosen of God, and sound into their ears
as a voice from Heaven. A 'divine instinct' may
sound more scientific, and less theological; but in
truth it would neither be an appropriate name for
what is a gift or grace accorded to but few, nor
would it be a more scientific, i.e. a more intelligible
word than 'special revelation.'

The important point, however, is not whether the
faith of Abraham should be called a divine instinct

or a revelation; what we wish here to insist on is that
that instinct, or that revelation, was special, granted
to one man, and handed down from him to Jews,
Christians, and Mohammedans, to all who believe in
the God of Abraham. Nor was it granted to Abraham entirely as a free gift. Abraham was tried and
tempted before he was trusted by God. He had to
break with the faith of his fathers; he had to deny
the gods who were worshipped by his friends and
neighbours. Like all the friends of God, he had to
hear himself called an infidel and atheist, and in our
own days he would have been looked upon as a mad-
man for attempting to slay his son. It was through
special faith that Abraham received his special revelation, not through instinct, not through abstract meditation, not through ecstatic visions. We want to
know more of that man than we do; but, even with
the little we know of him, he stands before us as a
figure second only to one in the whole history of the
world. We see his zeal for God, but we never see
him contentious. Though Melchizedek worshipped
God under a different name, invoking Him as Eliun,
the Most High, Abraham at once acknowledged in
Melchizedek a worshipper and priest of the true God,
or Elohim, and paid him tithes. In the very name
of Elohim we seem to trace the conciliatory spirit of
Abraham. Elohim is a plural, though it is followed
by the verb in the singular. It is generally said that
the genius of the Semitic languages countenances the
use of plurals for abstract conceptions, and that when
Jehovah is called Elohim, the plural should be translated by 'the Deity.' We do not deny the fact, but
we wish for an explanation, and an explanation is
suggested by the various phases through which, as we

saw, the conception of God passed in the ancient history of the Semitic mind. Eloah was at first the name for God, and as it is found in all the dialects of the Semitic family except the Phenician (Renan, p. 61), it may probably be considered as the most ancient name of the Deity, sanctioned at a time when the original Semitic speech had not yet branched off into national dialects. When this name was first used in the plural, it could only have signified, like every plural, many Eloahs, and such a plural could only have been formed after the various names of God had become the names of independent deities, i. e. during a polytheistic stage. The transition from this into the monotheistic stage could be effected in two ways —either by denying altogether the existence of the Elohim, and changing them into devils, as the Zoroastrians did with the Devas of their Brahmanic ancestors; or by taking a higher view, and looking upon the Elohim as so many names, invented with the honest purpose of expressing the various aspects of the Deity, though in time diverted from their original purpose. This is the view taken by St. Paul of the religion of the Greeks when he came to declare unto them 'Him whom they ignorantly worshipped,' and the same view was taken by Abraham. Whatever the names of the Elohim, worshipped by the numerous clans of his race, Abraham saw that all the Elohim were meant for God, and thus Elohim, comprehending by one name everything that ever had been or could be called divine, became the name with which the monotheistic age was rightly inaugurated, —a plural, conceived and construed as a singular. Jehovah was all the Elohim, and therefore there could be no other God. From this point of view the Semitic

name of the Deity, Elohim, which seemed at first not
only ungrammatical but irrational, becomes perfectly
clear and intelligible, and it proves better than anything else that the true monotheism could not have
risen except on the ruins of a polytheistic faith.   It
is easy to scoff at the gods of the heathen, but a cold-
hearted philosophical negation of the gods of the
ancient world is more likely to lead to Deism or
Atheism than to a belief in the One living God, the
Father of all mankind, 'who hath made of one blood
all nations of men, for to dwell on all the face of the
earth; and hath determined the times before appointed,
and the bounds of their habitation; that they should
seek the Lord, if haply they might feel after Him,
and find Him, though He be not far from every one of
us: for in Him we live, and move, and have our being;
as certain also of your own poets have said, For we
are also His offspring.'

Taking this view of the historical growth of the
idea of God, many of the difficulties which M. Renan
has to overcome by most elaborate and sometimes
hair-splitting arguments, disappear at once. M. Renan,
for instance, dwells much on Semitic proper names in
which the names of the Deity occur, and he thinks
that, like the Greek names Theodoros or Theo-
dotos, instead of Zenodotos, they prove the existence of a faith in one God. We should say they
may or may not. As Devadatta, in Sanskrit,
may mean either 'given by God,' or 'given by the
gods,' so every proper name which M. Renan quotes,
whether of Jews, or Edomites, Ishmaelites, Ammonites,
Moabites, and Themanites, whether from the Bible, or
from Arab historians, from Greek authors, Greek inscriptions, the Egyptian papyri, the Himyaritic and

Sinaitic inscriptions and ancient coins, are all open to two interpretations. ' The servant of Baal' may mean the servant of the Lord, but it may also mean the servant of Baal, as one of many lords, or even the servant of the Baalim or the Lords. The same applies to all other names. ' The gift of El' may mean ' the gift of the only strong God;' but it may likewise mean ' the gift of the El,' as one of many gods, or even ' the gift of the El's,' in the sense of the strong gods. Nor do we see why M. Renan. should take such pains to prove that the name of Orotal or Orotulat, mentioned by Herodotos (III. 8), may be interpreted as the name of a supreme deity; and that Alilat, mentioned by the same traveller, should be taken, not as the name of a goddess, but as a feminine noun expressive of the abstract sense of the deity. Herodotos says distinctly that Orotal was a deity like Bacchus; and Alilat, as he translates her name by Οὐρανίη, must have appeared to him as a goddess, and not as the Supreme Deity. One verse of the Koran is sufficient to show that the Semitic inhabitants of Arabia worshipped not only gods, but goddesses also. ' What think ye of Allat, al Uzza, and Manah, that other third goddess?'

If our view of the development of the idea of God be correct, we can perfectly understand how, in spite of this polytheistic phraseology, the primitive intuition of God should make itself felt from time to time, long before Mohammed restored the belief of Abraham in one God. The old Arabic prayer mentioned by Abul-farag may be perfectly genuine: ' I dedicate myself to thy service, O God! Thou hast no companion, except thy companion, of whom thou art absolute master, and of whatever is his.' The verse pointed

out to M. Renan by M. Caussin de Perceval from the
Moallaka of Zoheyr, was certainly anterior to Mohammed : ' Try not to hide your secret feelings from the
sight of Allah; Allah knows all that is hidden.'   But
these quotations serve no more to establish the universality of the monotheistic instinct in the Semitic race
than similar quotations from the Veda would prove
the existence of a conscious monotheism among the
ancestors of the Aryan race.   There too we read,
' Agni knows what is secret among mortals ' (Rig-veda
VIII. 39, 6): and again, ' He, the upholder of order,
Varuna, sits down among his people; he, the wise,
sits there to govern.   From thence perceiving all
wondrous things, he sees what has been and what
will be done[5].'   But in these very hymns, better than
anywhere else, we learn that the idea of supremacy and
omnipotence ascribed to one god did by no means
exclude the admission of other gods, or names of God.
All the other gods disappear from the vision of the
poet while he addresses his own God, and he only
who is to fulfil his desires stands in full light before
the eyes of the worshipper as the supreme and only
God.

The Science of Religion is only just beginning,
and we must take care how we impede its progress
by preconceived notions or too hasty generalizations.
During the last fifty years the authentic documents of
the most important religions of the world have been
recovered in a most unexpected and almost miraculous manner.   We have now before us the canonical
books of Buddhism; the Zend-Avesta of Zoroaster is
no longer a sealed book; and the hymns of the Rig-

---

[5] 'History of Ancient Sanskrit Literature,' by M.M., p. 536.

veda have revealed a state of religion anterior to the
first beginnings of that mythology which in Homer
and Hesiod stands before us as a mouldering ruin.
The soil of Mesopotamia has given back the very
images once worshipped by the most powerful of
the Semitic tribes, and the cuneiform inscriptions of
Babylon and Nineveh have disclosed the very prayers
addressed to Baal or Nisroch.   With the discovery of
these documents a new era begins in the study of
religion.   We begin to see more clearly every day
what St. Paul meant in his sermon at Athens.   But
as the excavator at Babylon or Nineveh, before he
ventures to reconstruct the palaces of these ancient
kingdoms, sinks his shafts into the ground slowly and
circumspectly lest he should injure the walls of the
ancient palaces which he is disinterring; as he watches
every corner-stone lest he mistake their dark passages
and galleries, and as he removes with awe and trembling the dust and clay from the brittle monuments lest
he destroy their outlines, and obliterate their inscriptions, so it behoves the student of the history of religion
to set to work carefully, lest he should miss the track,
and lose himself in an inextricable maze.   The relics
which he handles are more precious than the ruins
of Babylon; the problems he has to solve are more
important than the questions of ancient chronology;
and the substructions which he hopes one day to lay
bare are the world-wide foundations of the eternal
kingdom of God.

We look forward with the highest expectations to
the completion of M. Renan's work, and though English
readers will differ from many of the author's views,
and feel offended now and then at his blunt and un-
guarded language, we doubt not that they will find

his volumes both instructive and suggestive. They are written in that clear and brilliant style which has secured to M. Renan the rank of one of the best writers of French, and which throws its charm even over the dry and abstruse inquiries into the grammatical forms and radical elements of the Semitic languages.

April, 1860.

END OF THE FIRST VOLUME.

www.ingramcontent.com/pod-product-compliance
Lightning Source LLC
Chambersburg PA
CBHW032314280326
41932CB00009B/813